MACHINE GUNNER
1914-1918

PEN & SWORD MILITARY CLASSICS

We hope you enjoy your Pen and Sword Military Classic. The series is designed to give readers quality military history at affordable prices. Pen and Sword Classics are available from all good bookshops. If you would like to keep in touch with further developments in the series,

Telephone: **01226 734555**,
email: **enquiries@pen-and-sword.co.uk**,
or visit our website at **www.pen-and-sword.co.uk**.

MACHINE GUNNER
1914-1918

*Personal Experiences of the
Machine Gun Corps*

Compiled and edited by
C. E. Crutchley

PEN & SWORD MILITARY CLASSICS

First published in Great Britain in 1973 by
C. E. Crutchley on behalf of
The Machine Gun Corps Old Comrades Association.

2nd revised and enlarged edition 1975

Published in this format in 2005 by
Pen & Sword Military Classics
An imprint of
Pen & Sword Books Ltd
47 Church Street
Barnsley
South Yorkshire
S70 2AS

ISBN 1 84415 359 2

A CIP catalogue record for this book is
available from the British Library

Printed and bound in England
By CPI UK

Pen & Sword Books Ltd incorporates the Imprints of Pen & Sword Aviation,
Pen & Sword Maritime, Pen & Sword Military, Wharncliffe Local history,
Pen & Sword Select, Pen & Sword Military Classics and Leo Cooper.

For a complete list of Pen & Sword titles please contact
PEN & SWORD BOOKS LIMITED
47 Church Street, Barnsley, South Yorkshire, S70 2AS, England
E-mail: enquiries@pen-and-sword.co.uk
Website: www.pen-and-sword.co.uk

To the undying memory of officers and other ranks of
the Machine Gun Corps and the Regimental Machine
Gunners who gave their all—for their country—in the
Great War of 1914–1918, this book is reverently and
respectfully dedicated.

Contents

CONTENTS

Foreword

During recent years the work of recovering the Regimental and the Army records of the Machine Gun Corps, lost in two separate disasters, has been proceeding.

A new Corps banner of unique character was laid up forever in St. Wulfram's Church, Grantham, Lincolnshire, in 1967.

A Book of Remembrance, in which the records are set forth for posterity, was similarly enshrined in 1968. A reference copy has since been completed, and on 7 April 1972, at a special ceremony held in London, this copy was accepted by Sir Peter Masefield and Dr Noble Frankland, D.F.C., for the Imperial War Museum.

Upon the completion of the Book of Remembrance there came a renewed urge to compile a history of the Corps, based on the experiences of officers and men who served as front line machine-gunners in the most ghastly soldiers' war of all time. Old records and diaries were dug out, and dormant memories awakened, and from these sources this book has been compiled.

* * *

In March, 1973, the first edition was published as a private venture, and quickly sold out. As the demand for the book continued, the publishing house of Bailey Bros. and Swinfen Ltd. have undertaken to produce this second edition, which contains added reading matter and illustrations.

* * *

This book is not intended to glorify war—but to pass on the spirit and message of REMEMBRANCE in the hope that by so doing, it may help to point the way along the road to future world peace, more vital in this atomic age than ever before. If it succeeds in its object it will be because of the contributors whose names appear at the end of this book. To them I extend my warm thanks.

C. E. Crutchley

*   *   *

Royalties received from the sale of this edition will be given to the Machine Gun Corps' 'Boy David' Fund, which is affiliated to the Army Benevolent Fund.

Preface

By COLONEL SIR GEORGE WADE, M.C., J.P.,
Chairman, M.G.C. Old Comrades Association

Those who served in the First World War have many reminiscences. These are always full of interest, and the recollections of Machine Gunners are particularly so because of their unique function in active operations.

They were always at the centre of things. Wherever trouble most threatened, or an attack was planned, there they had to be, right amongst it all.

They had tremendous fire power, and the moment they started they were the targets of every enemy weapon within range. No wonder the Machine Gun Corps was nick-named the Suicide Club !

As they were so mobile and so much in demand they saw more of what was happening than any other Arm.

Machine-gunners had to be highly skilled, not only mechanically but tactically, and their devastating fire power gave them a deep sense of responsibility which never left them to the bitter end.

In a few years there will be no survivors of World War One to tell the story. Soon all their experiences which have not been recorded will be lost for ever.

All lovers of history should be grateful to the veteran machine gunner who has, while there is still time, painstakingly collected the memoirs of his comrades.

To old soldiers the following pages will awaken vivid pictures already etched deeply in their memories.

Comradeship such as could exist only between serving soldiers, and the bravery, the kindness, the sacrifice, the suffering, the agony will all come back. Even the smell of cordite and blood will return, together with the stale atmosphere of charcoal and earth which pervaded every dug-out.

Those who were not born when these stirring events took place will read between the lines of the grim determination which actuated the men of the Machine Gun Corps through long years of bitter warfare in conditions of extreme hardship, icy cold or insufferable heat, against enemies of many nationalities.

In those days every man was firmly convinced that we were fighting for Freedom, as indeed we were, but nowadays old soldiers wonder if those who enjoy freedom now appreciate what sacrifices were made to keep it, and what vigilance is still called for to preserve it.

Introduction

In World War One the machine-gun was the most deadly of weapons. When war broke out (August 4th, 1914) every British infantry unit had its own machine-gun section of two Maxim guns served by one officer and twelve other ranks. The section was divided into two gun teams. The men chosen to serve in the machine-gun section were mostly marksmen with the rifle.

Although the machine-gun officer had a certain amount of freedom relating to the training of his men, the Battalion machine-gunner enjoyed certain privileges. The Command Officer of a Unit usually had the first and last word in the placing of the guns in actual battle.

In the first year of the war the fire power of the Maxim gun (500 rounds per minute) gave vital support to attacking infantry and also in defensive actions. Even so, two Maxim guns supporting a battalion of eight hundred men, often on a wide frontage of varied depth, could not possibly be everywhere at once. The British High Command soon became aware of these limitations and it was decided to form a Corps of Machine Gunners.

THE MACHINE GUN CORPS

The Corps was created by Royal Warrant on October 14th, 1915, His Majesty King George V being Colonel-in-Chief. Its Infantry, Cavalry, Motor, and Heavy branches grew into formidable self-contained units in every theatre of war. A total of 170,500 officers and men served in the Corps, which suffered 62,049 casualties.

Very soon after the formation of the M.G.C. the Maxim gun was replaced by the Vickers machine-gun.

The Corps was continually recruiting from picked men. Both as an armed body, and as an association of men, it was therefore unique.

The story of the Machine Gun Corps is a record of front line soldiers, of those who accompanied the first wave of every assault and who remained to cover every retirement. Throughout the war years not a single day passed but saw the members of the Machine Gun Corps in the front line.

Where other Corps and Regiments have long records from which to cite their achievements, the Machine Gun Corps is possessed of but three swift years of history. These years are an epic of patience, cheerfulness, endurance, loyalty, sacrifice, courage and comradeship. Every month, indeed every day, the Machine Gun Corps had its Waterloo, its Balaclava, its Rorke's Drift. It was a Battalion with backs to the wall facing fearful odds; a company filling a breach; even a single gun team of six men, sometimes a single gunner alone among his dead, holding a vital flank.

There was a lad at High Wood with one arm hanging by a bloody thread who carried ammunition to a heavily besieged post.

There was a Company leader, whose command had been reduced by half, who at 'Third Ypres' turned defeat into a notable victory, who before relief buried all his dead, and who became Bishop wearing the Distinguished Service Order.

There was a driver at the Hindenburg Line who, the target for every hostile gun, shot through the stomach and belching blood, toppled his machine-gun limber with its precious load of ammunition into our beleaguered line and perished among his mules.

There was a gun team at Meteran at the top of a tottering windmill, who fought until the shell storm overwhelmed the shattered skeleton of masonry, and buried the gunners in its ruins . . . There was a groom on the Lys who rode the two miles' length of gun positions through the enemy's gun-fire, so that from the air a spotting pilot might mark his map.

There was a private on the Menin Road who, when officers and N.C.Os had become casualties, took command of his Company, added a Bar to his D.C.M. and gained his direct Regular Commission in the Field.

There was a signaller who, on many-times-mended lines, tapped out a message until overwhelmed by attack.

There was the M.G.C. Artificer whose fingers repaired intricate machinery, while a field dressing supported a shattered arm.

There was the lad at Arras who crept forward in the darkness, captured an enemy stronghold single-handed and turned the German machine-gun against the enemy's line, raking the parapets when our attack developed at dawn.

There are, too, the records of the missing, whose last history is unknown beyond the tale of the steady staccato of their guns when everyone else had retired.

Thousands of such actions add lustre to the history of the Machine Gun Corps.

Transcending all else was the comradeship of trench and billet, of camp fire and of tent.

Machine gunners knew the quality of comradeship : men in sodden Flanders beneath the scourge of Trommel Feuer; troopers who rode shoulder to shoulder at dawn before Damascus; Australians and New Zealanders on the beaches of Gallipoli; South Africans in the carnage of Delville Wood. Canadians bresting the ridge of Vimy . . . Men from the blue haze of an English countryside; the Scots, the Irish and the Welsh, from heathered hills and smoke-laden cities, wrestling with death on the Somme and the Hindenburg Line . . .

Bare-legged boys from shingled coves wading the mud morasses of Passchendaele; those whose cries echoed among the Dorian crags of Salonica and from the rocky peaks of the Khyber; men who found the enemy among the snow-capped heights of the Piave; and those who faced sand storms, thirst, and privation in the deserts of Egypt and Mesopotamia . . .

Men from the traffickings of an Empire's metropolis; those whose mother tongue was in every English dialect and whose calling was the field, the mine, the loom, the bench, the press and the counting house . . . Old soldiers who remembered Darghai and Magersfontein, and were familiar with the 'bat', the 'bhisti' and the 'blockhouse', and men who as youths knew only Haig's Final Drive.

Those who gripped hands at zero hour, and those who fell in mud and dust and rose no more.

Yes, men of the Machine Gun Corps knew the quality of comradeship.

*   *   *

Before formation of the Machine Gun Corps in October 1915, machine gunners of the Regular and Territorial Army carved an indelible niche in the history of their respective Regiments.

It would be true to say that these men paved the way for the formation of the Machine Gun Corps. As a tribute to them the opening stories in this book spotlight the vital contribution battalion machine-gunners made to Britain's fight for survival.

> We shall ever tell the story
> How their glory brightly shone,
> Who throughout a hell of carnage
> Set their teeth and carried on.

A 1913 Terrier Machine-Gunner Remembers

The sight of a carriage-mounted Nordenfeldt machine-gun at the Regent Street Polytechnic must have subconsciously influenced a young man who enlisted on December 5th, 1913, in the Poly. company of the 12th Battalion—the London Regiment, known as 'The Rangers'. That gun was one of two which went to South Africa at the turn of the century under the command of Lt. Colonel Alt.

As an eager recruit I pried into every activity of my new unit, and, though a mere rifleman, I became aware of a small sub-unit of the battalion attached to my company and designated the MACHINE GUN SECTION.

Its mysteries were not divulged to me at that stage. The recruit drills, company drills, route marches on Saturday afternoons and the Easter camp at Purfleet for musketry, passed all too quickly, leading to the event of the year : the annual camp. This was to be held at Lulworth Cove.

The parade of 'E' and 'F' companies, soon to become 'A' Company under the four company reorganisation, showed the Machine Gun Section, under the command of Lt. Worthington with Sergeant Norton and 13 other ranks. I had by now somehow learnt that it had two Maxim guns as its armament.

Though we marched proudly to Waterloo Station on Sunday, August 2nd, 1914, we never reached the camp. The train halted at Eastleigh and, after a suitable pause to dispel the rumour that the Germans had landed at Barking Creek, the engine was put on the other end and we were hauled back to London.

War with Germany was anticipated, and embodiment on a war basis followed within 48 hours.

On August 4th war was declared.

The details of infantry battalion training in those days have often been told, the machine-gunners part less often.

Some time in the autumn of that year I was designated as reserve for the machine-gun section and soon became aware of their intensive training. After battalion parades, many hours were devoted to learning how to rectify gun stoppages, how to fill ammunition belts, how to strip and re-assemble the guns, and their parts. We also did overtime, endeavouring to clip seconds off the average time for the various gun-drill movements. Morse code and semaphore signalling were also included in the curriculum. The guns, ammunition and equipment were carried in a box-like wagon drawn by two horses.

A Christmas Day to remember

After nearly five months of intensive training in England, we were declared fit for service overseas. Arriving in France on Christmas Day, 1914, we marched up the hill from Boulogne to the camp, where a site was allotted to the Battalion next door to No. 9 Hospital which dealt with cases of venereal disease. The miseries of those patients made a profound impression on many of us. The other memory of that port was daily fatigues on the docks in connection with shipping.

We learnt of the misdeeds of the units who had preceded us. Men under sentence in the charge of the Military Police did not wear caps, and I nearly got a beating for taking mine off during a break period.

Next came our first acquaintance with the French railways—the wagons for eight horses or 40 men in which we travelled to St. Omer, in northern France. Thence we marched to Blendecqes, where almost a month was spent in hardening up, living under rough conditions, and feeding in the way to be expected in the trenches. The then Prince of Wales passed by the place one day, but not much notice was taken of this event.

Trench digging had now become a major pre-occupation of the British Expeditionary Force.

First spell of front line duty

About the end of January, 1915, we moved on and up to Ypres. We had become one of two extra battalions in a brigade of the 28th Division, whose other units included the 1st Monmouths (T) and four regular battalions lately brought back from overseas duty. I may say here and now that I never saw a senior officer of the division from that time until May, when the battalion was withdrawn, and I have never ascertained the name of the commander.

Our first position was in trenches known as R, S and T astride the Ypres/St. Eloi roads, about three miles outside the ancient city, where the inhabitants still lived in their houses and shops. The position occupied was at canal level and the whole line was water-logged, dominated by the enemy who held trenches on higher ground. Fixed machine-gun positions were impossible and the gunners meekly accepted their role as carriers of rations and trench stores, leaving their guns in reserve.

Later in April the battalion moved to a new sector at the eastern apex of the salient near Zonnebeke and here the M. G. section was brought up to a supporting position in dug-outs on the embankment of the Ypres/Zonnebeke railway. Little of note occurred here and in due course the Rangers were moved to Velorenhoek/Frezenberg for an all too brief rest.

The second battle of Ypres

On April 24th, 1915, the Germans attacked the Canadians at St. Julian and used poison gas for the first time in the war. We were hustled from our rear billets to the scene of the battle and almost immediately ordered to take part in a counter-attack.

At this juncture our machine-gun section was in a position to observe from the flank of the battalion. What a sight to see across this open level piece of ground—the whole battalion spread out in extended order formation, as taught in the drill books, and advancing under a steady rain of shrapnel. Casualties were not heavy, but the commanding officer was one to go down wounded. A stop-gap line was established at the point of the deepest penetration of the Germans and we dug in for dear life. The machine-gun section took up positions, but worthwhile targets were few.

Having recovered from the initial shock of a gas attack, the Canadians and Allied troops gave little ground.

It was not many days later that the High Command resolved to shorten the line and withdraw from the indented salient. Again we marched to the new line and dug in.

Some 30 hours elapsed before the Germans decided to move into the salient we had evacuated. This they did in a somewhat brazen manner, and their movements on open ground were in full view of the Maxim guns. At one time a field gun was spotted being man-handled into position. We were able to get in enough fire to put it out of action and it was not heard of again. We stayed in our new positions until May 6th, when we were relieved and went back to the support line. Our rest spell was once again of very short duration.

On the morning of May 8th (a fateful day for British and Anzac troops) we were aroused with the news that the Germans had broken our line somewhat to the right of our former trenches, and a counter-attack was to be made from the flank to seal the breach. The machine-gun section had by this time been reduced to a one gun team, and we went in with the rest of the 12th London Battalion, suffering heavy casualties from German artillery fire which plastered the whole of the front and support lines.

Arriving at the old front line it was quickly seen that the Germans were pouring in through the gap. Our one gun went into action, inflicting heavy losses on them by enfilade fire. The range was about 2–300 yards; the machine–gun commander was one Lt. Dunlop (later Brigadier-General Sir John Dunlop). His leadership and courage was an inspiration to us. The enemy was held, but all the section and the gun became casualties. I got a Blighty-one.

On my way back to casualty clearing station, I encountered a battalion of the Warwickshire Regiment going up in support. Their efforts were successful, but I was told later on that day that the battalion came out of action fifteen men strong under a corporal.

2

The Defence of the Suez Canal

Soon after the outbreak of war in 1914, British regular army units based in Egypt were sent to France and their places taken by territorial battalions and Anzac units.

The defence of Egypt and the Suez Canal, so vital to the Allies, became the responsibility of Britain's part-time soldiers. It was a tremendous responsibility, but how well they faced up to it is described by a Lancs. man who served as a machine-gunner with the 1/10th Manchester Regiment, 42nd Division (East Lancs Territorials).

We left Southampton on the morning of September 15th, 1914, on board the mail ship *Avon*, and as we moved out the lads sang : 'Homeland, homeland, when shall we see you again?'

The majority on that ship never did.

The day before embarkation everyone in the battalion had been vaccinated, and the password was 'Mind my arm mate' as the old boat tipped us around, especially when we reached the Bay of Biscay. It was then that sea-sickness superseded sore arm worries, but by the time we docked at the Egyptian port of Alexandria everyone was in high spirits and fascinated by the discovery of another sort of world. Not many of us had been any further from home than Blackpool, and a few weeks ago most of the battalion had been working in mill or office at Oldham and other Lancashire towns, little dreaming that very soon they would be pitched into a war, and sailing to places seen only as red patches on the map of the world.

It seemed, as I helped unload our machine-guns and equipment from the troopship, that I was experiencing a fantastic kind of dream.

From Alexandria we moved to Cairo racecourse, where we camped. During off-duty periods we enjoyed ourselves until the arrival of Anzac troops. Then up went the prices in Cairo shops and cafes, which put a damper on our trips into that city. You see, the Aussies were paid six shillings and ninepence per day, compared to the British Tommies' pay of one shilling per day, reduced to sixpence per day for many of us who made an allotment to parents. What a cheap army we were!

In late October our machine-gun sections moved to the banks of the Suez Canal, where we dug trenches and machine-gun emplacements at various points. We slept rough and did lonely night sentry duties. This experience certainly toughened us up, and after a few weeks we no longer looked like part-time soldiers.

A few days before Christmas 1914, we accompanied the 1/10th Manchester Regiment back to Cairo, where we had Christmas dinner. Six men to a turkey, and all the trimmings. My machine-gun section filled a dixie full of beer. The cost, per head, a mere 9d. Not a bad old war I thought, for some of us. I little visualised what the future held in store.

A few days after Christmas we travelled to a place called Tell-el-Kebir, where we did a short spell of duty. I remember seeing the graves of 400 British soldiers who died during the Egyptian campaign of 1882—a grim reminder of past wars. From Tell-el-Kebir we were hurried back again to the Suez Canal area and took over from an Indian unit at a place that had no name, merely a map reference of 50 point 8. The desert stretched out as far as the eye could see.

The Turks Attack

We were up and down the banks of the Suez Canal like yo-yo's, until January 26th, when our machine-gun section settled in an isolated spot a few miles north of El-Kantara, a scruffy little village about twenty miles from Port Said.

In the early hours of January 28th, 1915, we got an inkling of what was to come. I was on gun sentry duty at the time and thought I saw strange figures moving about outside the barbed wire perimeter. Must be my imagination, I thought and after a moment or so continued my patrol. Then I heard a distinct sound of metal scraping against metal, like someone trying to cut the wire entanglements, and that decided me. I aroused the guard sergeant with the words : 'Come on, the bloody Turks are here!' 'All right' he said calmly and, after a leisurely stretch, ordered, 'wake up the lads and no talking.'

We manned our two Maxim guns, and sent a chap out to the wire perimeter to investigate. Immediately a great commotion took place on the other side of the wire in front of us. Someone shouted, 'No fire! No fire! Friends.' It was a party of Indian Lancers, some of whom were wounded and half dead from thirst.

We got them inside and emptied our water bottles and attended to their injuries. The Lancers had been in a brush with Turkish advance patrols in the Sinai Desert.

Later that day a British Royal Flying Corps pilot reported having seen a Turkish force of several thousands with field guns, moving across the Sinai desert. Other enemy columns had also been located approaching the Canal defences over a wide area. Incidentally, the Suez Canal is 99 miles in length, and has a minimum width of 135 feet. Quite a stretch to keep an eye on.

Early on the morning of January 29th a Turkish force attempted to rush Indian outposts at El-Kantara but was repulsed. The Fourteenth Sikh Battalion lost one officer and 30 men in this sharp engagement.

In the late evening of February 1st an estimated two divisions of Turkish infantry supported by field guns, prepared to attack defences at Kantara, and also at Ismailia, an important point in the Canal defences situated on Lake Timseh, about half way between Port Said and Port Suez.

In the early hours of February 2nd, 1915, the attack began, the main thrust being made about four miles off the Ismailia ferry, but a violent sand storm held up operations.

During the hours of darkness on February 2nd, Turkish army engineers managed to get about 30 galvanised-iron pontoon boats right down to the edge of the Canal without detection; but the moment they began to push their boats into the water, Maxim guns attached to a mountain battery opened up and the guns from British warships on the Canal joined in the fray. The Turks brought several batteries of field guns into action from the rising ground west of Kataib-el-Kheil, and two battalions of Anatolians made a gallant effort to hold a bridgehead at Ismailia, but British artillery, Maxim gun and rifle fire routed them; by the middle of the afternoon of February 3rd, the Turks were in full retreat leaving many dead : a large proportion of whom had been killed by shrapnel.

As the fighting died down around the Ismailia ferry, it also fizzled out at El-Kantara where our Maxim guns had been in hot engagements, but we escaped serious casualties.

Next morning, February 4th, we took out a gun to support a Gurkha patrol searching for snipers hidden in the bushy hollows on the East bank. Subsequent operations were merely rounding up prisoners and bringing in to Kantara military equipment left behind by Turks fleeing as fast as they could into the wastes of the Sinai Desert.

British losses in the first battle of the Suez Canal amounted to

111 killed and wounded. Turkish losses were put at 2,000. The Turks had fought bravely but they had no chance at all.

To reach the Suez Canal they had crossed 120 miles of the Sinai Desert, through sand and terrible heat where water was non-existent. No mean achievement, as a British force was to discover when, later on in the war, they crossed that very same stretch of desert. But that is another story.

After the end of the first Suez battle. The 42nd East Lancs. Territorial Division, was given a rest (in relays) until early April 1915, when we went to Port Said to prepare for that ill-fated Gallipoli Campaign.

3

Gallipoli

Three plans had been put forward during the winter months of 1914 with a view to ending the stalemate on the Western Front.

Winston Churchill (1st Lord of the Admiralty) presented a plan to attack the Dardanelles by land and sea.
Lord Fisher (First Sea Lord) wanted to open up the Baltic.
Lloyd George (Chancellor of the Exchequer) was in favour of a Salonica landing.

At first Lord Kitchener (Secretary of War) was opposed to any plan that would take troops from the Western Front, but eventually Churchill got his way and on February 19th, 1915, at 9.51 a.m., British and French fleets bombarded the outer forts of the Dardanelles.

Then for a whole week very stormy weather caused a suspension of the bombardments, but on February 25th the bombardment was resumed and minesweepers cleared the entrance to the straits. On February 26th marines and bluejackets were landed to blow up the guns in the abandoned forts on both sides of the sound. The landing-parties met with little resistance. It was later established that at this date Achi-Baba, the key hill on Gallipoli, could have been occupied and held with a very few troops indeed, but naval experts still believed that the assembled armada of Allied warships, which included Britain's super dreadnought, the *Queen Elizabeth*, could accomplish the forcing of the Dardanelles on its own. But we had, as is were, sent a postcard to the Turks of our intentions, and the Turks brought up large numbers of Howitzer guns, on both shores. Minesweepers, mostly operating during the hours of darkness, were picked out by glaring searchlights and raked by the fire of the Turkish field guns.

On March 18th, the Allied fleet made its greatest attack on the strait. It was a disastrous affair. The *Bouvet* (a French battleship) and the British battleships *Ocean* and *Irresistible*, were sunk. Four other attacking vessels were seriously damaged.

After this serious set-back, the entire fleet steamed away and never came back until the first landing of the troops on April 25th, 1915.

In the five weeks that elapsed between March 18th and April 25th, field defences on the peninsula had been strengthened with feverish activity by the Turks under German supervision. Turkey had by this time mobilised 800,000 men, and a big proportion of these troops was now ready to fight on the Gallipoli peninsula.

For all practical purposes, at the time the Allied troops landed on the peninsula, they were faced with the bulk of the strength of the Turkish Army, under the Generalship of Field Marshal von Sanders, a German officer of noted ability.

THE GALLIPOLI LANDINGS

At dawn the attack began. There were six landings by British and Anzac troops; five at the tip of the peninsula, and one at Anzac Cove. All were terrible and bloody. At no point was the advance inland more than a mile.

At Anzac Cove, Australians and New Zealanders hung on to the edges of precipitous cliffs. The fighting was even fiercer at Cape Helles, where the attack was led by the famous 29th Division, who had already fought in France.

The landing from V beach will remain even more memorable for two main reasons : the running of the troop ship *River Clyde* almost on to the beaches, and the vital part played by 12 Maxim guns manned by men of the Naval Division on the troopship.

A machine-gunner who was there gives his account of the landings :

Over two thousand troops were aboard the *River Clyde* when at dawn on April 25th, 1915, she slowly steamed towards shore. The idea was to approach close inshore without being exposed— a sort of 'wooden horse' strategy, similar to that used by the ancient Greeks at the siege of Troy.

The steel sides of the ship afforded protection to hundreds of our men crammed between the side decks. Great doors were cut into the ship's sides, to allow a speedy disembarkation, and wooden gangways were slung from ropes down from these doors, to enable men to pass down in single file and either jump into the water, if not too deep, or on to lighters which the ship had towed in with her. The bridge of the *Clyde* was converted into a miniature fortress from where the twelve Maxim guns would operate. The gunners were protected by steel plates.

After a rapid bombardment from the battleship *Albion*, and a covering fire from our machine-guns, the first batch of men left the ships and got into the steam pinnaces and boats. Most of those in the boats were Dublin Fusiliers and Naval men, who suffered severe casualties from enemy rifle and machine-gun fire, which swept the foreshore. The survivors crawled along the front of the beach to a sandbank several feet high, which gave them some protection from the murderous gunfire sweeping the beaches.

Meanwhile the *River Clyde* had drifted further than had been intended, bow-on close to a reef of rock. The water here was too deep to allow men to wade ashore. A steam hopper was brought up and then run ashore to provide a gangway from the wooden gangways on either side of the ship. During this time the troopship was subjected to a whirlwind of rifle, machine-gun, and pom-pom fire, the bullets rattling against her sides like huge hailstones. The troops on board were now well aware that it meant almost certain destruction to leave the ship.

However, later that morning about two hundred men, led by their officers, dashed down the gangway to the starboard side and attempted to reach the reef. Some became casualties on the gangway; others were killed or wounded as they reached the hopper; others on the reef, and many of the survivors, no sooner reached the beach than they also became casualties. The few survivors lay under the shelter of the sandbank, hardly daring to move. Annihilation of the entire force was threatened now if any further attempt to disembark was made.

The battleships *Cornwallis*, *Albion* and *Queen Elizabeth*, opened a terrific bombardment on the fort of Sedd-el-Bahr, and on the Turkish trenches in the hills which rose up from the beaches opposite our ship, like so many eerie monsters waiting to devour us. The continued heavy shelling from our ships eventually silenced the Turkish batteries, but until well into the evening it was still almost certain death to pass down a gangway on the *Clyde*. From the start of the attempted landing about 1,000 men had left the troopship, in one way or another, and nearly half had been killed, wounded, or drowned.

For the best part of that day, after the first costly landing attempt, over 1,000 men were packed together on the *Clyde*, unable to land. The position looked pretty hopeless until our 12 Maxim guns, sheltered behind steel plates, opened a concentrated fire on the Turkish position at the foot of the hills. Each gun fired 500 rounds per minute, which meant that some 6,000 bullets per minute were landing among the Turkish troops occupying the foothills. It proved too much for them, and at about 8 p.m. that night (it was still daylight) the thousand men on board walked down the gangway without a casualty and reached the cover of the sandbank at the foot of the hills.

THE BATTLE OF KRITHIA

Krithia is a village of Gallipoli. It is about four miles from the end of the peninsula, and was the scene of severe fighting in 1915. A machine-gunner of the 1/10th Manchester Regiment, who took part in this momentous battle recalls his experiences :

The first attack on Krithia was made on April 28th, 1915, only three days after British troops had landed on the Peninsula. The attack failed to dislodge the Turks. The next assault was made on May 6th–8th. It also failed. I well remember both battles, but outstanding in my memory is the third battle of Krithia which commenced on June 4th and continued until June 8th. As soon as it was dark on June 3rd, we began to dig a gun pit in no-man's-land. Infantrymen of the Hampshire Regiment dug near us. We had not been at it very many minutes, when Johnny Turk opened fire with rifles and machine-guns. One of our guns was rushed to the right flank of the digging party, and its fire helped to keep down the casualties, but by early morning on June 4th the place was a shambles.

Two particular incidents stand out in my memory of that tragic night of June 3rd, 1915. During the digging a sergeant of the Hampshires was urging his men to dig faster, when the man digging directly behind him accidentally (I think) stuck his pick into the backside of the sergeant, who gave a terrific yell. This incident caused a flutter of laughter from those who witnessed the incident, but almost immediately the merriment turned sour when the man next to me was shot through the nose.

We abandoned our no-man's-land positions just before dawn on June 4th, crawling back to the original trenches occupied by the main body of troops. Stretcher-bearers brought in many wounded. We prepared our machine-guns for the attack which was to begin at 12 noon. What a time, right in the heat of the day, but so it was planned.

At 10 a.m. June 4th, 1915, every British and French gun on

the peninsula poured shells of various calibres into the Turkish trenches. Battleships off the northern coast battered the enemy's right, while a French warship, in the entrance to the Dardanelles, bombarded the left of the Turkish positions. A continual rain of 18 pounder shells and French 75's exploded along the parapets of the Turkish trenches. Some of these shells burst too near to us for comfort as we crouched low in our trenches, which we had dug to a depth of some 12 feet. For ninety minutes there was no let-up by our guns. At times the Turkish positions were invisible behind a thick curtain of white billowy smoke and flame.

In Krithia, a tower, which had somehow escaped previous shelling, came toppling down, and from where we were it looked as though the whole of the village was on fire. The air was rent with the shrieks and whistles of shells passing over our heads towards the Turkish lines.

Just after 11.20 a.m. the shelling ceased. Then, acting on a pre-arranged plan, our infantry showed their bayonets above the parapets and gave a loud cheer, but stayed where they were. It was always the drill, on both sides, for front line infantrymen to take shelter in reserve dug-outs during a heavy bombardment, and return to front line trenches directly the shelling ceased, in readiness to meet attacking infantry. The Turks did exactly this, and were badly caught out, for at 11.30 a.m. our guns opened up again with an even more intense bombardment, which continued until a few minutes before 12 noon. A brief uncanny silence followed and then the infantry leapt from their trenches and ran hell-bent over the 200 yards or so which separated our trenches. My machine-gun team went over with the first wave and we set up our gun in a captured trench, alongside a platoon of the Manchester Regiment. Turkish dead were piled up in the captured trenches.

A second wave of East Lancs (42nd Division) quickly followed upon our heels and went on to capture the Turkish support lines some 500 yards further ahead.

A third wave followed the second, to fill up casualty gaps and press home the attack. An interval of about fifteen minutes elapsed between the second and third wave assault. Dazed and badly mutilated by the British shelling, Turks could be seen running panic-stricken along communication trenches to their reserve positions. By early afternoon the 1/10th Manchesters had reached a point only half a mile from Krithia, but there the advance ended.

Several Light Armoured Motor Battery cars, having successfully negotiated rough tracks leading from Sedd-el-Bahr and

c

Cape Helles, dashed up to the battle area near Krithia and opened fire with their machine-guns on the retreating Turks, but this forced them to retire along the road they had come.

The quick success of the 42nd East Lancashire Division (T) in the centre of the attack, had not been matched by the Divisions operating on our flanks. News came through of heavy casualties suffered by the Naval Division, especially the Collingwood Battalion who were almost wiped out.

About 4 p.m., just before the sun began to dip behind the top of Achi-Baba, we received orders to return to our original trenches. Flanks were exposed and Turkish guns from the heights above soon made our positions untenable. Another gunner and myself brought back a single Maxim gun through communication trenches where the dead and seriously wounded lay around like so many bundles of old clothes. The sun was beating down on us with added ferocity. Most of us had already emptied our water bottles, and there was no chance of a water party fatigue reaching us. Our tongues became horribly parched, and we longed for the night to arrive. When it did, the battle faded out, as though a magic wand had been suddenly waved over the entire area.

The peaceful night was superseded by a very turbulent dawn. It was barely daylight when the Turks, having recovered from their shocks of the previous day and heavily reinforced, launched an attack on our lines. We held on until the night of June 8th, when another Brigade took over from us.

A roll call was taken. From about 800-odd 1/10th Manchester Battalion who first entered the trenches around Krithia, only 150 remained, plus one machine-gun served by a sergeant and myself.

The Brigade, being in no fit state for further immediate front line duty, was withdrawn and shipped off to the Island of Mudros for a rest spell and to get made up to strength again in numbers.

The 42nd East Lancs. Territorial Division, by its contribution to the Defence of Suez, followed by the heroic Gallipoli 'Lancashire landing' and subsequent fighting, made history of a nature which ranks among the most distinguished of Britain's Territorial Army.

SUVLA BAY

When it became apparent that it was impossible to make any further progress from the Anzac side of the Peninsula, another landing was planned to take place at Suvla Bay, an inlet on the west coast of the Gallipoli peninsula where the Gulf of Saros joins the Aegean Sea.

It was hoped that a force landed here would succeed in taking the Anafarta Hills and link up with the Anzacs on its left. The landing took place on August 7th, 1915, and was a complete surprise to the Turkish High Command; 10,000 British troops got ashore on the very first day of the attack on the hills surrounding the Bay, and met with little opposition. But when the Turks discovered what was happening the scene changed rapidly, and eventually the Suvla battlefields became as bloody affairs as those at Anzac Cove, Cape Helles, and the rest of the Gallipoli Campaign.

A machine-gunner of the 4th Northamptonshire (T) Regiment tells his story :

We left Devonport, quietly and without any farewells, in the early hours of a July morning on board the *Royal George*, a Cunard liner turned troopship. It was a hush-hush affair, for German submarines were now taking a very active part in the war. We had no knowledge of our destination, but guessed it was 'out East' as we had been issued with tropical kit. As far as Gibraltar it was a rough trip, so rough in fact that the neat tables were deserted, although covered with food no-one wanted to eat. During the hours of darkness the ship was completely blacked out, and in the prevailing silence it was as though we were sailing on a ghost ship.

All was peace as we sailed on through the Mediterranean. On deck night duty I could hear the waves breaking against the ship's sides and then recoiling into endless space. It made the ship seem so small, so trivial. I remember thinking at the time that this mighty expanse of water which was bearing us towards the war was in a way humouring us by permitting our passage. It was as though the lapping waves were saying : 'You and your wars will pass away but I shall be here always.'

We passed the daylight hours—after morning fatigues and boat drill—on the deck playing cards, Housey-Housey and Crown-and-Anchor. For a time these pastimes and the warm Mediterranean sun helped to create an atmosphere reminiscent of a holiday cruise. We knew that our mission was to go somewhere to kill or be killed, but in such circumstances it seemed most unlikely.

Then one morning, there came a reminder of the harsh truth. A German U-boat was sighted. We all saw it. It was on the surface and appeared to be refuelling. We had no naval escort—but we were not attacked. Fifteen hours later, the *Royal Edward*—sister ship to our trooper—was attacked, and sank with heavy loss of life.

Now the secret of our final destination was secret no longer. Orders were issued and water bottles were filled from the ship's supply (we did not know then just how valuable that water was to become). Iron rations of bully beef and biscuits were drawn, and extra ammunition handed out.

Then we transferred to a destroyer, being packed on the decks like sardines in a tin. Silence was the order of the day as she slid through the calm sea, the only noise being the swish of the wake and the faint thud of the screws.

Dawn was breaking as we jumped from the decks of the destroyer into the small boats. A silky mist covered the sea as we drifted towards the beaches, where the gates of hell had already been opened to receive us.

Many battleships lay off-shore pounding with their guns into the Turkish positions on the hills, which rose up from the beaches like so many eerie monsters waiting to devour us.

As soon as we touched the shore we made for any cover that was available. Only a short way inland the other battalions of our brigade—the 1/5th Bedfords, and the 10th and 11th Londons—were fighting for their lives. Gradually our C.O., Colonel Curtis, assisted by Major (later Major General Sir) John Brown, regrouped us. Moving over a ridge, we came into view of the Turkish observation posts. Seconds later a shell burst among us with a sickening din. This was our baptism of fire. The bombardment from our battleships had caused heavy casualties among the Turkish infantry but they were still there waiting for us on the hills above.

I remember reflecting that I had no personal grudge against the Turks lining the hills we had to take. Yet at any moment, I knew I might find myself trying to stick a bayonet into one of them and that he would be endeavouring to do the same thing to me. It was now a matter of self-preservation. We had to make use of everything we had learned in our military training in England, to get the better of the so-called enemy.

We were getting our first sight of the horrors of war. We met the wounded coming away from the front line and I saw a boot sticking out of the ground attached to part of a Turkish soldier's leg.

Then darkness came to shut out the horrible sights. We spent the night digging trenches in anticipation of a Turkish counter-attack. We had no exit, for only the sea was behind us. As we dug, a fresh battle flared up on the Anzac side of the Peninsula. Very lights lit the night sky and the rattle of machine-gun fire echoed across the hill.

Eventually, the Very lights fizzled out just like fireworks on Guy Fawkes' night in England. Then I watched the shells exploding as I dug. Dawn came. A Turkish observation plane circled high over our trenches, then suddenly swooped low and sprayed us with machine-gun bullets.

As the sun rose so did the temperature. It was then that my machine-gun officer detailed me and another gunner to get some boxes of ammunition from a dump at the bottom of the hill. It was not an easy journey. Turkish snipers seemed to be everywhere and every time we toiled up the hill we were shot at. But we were lucky. For the moment the gods of war were smiling on us.

An Australian patrol caught a Turkish woman sniper who had the identity discs of several British soldiers hanging round her neck. They shot her, and that shocked me for I thought she was a brave person doing only what many British women would have done to invaders of our land. But I kept my mouth shut for I knew that in war everyone is affected by its lunacy.

For the most part our food was bully beef and hard biscuit washed down with the stale warm water from our bottles.

Almost as bad as the Turkish gun-fire were the thousands of flies and the terrible heat. The flies gave us no rest at all and you were lucky to have a mouthful of food which was not covered with them. Then there were the crickets whose non-stop chirruping filled in the gaps between the gun-fire, and from the hills all round us wafted the sickly perfume of wild thyme.

That's what life was like on the first two nights after our landing in Suvla Bay. And it didn't change much for the next 125 days. Then we were evacuated, the battalion decimated by shot and shell and the ravages of dysentery.

While this was going on, General Birdwood's forces became engaged in a desperate struggle to obtain possession of the ridges running north-east of their positions.

The main objective was the crest of Sari-Bair, the commanding ridge overlooking the Dardanelles which gives access to the highest peak of all, the frightening height of Koja-Chemen, split down the middle by a giant ravine. No troops were ever called

upon to attack over more rugged and dangerous country, but
even so, Anzac and Gurkha infantrymen almost reached their
objective. The 6th Gurkha Battalion actually reached the crest
of the plateau on the night of August 8th, and held on all next
day, being relieved on the night of the 9th by the 9th Gurkhas.

MUSTAFA KEMAL

At dawn on August 10th, 1915, six thousand Turks, led by
their fanatical but brave commander, Mustafa Kemal, made a
tremendous assault on the Anzac Corps positions from Hill Q,
and Chunuk Bair. The all-night Turkish artillery bombardment
ceased at 4.30 a.m. as masses of Turks charged down the slopes of
Chunuk Bair, intent on driving the British into the sea. An early
morning mist, intermingled with the remains of cold, dewy night
air, drifted around the hills, giving a ghost-like appearance to
Turkish and British troops locked in battle.

Very soon the warmth of the sun dispersed the mist, and the
Turkish masses, now half-way down the slopes of Chunuk Bair,
became clearly visible. Every Anzac gun on the peninsula
opened up. The Turks were sweeping all opposition aside, but
they were caught in a trap. The slaughter was terrible. The dead
lay in heaps as battalion after battalion came on, yelling and
shouting like madmen.

Huge shells from British battleships exploded among the massed
ranks of the attacking Turks. Great pieces of earth mixed up
with human bodies were seen hurled into the air and then dashed
to the ground or down deep ravines. Even this artillery fire might
not have stopped the Turkish advance, had it not been for the
concentrated fire of a battery of ten machine-guns belonging to
a New Zealand brigade which maintained a rapid fire until the
gun barrels were smoking with heat.

Enormous losses were inflicted on the Turks, and only a mere
handful of Kemal's six battalions ever got back to their own side
of the Chunuk Bair.

MASSACRE AT THE FARM

Around a place called 'the farm'—a tiny plot of pasture with
a shepherd's hut in the middle, perched on the edge of a moun-

tain-like ridge—the fighting was savage. Masses of Turks swarmed down to the farm, which was held by British troops. Fierce hand-to-hand struggles and bayonet fighting took place on a scale seldom seen before. Officers of high rank fought alongside private soldiers. Among senior officers killed was General Baldwin.

A machine-gunner describes the massacre :

> Fallen men lay strewn all over the place—we saw bodies lying four and five deep on barbed wire entanglements, and Turkish survivors of the attack retreating, followed by relentless death. It was a terrible sight.

By midnight on August 10th, 1915, Kemal's effort to drive the British into the sea had failed, but it was a near thing, when the Turks at one spot reached within half a mile of the Anzac beaches. The massed New Zealand machine-gun fire had in no small way prevented Mustafa Kemal from achieving his objective.

Of the 20,000 assault troops General Birdwood committed to this gigantic battle only 8,000 were left when night closed in on August 10th.

*   *   *

The gallantry of the April landings, the grim struggle for control of the hills of Suvla, and the Australian attack on Sari-Bair were of no avail.

Between December 29th, 1915, and January 6th, 1916, the Gallipoli peninsula was evacuated, but 50,000 British and Commonwealth young men had died on those blood-stained hills during a campaign that lasted barely nine months. And of course thousands upon thousands of brave Turkish young men shared the same fate.

4

On the Western Front

Every front line soldier serving on the Western Front hoped he would be lucky enough to spend Christmas Day in billets. Of course only a small percentage were able to do so, but one machine-gunner was lucky :

I was in the machine-gun section on the 11th Inniskillings, 36th Ulster Division, attached to 'B' Company. On Christmas Eve, 1915, we were relieved at 8 p.m. and marched through the mud down Jacob's Ladder, from the old cemetery on the left of Beaumont Hamel, to the main Martinsart-Asnex road.

When we were about to turn left to our billets in Martinsart, a messenger from HQ met us with the information that our billets had been taken over by a football team and supporters from 108 Brigade for the inter–brigade football match at Martinsart on Christmas Day.

Transport was awaiting us, we were told, and the messenger would guide us to our temporary billets. So off we set and in due course all were billeted in barns, etc., except our machine-gun section and about 26 men of 6 platoon. We were marched on, and eventually arrived at a cluster of houses and a very large barn attached to a farmyard complete with pond. We were very tired, but not too tired to notice that there were seven ducks swimming on the pond. After a drum-up (tea) very soon all was quiet, so six of us slipped out of the billet, and quickly captured the seven ducks, silenced them, and safely deposited them until the morning.

Reveille with a difference

Reveille on Christmas morning was not by bugle, but by the Frenchman (late owner of the ducks) and he was making some noise. A chap in our machine-gun section could speak French like a Frenchie, so he held a discussion with the farmer and tried to calm him down. It was no use. 'I am going straight to the General,' said the irate farmer. I noticed that the Frenchman was smoking an empty pipe, so I filled his pipe and he quietened down a little. It was then I remembered that we had a platoon issue of tobacco in our gun limbers, but nobody would smoke it as it appeared to be made of rubber cuttings and weeds, and when smoked left a smell around like a blacksmith shoeing a horse. I nipped down to transport lines, got a tin of this vile tobacco and offered it as a peace-offering to the French farmer. He opened the tin, carefully examined the contents, and then gleefully accepted the gift.

In a few moments we had collected the entire stock of issue tobacco (about 40 4 oz. tins) and handed them over. So great was the farmer's satisfaction that he decided to consign the General —who was to be his ally—to warmer climes. Off he went and was soon back with about 10 stone of potatoes, several turnips, a crate of honey and a barrel of French cider. The seven ducks were roasted in clay castings, and what a Christmas dinner we prepared.

We invited the French farmer and his wife as guests, and to our delight—and surprise—they accepted, but the only drawback was he would not stop smoking that awful tobacco, which he declared was much better than the sample I had given him. To sort of ease our conscience a little more we presented Madame with a few tins of bully-beef and Ticklers jam.

When we left on January 26th, for another spell 'up there' the farmer and his wife conveyed us to the main road, a distance of four kilometres.

For us it had turned out to be a Christmas of goodwill, and we sang as we marched towards the trenches, where man's inhumanity to man continued.

RELIEVING THE GURKHAS

Just after Christmas 1915 the weather was absolutely bitter with a wind which cut like a knife made of ice.

We had to take over from the Gurkhas a stretch of line where months before there had been heavy fighting at the battle of Neuve Chapelle. Bodies lay everywhere and even dangled from the wire. The ground there was waterlogged, no trenches could be dug, and the defences were only parapets with the occasional parados. There were no dugouts, just corrugated shelters here and there.

The rats there were the largest ever, and so fat with feeding on the bodies that they could only waddle along. They were pink in colour because they had hardly any hair on them, and when you cornered one it screamed like a frightened child. If you socked one it only lay about and added to the general all pervading smell of death. Nothing was safe from the robbers.

I was writing a letter on one occasion when the light began to flicker and I looked up just in time to see a huge rat carrying off the lighted candle. If you went to sleep with a biscuit in your pocket you woke up to find your pocket bitten away and your biscuit gone!

The trenches were knee-, and sometimes waist-deep in very sticky, stinking mud, with the occasional submerged body tripping you up as you made your way round.

Icicles festooned the machine-gun positions, and crosses marked places where heavily burdened soldiers had fallen down and been drowned in the mud at night.

The poor Gurkhas were in a desperate condition, frostbitten and unbelievably exhausted.

None the less they handed over all the SAA and trench stores, wished us good luck and, supporting each other, staggered off through the mud to the communication trenches and way out.

Half an hour later, a Gurkha runner came back with a message from their Commanding Officer to say one of his men had gone beserk on the way out, killed two of his comrades with his kukri and made his way back to our trenches! would we shoot him on sight!

After dark when making our rounds we were far more scared of that one Gurkha than the whole German Army, and could see him in every shadow. However, he was never heard of again.

THE SOMME OFFENSIVE OF 1916

Twenty-six British and fourteen French Divisions took part in the great Somme offensive which began on July 1st, 1916, and continued until early November of the same year. The main object of this momentous and ghastly affair—when 60,000 British soldiers became casualties on the first day of the attack—was to ease the terrible strain on the French army, slowly bleeding to death defending Verdun.

The Somme offensive was fought over a 25 miles frontage, north and south of the Somme river. Only seven miles was captured and the cost was terrible, there being three-quarters of a million British and French casualties. The Germans have since referred to the Somme battles as the 'bath of blood' for it was an orgy of slaughter unparalleled in human history.

Ordinary soldiers wondered why it was allowed, but it was 'not theirs to reason why.'

Throughout the Somme battles the Vickers machine-gun was the main front-line weapon of the British forces, and so remained until the end of the war.

If it were possible to record every action fought by machine-gunners in the Somme battles, it would fill a book in itself.

Here is an account by an N.C.O. of 168 Machine Gun Company of his part in the offensive :

Our part in the battle began a few days before zero hour on July 1st. One of our regular duties was to go out at night time, over the top from the Hebuterns side of Gommecourt Wood, and put up a barrage of overhead fire on German communications, ration parties, etc. This was supplementary to the British artillery harassing fire.

I used to take a four-gun section to a registered spot with about 3,500 rounds of belted ammo, and keep going until all was expended. It was no picnic, and when it rained, which it often did, the whole lot—men, guns and equipment—got into a frightful muddy mess which took a good deal of our rest time to clear up.

The great day approached, and throughout the night of June 30th, the British artillery bombarded the German lines.

The news got round that the 'Rangers' (my old battalion) and the London Scottish were to be the assault battalions in our section. Two of our machine-guns were to go over the top with the first wave of the London Scottish and two with the second wave. My role was to serve two guns in a newly-dug trench in dead ground in front of our normal lines, where a dug-out had been constructed under the wire, with two forward openings for machine-gun emplacements.

Here we could supply overhead fire in support of the assault waves on July 1st. And so it came to pass.

The preliminary bombardment had alerted the Germans to the imminent attack and they fairly plastered the whole of our line in retaliation. At daylight the first wave went over and I saw the machine-guns with the London Scottish leave.

There were two corporals as No. 1's, each carrying tripods; they returned later in the day and each was awarded the Military Medal for his work. Our own two guns were not called forward.

We kept on steadily throughout the day, though somewhat disrupted by the damage done by enemy fire, necessitating the rebuilding of the gun emplacement. One lucky shot was to send the gun, tripod, and all its platform slithering down the steps of the dugout, but no one was hit, and after a time repairs were effected. For my share of the day's work I collected three 'highly commended' cards (from G.O.C. Division, Brigadier General, and Company Commander).

In later years I have often been asked what the trenches were like and how the High Command obtained the vital information from the front on which to base their fateful decisions.

I have always wondered this myself. I do remember my company Commander and his Warrant Officer coming round, also a frightened cinema operator, who put his camera over the top of a communication trench, took a brief exposure and then scuttled away for dear life, but I cannot recall ever seeing a senior officer, much less a general, in any part of the line which I was occupying. Communications were appalling and chiefly made by the two-footed runners—heroes every one.

Reading later of the optimism of the General Staff about the destruction of enemy wire and dug-outs, one can only conjecture they thought of German dug-outs as of similar type and strength to our puny affairs. A grave misconception.

We were relieved after the first day of the Somme offensive, and no wonder, considering the casualties the division suffered in what was afterwards learned was merely a diversionary attack.

We went back to rest billets, being in no fit state to take any further part in the offensive. The next two months were spent regrouping and receiving reinforcements.

MEMORIES OF THE SOMME

(July 1st to October 1916, by an N.C.O. of X100 Machine Gun Company)

The whole of the Somme battlefield was blazing with fire when our draft of machine-gunners set off for the line in the last hour of daylight. Our limbers went off at five-minute intervals straight up the metalled road to the line. Tattered poplars still lined it on both sides. Shell-holes had been filled with rubble, which assisted our transport to keep going safely. As it grew dark we passed through the zone of field-batteries, the guns banging away ear-splittingly to left and right. The whistles of the approaching enemy projectiles were faint and intriguingly harmless, and the bursts came nowhere near us. Indeed, the whistles could scarcely be heard above the clamour of our own barrage and the rumble of our wheels.

It was a beautiful night, cool and star-lit, and the scene was continually lit by sheet-lightning, sudden balls of glowing orange, and twinkling sparks of red. The fitful landscape appeared in romantic flashes, with no suggestion of waste or ruin.

We came to a small hollow at the foot of a brief and gentle rise, a place called Frenchy's Cross. A solitary grave stood by the road-side, marked by an ornate white-painted wooden cross, and bearing a date in October, 1914. Beyond here and to the top of the rise the ground was incredibly battered and strewn with splintered debris. The stench of many corpses was overpowering. The front line was a thousand yards ahead.

A Guide joined us. 'This way; single file' he commanded—and led us into a communication-trench that wound its way towards the hamlet, well clear of the road. In places the sides of the road were down, and the bottom undulated over debris that had been trampled smooth. It seemed a terribly long way, and just as I began to notice ragged bits of timber and fragments of wall above the trench, there came a steady series of low whistles. They were easily distinguishable above the barrage, and each was followed by a 'pop'.

'Gas shells,' came the muttered warning down the line of carriers.

We dumped our loads and drew the face-piece of our respira-tors from the satchel on our chest. The face-piece was the new kind with a nose-clip. We kept on halting, dumping our loads, and sniffing past the edge of the mask to see if we dare take it off. At last our Guide scrambled out of the trench, took off his respirator, and said it would be better if we kept on top, above the gas. We set off again, but now had to climb in and out of every transverse trench, occasionally getting whiffs of the eye-sting-ing, throat-irritating gas.

After one of these episodes the second bomb-carrier cast down his load and sat on the parapet and burst into tears, declaring he could go no further. The gas shells went *wheew-pop*, and the fire from an enemy machine-gun was much sharper now. We shared some of the poor chap's load and persuaded him to keep on. 'Silly turd,' said the Guide, unemotionally. 'It's a quiet night really; and nice and dry.'

We had to push our way through bits of occupied trench. There were troops everywhere; some on the move, and some in residence. At every encounter the residents resented our intru-

sion, and angry N.C.O.'s told us to make less noise, to hurry past
danger-points, to beware of dead and wounded lying in the
trench, and to keep low. At one deserted place two bodies blocked
the way. We began to put them over the top when there was a
sudden burst of machine-gun fire. The Guide gave a loud cry and
fell. 'He's got officers' rations,' said someone, and went to remove
the load from the huddled figure. The Guide, however, arose
cursing, and said no one was going to pinch his officers' rations,
which indeed had been the predatory intention. The bulky sandbag he carried contained delicacies such as jars of tongue and
tins of peaches. An enemy machine-gun bullet had hit the nose-
cap of his slung rifle, shattering it and throwing him to the
ground with a numbed shoulder.

At last we came to an empty stretch of old but well-revetted
trench. The Guide led us to the timbered entrance of a shelter
built with parados. Inside was a shallow pit about ten feet
square, roofed with sagging smoke-blackened timbers covered
with a thin layer of earth. The sides were lined with narrow wire-
netting bunks. 'It's a good place,' said the Guide, proudly. There
was a brazier for heating and cooking, and other primitive amenities. Built as a company headquarters by the French when the
line was first stabilised in 1914, it was still serving its original
purpose. It was in the complex of support trenches, about two
hundred yards behind the front line.

'We've got nothing to do till the lads go over the top,' announced the Guide. 'The O.C. is in a dug-out a bit further along.
He's got a buzzer to Brigade H.Q. and he'll send a runner if he
wants anything.'

I had arrived. The barrage roared on. I lay down on one of
the bunks and was instantly asleep.

*   *   *

When I awoke it was hardly possible to hear oneself speak.
Jock Cohen was shaking my shoulder and shouting in my ear,
'It's stand-to, Corp,' I sat up and gratefully took the mug of
gunfire (tea) he was offering.

The ground pulsed like the deck of a ship, and black dust was
coming down from the timbers overhead.

Outside it was just light enough to see a part of the enemy
lines. The whole earth spouted, making an unbroken curtain.
The air above us seemed to be roofed-in with the unceasing rush
of projectiles. I stood half out of the trench, awed and fascinated
by the sight and sound. Surely nothing could be left alive over

there. Nothing seemed to be coming back at us. A signal-light rose serenely out of the erupting landscape and hung in the paling sky.

Now I could sense a traffic in the air going the other way: enemy shells were falling in the hamlet behind us and among the massed field-guns. The maelstrom in front continued, but after a while I perceived that the curtain of fire had moved. It had crept eastwards, and where it had been there was now a less-solid flurry of enemy shells falling among a few moving figures. I looked for a long time.

At last I was called to breakfast: a rasher of bacon, a wedge of bread, apricot jam, margarine, and tea, all flavoured with scraps of hessian from the sandbags in which the rations had been carried. We still waited for orders to move. The sun was shining, and suddenly I heard a bird sing. THE BARRAGE HAD STOPPED. I jumped up and looked forward. The landscape was utterly still in the sunlight, greatly scarred and littered, but still showing green in places.

Into the Attack (July 4th, 1916)

At about ten in the morning a runner arrived in the trench with orders. The bomb-squad was to leave its heavy kit and go up in fighting-order and report to number two section: the runner would show the way. We gave him tea before making a start. He had nothing to say about the battle, except that we had not gone far as yet. He led us along the trench to where it met the road from Frenchy's Cross—a surprisingly short distance. We walked along the road towards the enemy, well apart and in single file. The silence was almost complete; one could hear insects in the patches of rank grass beside the long-unused highway.

We continued forward along the scarcely distinguishable road till we came to the bottom of a dip in the middle of no-man's-land. At a place where the bank in a field was rather higher than its surroundings, we came on a sprawled group of infantrymen. 'Get down, you bloody fools,' said their sergeant in an angry whisper. 'You've come all the way in full sight of Jerry.' This spot had been their jumping-off point at dawn. A broken trail of white webbing still led to it from a gap in our barbed-wire.

Shocked, I asked where the enemy were.

'There was no one in his front line,' explained the sergeant. 'His front line was no longer there. We were caught by the machine-guns in his support line, and that's where they still are, looking straight down on us. Why they didn't wipe you out I don't know. I suppose everybody's knocked-off for a cup of char. Here's something better.'

He handed me a nearly empty petrol tin. I tipped it to drink, and nearly choked. The contents were neat rum sickeningly laced with the original petrol.

'Give the others some,' urged the sergeant. 'We don't want any more : it was the ration for the whole company, and didn't come up in time.'

'Where's the rest of the company?' I asked.

The sergeant pointed. I knelt up and looked. Not far away there were hummocks of churned ground where the enemy front line HAD been. Nearer still the pale soil was churned up into encrusted clumps and tangles and stumps of half-destroyed wire, and among the remains were fantastic khaki dolls in all attitudes from fully prone to grotequely upright. From the wire to the enemy front line, and beyond, the bodies lay in decreasing swathes so that the top of the insignificant ridge, no more than three hundred yards away, was unencumbered.

*   *   *

As the days, weeks and months passed, we who were spared began to know something of the truth about this long-drawn-out battle; but we did not suspect that the British dead totalled a quarter of a million. We did hear that the ambulance-trains were re-timed to arrive at Charing Cross only during the small hours. After the war, one set of official figures recorded 800,000 British casualties in the four months of the Somme 1916 offensive—and the proportion of dead was always about one in three.

We were involved not in a GREAT PUSH, but in 'stunts'—grandeloquently-heralded attacks that petered out in bloody futility. In the end the word was applied to all offensives.

We often knew that a stunt was coming by the massing of lines of tethered horses in all the back areas. The ominous phenomenon recurred throughout 1916, 1917, and 1918. The cavalry was being assembled to exploit an imagined break-through.

Almost to the end our masters clung to an astonishing belief : bullets, they maintained, had little stopping-power against a horse. If only the wretched infantry could breach the line, the cavalry would be in 'Lille' in a matter of hours. The realities of positional warfare and the supremacy of the caddish machine-gun were calmly discounted, and the sacrificial role of the infantry taken for granted.

I was in headquarters dug-out one afternoon. It was our third

day in the line following a rest period, and there was to be a
stunt in the morning. From the previous day's sniping I knew
that we faced a sector strong in defensive weapons. I was thankful not to be going over the top with the first wave.

No one was about except the duty signaller, who had a line
to the command post of the infantry battalion. Suddenly he
motioned me to take the spare headphone, whispering in an awed
voice, 'It's the Corps Commander.'

'I'm up with the Division,' the voice was saying, 'What is
your trouble?'

On the buzzing, crackling earth-return line I heard the infantry C.O. giving an account of local enemy dispositions: he was
deprecating the orders of the attack.

The reply was a reiteration of the orders. 'What's the matter
with you, man? Cold feet?'

The line crackled on for a while. 'You must expect losses,' said
the voice finally, 'There's nothing to worry about; I'm putting in
masses of stuff behind you.'

The signaller and I looked at each other. We, and many more,
were the 'stuff' that would be put in after the immolation of the
first wave.

No other experience throughout the war made a deeper impression on me.

*   *   *

By mid morning of the next day the survivors of the first and
second waves were back in our front line, but the line was no
longer continuous. An enemy counter-attack had made a lodge-
ment in our trenches somewhere to the left. I was told to take
a gun forward to stiffen the front line, and then bomb left-handed
along the trench to clear it of the enemy.

We got there all right, and laid the gun on an S.O.S. line to
deny the ground between the enemy main position and the part
of our line held by the intruders.

It was during these operations that my luck gave out. I felt a
numbing blow on my foot and severe pins and needles in my leg.
A shell burst very close with a great 'crump', followed by the fury
of explosions all around. I lay on my back with my arm over my
face to keep off the falling earth, and waited for the bombardment to subside. After a long time the shelling became intermit-
tent, and our artillery seemed to be playing a part.

I tried to sit up, and found that my left leg was quite stiff. The
heel of the boot was torn off, and from ankle to knee my calf was
a ragged pudding of congealed red jelly kept together by the half-

D

shredded puttee. I supposed my leg to be shattered, but in fact all I had was a dozen superficial wounds, some torn muscle, and a hole through the flesh of the ankle. The burst of machine-gun bullets had skimmed the calf of my leg as I lay on the edge of the crater. I sat in a shell-hole as in an armchair, the leg stretched before me. It was best to leave it alone, I thought. The puttee was holding, and the blood was well clotted.

Two stretcher bearers came out for me directly it was dark. It was not far to the collecting point, and I got there helped by two men with arm wounds on opposite sides. The collecting point was littered with badly-wounded cases, and everyone was on edge, expecting the Evening Hate (shelling) at any moment. Helping each other, we bypassed the diagnostic-disposal process, and got straight into the queue for the ambulance-train.

Twenty-four hours later we were in hospital in the north of England. It was like heaven on earth.

*   *   *

A gunner who served with 50th Company, 17th Division, tells his story :

I shall never forget the Somme. After a few quiet weeks at Armentières, we marched to the rear of the Somme battlefields, where thousands of troops were bivouacking, waiting for the day, July 1st, 1916. The weather was most comfortable, but uppermost in my thoughts was the coming big push.

This air of expectation cast a shadow over everything. At night the sky was lit up by the flashes from hundreds of British artillery guns, firing shells of all sizes. It seemed impossible for anything to survive in Jerry's lines.

At dawn on July 1st, 1916, we were marched, in full battle order, to a point at the rear of Fricourt, where we occupied places in a sunken road, remaining there all that day.

The 50th Brigade, of which we were part, made attack after attack, only to be cut down by German machine-guns which could not be located. Casualties were particularly high among the East and West Yorks and the Dorsets.

It was not until next day (July 2nd) that the German machine-gun post, which had held us up, was silenced for good. After that we advanced with fair progress and later that day Fricourt was captured.

All that summer we were fighting on the Somme; two weeks or more in the line, and then out for a rest for a week or so.

As each spell 'up front' came and went, I lost more of my chums. Rations were never certain to reach us and we were obliged to take cover, often for long periods, in mere grooves in the ground, from which we operated our guns.

As the battle fizzled out, it became like a ghastly nightmare. I remember seeing the body of a soldier (unknown regiment) who had been killed in the early days of the Somme and each time we went up the line, the body was in exactly the same position, and left there until it eventually became a skeleton. Another thing I well remember, I spent my eighteenth birthday in Trench P.2.A.

Among the numerous machine-gun companies that went into action on the first day of the Somme offensive of 1916, was the 10th Brigade M.G.C. The commander of this company, who later on became a Brigadier, says :

Towards the end of 1915, I think in November, I took my machine-gun section of the 1st Battalion Royal Irish Fusiliers, together with the M.G. sections of the Royal Warwickshire's, 2nd Seaforth Highlanders, and the 2nd Royal Dublin Fusiliers, to form the new 10th Brigade Machine Gun Company.

For six months we followed normal trench routine until we withdrew to rest areas to prepare for the Somme.

On July 1st we went into action between Serre and Beaument Hamel and had a very bad day with four officers killed and one wounded out of nine, with a corresponding loss of N.C.O.'s and men.

Licking our wounds, we were moved to the Ypres Salient— hardly the place for a rest cure—where we remained for two months. I remember the Corps Commander, Hunter-Weston, come galloping round in a flurry of red to say goodbye to his troops.

Back we went to the Somme where we went in again in front of Les-Boeufs and had another dreadful day, or rather night, in October. We suffered badly and were pretty well crippled. For the next few months mud was a worse enemy than the Boche, until spring came again, but by that time there were very few survivors of my original Machine Gun Company.

WITH 100TH MACHINE GUN COMPANY AT HIGH WOOD

The great British Somme offensive of July 1916 had been in progress for 14 days when the 33rd Division, which included the

100th Machine Gun Company, was ordered to attack a German strong point at High Wood.

The following extract from The History and Memoir of the 33rd Battalion Machine Gun Corps describes this action :

At dawn of July 15th, 1916, a thick ground mist covered the whole of the valley lying east of the village of Bazentin, completely obscuring High Wood and Martinpuich.

The 100th Infantry Brigade concentrated in the valley about 800 yards east of High Wood. There was no cover of any sort to help the attackers across one mile of no-man's-land.

The first Battalion of the Queen's Regiment was ordered to attack on the left, and the 9th (T) Battalion H.L.I. on the right, the attack being supported by the 16 (S) Battalion K.R.R.C. with the 2nd Battalion Worcester Regiment in reserve. Each battalion in the forward wave was supported by one machine-gun section (four guns), that with the H.L.I. (Glasgow Rangers) under Lt. Huxley and that with the Queen's under Lt. Heseltine. Under cover of the mist the transport was able to get forward to the area of concentration.

Meanwhile the 98th Brigade with its machine-gun company was concentrated in positions in the eastern outskirts of Bazentin-le-Petit. At 9 a.m. the mist rose. The attack was ordered at 9.30 a.m. Under cover of a weak bombardment the attack swept forward, to be met on both flanks by murderous machine-gun fire from the Wood itself and from Martinpuich. Both the Queen's and the H.L.I. were practically annihilated. Lt. Heseltine was seriously wounded and Lt. Huxley was killed. At the same time, an enemy bombardment of great intensity was opened.

By 10 a.m. the attack was held up. Captain Hutchison then moved forward the remaining two machine-gun sections under the hottest fire to within 150 yards of the wood, to engage the enemy who were posted in the trees. He then rushed forward two companies of the 16th K.R.R.C., who had no officers left, in support of the guns. This fire inflicted heavy casualties upon the enemy, particularly the guns of Lt. C. L. Davey, Sergeant Barnes, and Lt. Vaughan-Williams, who broke up a strong enemy counter-attack on the wood. During this engagement Vaughan-Williams was killed.

By 12 noon the Worcestershires were able to obtain a footing in the wood, and the 98th Brigade began to come up on the left, and fill the gap in which the 1st Queen's had been wiped out. The casualties of the 100th Machine Gun Company now numbered five officers and forty-four other ranks.

The Brigade on the right was now showing signs of weakness and began to dribble back. An attempt was made to hold them, but the opposition was too great. This exposed the right flank of the 100th Brigade on the south-east side of the wood.

The situation was most desperate and at 3 p.m., owing to the very heavy casualties of the Brigade, it was thought that the ground won could not be held. The complete teams of six guns of 100th M. G. Company were casualties. These guns were gathered up by Captain Hutchison, Lt. Davey, Lt. Williams, Sgt. Barnes, Private Smith and Private Diskin and got into action as a battery guarding the right flank of the Brigade, whilst the remaining guns were disposed in groups covering the whole front. No further support came. It was apparent at 5 p.m. that the whole attack had been a costly failure.

During the night the remains of the 100th Machine Gun Company, with its guns, occupied a small trench just west of the wood. The German bombardment became so severe that it was decided to retire still further. Had this decision not been taken there is no doubt that the company would have perished to a man.

On the morning of the 16th, the 19th Brigade relieved the 100th Brigade and what was left of us returned to defensive positions on the north side of Mametz Wood.

The following awards were made for the action : Military Cross : Captain Hutchison, Lieutenant Davey; D.C.M. : Sergeant Barnes (and direct Commission in the Field for Gallantry); D.C.M. : Private Diskin; D.C.M. : Private Bradbury; M.M. : Private W. Smith.

Fighting of the bitterest nature followed, in which both the 19th and 98th Brigades were involved. The Cameronians and the 5th Scottish Rifles in particular sustained very heavy losses.

It was apparent that the attack was held up, and the retention of the ground gained became more and more costly owing to very heavy shell fire. Trenches and communications were dug by night by the 18th Middlesex Regiment (Pioneers) only to be obliterated by daylight. It was possible to sit on the western edge of High Wood and actually see the heavy shells in the air for about the last 40 feet of their descent before the deafening roar of their explosion and the upheaval of earth and roots and clouds of brown earth.

Early in August the Division was relieved for a short rest and bivouacked in the battle area around Mametz Wood.

The 100th Machine Gun Company was ordered to place guns in the 1st Division area, Contalmaison, to reduce the fire from

Martinpuich, flanking our High Wood position. Sniping in this area was very severe and the German snipers exceedingly bold.

Lieutenant Hyland, in charge of the guns, was killed whilst searching in broad daylight for these snipers in no-man's-land.

The First Machine-gun Barrage

The 33rd Division, having been reinforced, resumed the offensive upon High Wood and the high ground between High Wood and Delville-Wood on August 18th. During the interval which had elapsed between the 15th July and this date, the Germans had considerably strengthened their positions; and it was necessary for minor operations to seize certain important trenches before a general attack was made. This done, an attack on a wide front was planned for August 24th. It is believed that, for the first time in the history of machine-guns, a machine-gun barrage was planned to cover this attack, the guns employed being those of the 19th and 100th Machine Gun Companies and of the 14th and 23rd Divisions.

Both the 19th and 98th Brigades had already obtained tactical advantages at High Wood and in the recapture of Orchard Trench, Black Watch Trench and the snipers' post east of Black Watch Trench. Sergeant Beard of the 98th Machine Gun Company was awarded the Military Medal for gallantry whilst assisting the 2nd Argyll and Sutherland Highlanders in a further attack through High Wood.

The 100th Brigade was ordered to carry out the attack on the 33rd Divisional front. For this attack six machine-guns were grouped in Savoy Trench, from where a magnificent view was obtained of the German line at a range of about 2,000 yards. These guns were disposed for barrage. On August 23rd and the night of the 23rd-24th, the whole Company was, in addition to the two companies of infantry lent for the purpose, employed in carrying water and ammunition to this point.

Many factors in machine-gun barrage work, which became common knowledge later in the war, had not been learned or considered at the time of the firing of the first machine-gun barrage.

In the orders of the 100th Machine Gun Company's barrage of ten guns, Captain Hutchison (O.C.) requested that a rapid fire should be maintained continuously for twelve hours, to cover the attack and consolidation. The gunners did that, and the Vickers gun proved its stamina.

During the attack on the 24th, 250 rounds short of one million were fired by ten guns : at least four petrol tins of water besides all the water bottles of the Company and the urine tins from the neighbourhood were emptied into the guns for cooling purposes; a continuous party was employed carrying ammunition. Private Robertshaw and Artificer H. Bartlett between them maintained a belt-filling machine in action without stopping for a single moment for twelve hours.

At the end of this time many of the N.C.O.'s and gunners were almost asleep on their feet from sheer exhaustion. The gun team of Sergeant P. Dean, D.C.M., fired just over 120,000 rounds. The attack was a brilliant success, and all objectives were taken within a short time. Cpl. Smith, M.M., was awarded a bar to his M.M. Cpl. Hendrie, Lcpl. Sorbie and Gunners McIntyre and Ogden (both the latter being runners) were all awarded the Military Medal.

Prisoners examined at Divisional and Corps H.Q. reported that the effect of the machine-gun barrage was annihilating, and the counter-attacks which had attempted to retake the ground lost were broken up whilst being concentrated east of Flers Ridge and High Wood.

In this action the M.G.C. Transport men did sterling work, facing the perils and horrors of the valley of death and the green dump, the valley being continuously soaked in gas, and an unceasing bombardment being maintained upon its whole length. The casualties were not heavy on this occasion but Sergeant Oates was killed—a great loss.

The operations ended with the capture of Delville-Wood, but the north-east corner of High Wood still remained in the hands of the Boche.

At the end of September 1916 the Division was withdrawn from the forward area and proceeded by train to Longpré to the Longpré-Airaines area, where we were billeted for a rest period.

CARNOY VALLEY

It was during the Somme offensive in 1916 that we, the 166 Machine Gun Company, found ourselves in trench dug-outs in Carnoy Valley. The trench, like the valley itself, was in enfilade (or end on) from the German line about 1½ to 2 miles away. The dug-outs were what the Army called 'baby elephants' being half hoops of channelled steel bolted together to form an arched protection from the weather and also from shell splinters. As an aid to some precarious protection from a small shell-burst they were covered with earth about a couple of sandbags thick.

These 'baby elephants' were adjacent to each other, and were open-ended into the enfiladed trench. We were in reserve at this position for a week or so.

Each morning, as daylight came, we could see and count a line of German 'sausage' balloons, each with its observer equipped with powerful field glasses, and in telephone communication with the ground crews. They were, of course, captive observation balloons.

One day, in company orders, we heard with dismay that, owing to our being confined to the trench dug-outs, it was necessary that we had some exercise so, for half an hour each morning, we were to parade in the open valley and perform physical exercises. I was appalled at this asinine order.

So the next morning at 7 o'clock we scrambled out of the trench and lined up for physical jerks. There in front of us were half a dozen German balloons. I felt like a fly under a microscope, and wondered how long it would be before a German battery gave us a good strafing.

I told my section to be ready to make a dive for it. We performed our antics for three or four mornings, and we were not molested by the Germans. But one afternoon, as we sat in our dug-outs, a 5.9 inch shell shrieked towards us and exploded at the end of the trench nearest to the front line, and about five yards to one side. A few minutes later, another shell screamed over and landed about fifty yards further along the trench, and on the other side. After a further interval a third shell plummeted over, still further along the trench and on the side where the first one had dropped. We knew then that we were 'registered'. No further shell came over.

That night, much to our relief, another machine-gun company took over from us, and we moved back to the Pommiere Redoubt area about three or four miles to the rear.

The next day we had a report that the dug-out in Carnoy Valley had been violently shelled after midnight, and the company which had relieved us had been decimated.

Our feelings were very mixed. We felt thankful that we had been relieved the previous night, but we also felt great sorrow for the poor fellows who had been killed as a result of our foolhardy P.T. exercises in the open valley.

It could be argued that the shelling might have taken place, P.T. or no P.T., but we veterans knew that it was foolish to flaunt our presence in the manner we did, and in broad daylight. If P.T. had been deemed essential, we could have performed our exercises at night. The tragedy was that we, who inspired the shell attack, escaped the consequences, and some other poor fellows suffered.

I shall never forget Carnoy Valley.

(By an ex-gunner of 166 M.G.C.).

THE SICK PARADE, AND NUMBER 9

In modern times the word 'pill' hits the headlines of the press. Veterans of the Kaiser's war were well acquainted with another kind of pill, Number 9, which was always much in evidence. Old sweats used to say that the way to Blighty was paved with Number 9's, for the infantry medical officers were never without ample stocks.

Number 9's were expected to cure trench feet, the aching tooth and ingrowing toe nails, to lower the temperature, restore lost appetite, regulate the pulse, heal the boil on the official place and cure scabies. Indeed the Number 9 was the M.O.'s answer to the soldier's prayer, always provided the soldier had the faith that removes mountains, for the Number 9 would remove anything. Whether it endowed the sick soldier with synthetic courage to face the Medical Officer at 7 a.m. was extremely doubtful, for the M.O. could scarcely be in a happy frame of mind at such an early hour, knowing that he had to deal with 30 or 40 men who could usually be relied upon to put forward ingenious reasons enabling them to qualify for a ticket to Blighty.

Before the formation of the Machine Gun Corps, machine-gunners wishing to report sick paraded with the battalion in which they served, but when the M. G. Corps was inaugurated machine-gunners were divorced from their usual M.O. and there was no establishment for an M.O. with a machine-gun company. They were expected to report to the nearest unit.

No parade (sick) would be complete without the lead swinger. Many and varied are the stories relating to him. A machine-gunner who served with No. 184 Company, recalls an episode in which he featured :

In our lot was a real old soldier (South Africa and Indian Frontier) and when he discovered that the nearest Medical Aid Post was four miles distant, he gathered together a few of us younger old soldiers and propounded an idea which we thought a good one.

Several of our gun section reported sick and after breakfast swung off through the French countryside, without a care, and singing at the top of our voices :

Have you seen the Sergeant Major?
I know where he is, I know where he is, I know where he is,
Have you seen the Sergeant Major?
I know where he is,
He's hanging on the old barbed wire !
      Chorus (ff.)
We saw him, we saw him,
Hanging on the old barbed wire,
We saw him,
Hanging on the old barbed wire.

Confronted with a sub-section of very healthy young Emma Gees (nickname for machine-gunners) all trying to look ill, the M.O. said 'The M.G.C. never report sick when on duty in the line. The only time I see them is when they are carried in wounded, or when they are out on rest', and this most understanding man marked us all M. & D. (medicine and duty). The medicine was of course a Number 9.

An hour's march there, an hour's waiting, a surreptitious hour in the Estaminet (small restaurant) and an hour's return journey, landed us back just in time to be detailed for a ration fatigue party.

In the Battalion word soon got around when a new M.O. arrived. He might be sympathetic, but it was harder for a camel to get through the eye of a needle than for a bold hero, without a wound and without batting an eyelid, to get a ticket for Blighty ! The M.O. might appear to be sympathetic and listen, without any sign of having weighed up the hard luck story, but when the pulse was normal and the temperature O.K. he knew there was nothing wrong that the famous Number 9 couldn't put right. 'Come back in the morning if you don't feel any better' was the usual instruction. What that doctor and his orderlies didn't know about the healing properties of Number 9 was nobody's business. One thing was certain, it was no use going to the Shop Steward or going on strike.

Not all the artful dodges happened on official sick parades. In April, 1916, while in the Ypres area, a certain infantry soldier had 'a touch of gas', and two stretcher-bearers were carrying him down the Ypres road when Jerry strafed the area. The stretcher-bearers put the victim on the roadside, and sought cover in a nearby ditch. When the shelling died down they emerged from the ditch only to discover that the stretcher and occupant had disappeared.

Weeks later it was learned that the sick hero was in Blighty lecturing the second-line men on trench warfare. How did it come about? Apparently the 'gas' patient carried the stretcher to the field hospital, lay down on it outside the dressing station, and was soon on the way to Blighty.

P.S. It is only fair to say that the sick hero was not a machine-gunner.

WITH 142 MACHINE GUN COMPANY IN FRANCE

(August–September 1916)

I have had the use of Jimmy Wells' diaries as well as those of Lieut. Morris (those that were not lost), together with a lecture of friend Lewin, and these, together with the Divisional History, are the sum total of my references. In order that I may not be accused of having inside information not available to other authors, I am attaching a full record of the Company's movements, so far as I have been able to trace them. I should like to express my thanks to those named for having so willingly placed the documents at my disposal.

Just one other point. We were all pals together, and recollections cannot be given truly without personal references. Will all those mentioned in the pages following please take the references to themselves in a kindly way, and accept any roasting in the same spirit as they took their chaffing in the old days. And now, gunner, 'carry on'.

J. Gadsby

Having been in France only a few months with the 47th Division, during which time I ran across a pack of trouble in consequence of my dislike of too rigid discipline, I found myself detailed to join the 142 Machine Gun Company. I cannot say that I shed any tears on receiving the instructions. Note how carefully I am making distinction between orders and instructions. Instructions sounds better, and tends to make one feel something more than the very minute cog in the gigantic machine that one really is. I had no friends to mourn, and no particular chums. So although the instructions, blessed word, gave the officer imparting them a truly great satisfaction they left me quite unmoved. So I packed up, said goodbye to the farmyard hen, consoled myself with a soldier's farewell, albeit under my breath, and trudged a few miles to Lahoussoye, to join my new crowd, the fourth unit I had served with. Rumour had it that I was booked to carry ammunition during attacks, and if I survived this 'hard labour' I was to rejoin the 24th Battalion.

I cannot say that I was at all impressed with my reception, either at the Orderly Room or in the billet.

I was received by a very martial Sergeant Major, who did not give me the impression that I was conferring a favour on his Company by my presence. In fact I am of the opinion that he thought I should be a darned, but unfortunately necessary, nuisance. I was, as he was later to find. But I forget myself. It is necessary to give names, and this gruff being with the overgrown Chaplin moustache was one Sergeant Major A. J. Brian, known, as I was later to discover, amongst O.R.'s, (other ranks, not orderly rooms) as 'the old man'. First impressions are often misleading, and looking back now I think he fully deserved this rather affectionate title.

I was handed over to a Signaller who indicated the billet I was to grace with my presence, and he also informed a Lance-Corporal that I was attached to his team.

My first hour or so with the Company was hardly an auspicious start, and I found myself still in trouble. Having acquired a fairly clean bit of the mud floor I deposited my worldly possessions thereon, and wandered over to watch a card game in progress. This ended in a short time, and one of the players began showing a few card tricks. Before I go further perhaps a word of explanation should be given. Although I had been in the Army some 15 months I had never shown any tricks, although in 1913 I had appeared at our largest Music Hall in Chesterfield, and dozens of times since 1909 at concerts, dinners, and so on. But seeing a fellow artist must have awakened something, and prompted me to ask if I might show a few tricks. I was hardly prepared for the reception I got at the hands of my co-deceiver. 'What! you show us tricks. A country b——d like you.' Now unless the marriage and birth certificate I have are forgeries I am certainly not one of those, and this was a brand new epithet as applied personally, and one which I was not, at that time, accustomed to. High words and threats followed, and I almost had my first Company fight, and possibly hiding. At any rate we were restrained from physical violence on each other, and I was persuaded to carry on and show a few tricks, which I did, and this was the first of many dozens of times that I did my best to amuse my gun team.

Now a countryman joining a London unit is at a decided disadvantage. Londoners are naturally very proud of their city, and of their own close connection of the world's première port, and they are apt to look down a little pityingly on those from outside. I am not blaming them for that. Reverse the position and I should most probably do the same. But it is a great mistake to suppose that everyone living outside London is necessarily ignorant. In many ways perhaps we are rather lamblike* (I was wearing a 24th Battalion cap badge, remember) but quite a few have their buttons sewn on in the right places.

My first exposition of card tricks did a great deal to close the gap that at first is bound to be present if a lone country man is let loose among Londoners.

I was received with good-natured tolerance and, owing to the efforts of the Lance-Corporal, was made to feel more or less at home. That is, if one can possibly feel at home in a leaky barn with a floor remarkable only for the number of protuberances to the square foot, and its concrete-like softness. This Lance-Corporal was the first of many real friends I made and more important still, kept, in the 142nd Company.

He was pleasant, conscientious, not so witty as many cockneys I met, but still blessed with a quaint dry humour of his own, and altogether a real fine chap, and I was fortunate to be posted to his gun team. Ted Venis and I shared many hardships, and many a good time, and I never found him wanting, and to-day he still has the respect born that night in August, 1916, in the residence where awake or sleeping one got the effluvia of a rotting dung heap situate half right, distance eight feet, from the doorless entrance to our home.

The remaining fortnight or so spent at Lahoussoye was productive of little excitement. There remains just a vague recollection of the never-ending parades and field practice attacks which I am afraid did not interest me much. The floating about of aeroplanes dropping messages, the purport of which one never knew, failed to arouse enthusiasm, and the only thing one existed for was to lug boxes of ammunition here, there, and any old where, at the behest of one, two and three stripers and pippers. What it was all about no one seemed to know or care. Just 'muckin us

* Cap badge of 24th Battalion was a lamb.

abat' I think, to make us fit, and eager to do anything to ease the monotony.

Nothing was done to satisfy any curiosity I may have felt as to the mystery of the machine-gun. I suppose as a spare number it never struck anyone that there might come a time when a pseudo machine-gunner might, through necessity, have to fire the gun. Thank goodness they were right. I didn't.

But I did get to know one or two of the Company I was in immediate contact with. Venis, my guiding star, I have already mentioned. Then as number two we had Bill Ford. I stood about six feet, and Bill could give me an inch or two. Yet because of his excessive leanness Bill looked a foot taller. Number three was Tommy Newsum, a laughing Lancashire lad with whom one could never have a wrong word. He was the inventor of the 'duck-board crawl', and incidentally the quickest man I ever knew in stripping and re-assembling a machine-gun lock. I am writing many years afterwards, but I believe he could do the whole business in under ten seconds. Far fetched, you ex-gunners will say, but I shall refer to this special feat of his later, and the trouble it caused us.

Sam Giddings was our number four, a braw likeable Norfolk boy, who could laugh at his own misfortunes as well as yours, a rare accomplishment. Number five was Abrahams, our little Abe, of whom we thought so much that we willingly shared his un-leavened bread. A real likeable happy crew, and I felt myself perfectly comfortable with them. These were my comrades for many months, and I should go a long way before I found better. For the first time in my Army life in France I had found some-one I could really pull with, and I contemplated my leaving them at the conclusion of my 'attached' duty with a feeling of regret. I liked our fresh-faced Sergeant too. It struck me when I first met 'Punch' Lovel that he was out of his place here. He should never have worn khaki. He seemed to me to be the ideal type, with his fresh complexion and clear-cut features, for an officer on some man-of-war. Strange how these impressions strike one and stick. I also liked our Section Officer, Lieut. Ivory. He was a different type from those I had previously served under in France. Unstarched and human will best explain my meaning. And you got the impression that you were trusted.

The war to many of us was an episode—an unpleasant period of voluntarily giving up your liberty, and submitting, willingly or reluctantly, depending on the personality of your officer, to doing anything considered necessary to enable you to do your bit to-wards putting a scotch on the aims of Germany.

The Army as a career, or as a means of advancement, was the last thing one thought of. My own enthusiasm, willingness, even anxiety, to do my bit, was stifled early by the rather crude handling of inexperienced officers.

Admittedly a Tommy was unimportant, and his loss would never be felt. But so is every blade of grass in a field if taken separately. But we get haystacks. And so in these isolated unimportants lay the real strength of the British Army when considered in the aggregate. And I do think that it was mistaken policy that so many officers felt it their bounden duty to take any, and every, opportunity of impressing on the poor Tommy his utter uselessness.

The interest in his men's welfare shown by Lieut. Ivory, revealed by many little acts of thoughtfulness, revived a little of the willing spirit in me that had lain dormant far too long. You instinctively felt that you had a part to play, that here was a man who trusted you to play it, and that you would be letting him down badly if you failed. And because of that trust in us we were less likely to fail than if browbeaten and repeatedly told that we were less than a minus quantity. It was a new and a pleasanter atmosphere, and one in which I felt I should thrive.

*   *   *

All good things come to an end, and compared with what was to follow, our rest at Lahoussoye was good. About the 6th of September we moved forward through Albert.

I well remember marching through the desolate town, and I picture a ruined, burnt-out factory with twisted cycle frame still on what little of the walls was left standing. There was a statue of the Virgin and Child looking as if it would fall. As we marched underneath we discussed the legend that whichever side was responsible for bringing down the statue would lose the war.

What concerned most of us was not so much who won the war, as when it would be won. What untold misery had its cruel, bloody, course of over two years caused, and what would it cause before it was ended?

We marched through Fricourt and on to some old trench system. Here we were told to get down for the night. Out in the open here were a number of tents which sheltered a battalion of Northumberland Fusiliers. One or two of these tents I discovered to be unoccupied. In company with another gunner, Hodgkinson, I managed to find some half dozen blankets, and blankets and a tent are preferable at any time to bare trenches, plus ground sheet and greatcoat. Before long we were well in the land of nod. I awoke some hours later with a feeling that all was not well. Emerging from our shelter we found that the Company had moved off suddenly. Luck was on our side, however, and we had not gone far in the direction indicated by one of the Fusiliers as that taken by the Company, when we halted a passing limber, and found it was one of our own. We hung on to this, and eventually found the Company in a big field. Here in the open within a few miles of the front line were huge fires surrounded by sleeping forms. Besides one particularly big fire sat Punch, grimy and rather forbidding looking. I reported to him. He said little, but it was very much to the point. My apologies were accepted, but his looks conveyed that it was no more than he expected of me.

Blackwood

Well here we are at Blackwood, I believe that is the name, and here I must make myself comfortable. I have an inherent dislike for the sky as a roof, especially when I can find something a little nearer, and on a scrounge round I discovered a dinky dry dug-out. And here I deposited myself and slept the sleep of the just. I recollect awaking in daylight once or twice, but I fell asleep again without any real effort. As I had no issue watch, and had never been on a course to receive instructions to enable me to judge the time by the position of the sun (and I could not see the sun through several feet of earth anyway), I had no idea of the time. Have I missed a parade? Or a fatigue? Well, what matter? I could be sorry!

An uncomfortable gnawing inside me at length prompted me to try to find a remedy. Another shock. The birds had flown. Birds? Rather a new name for the Company. If one on scouting around finds the rear Company Headquarters situated in what appeared to be a moving pigeon caravan it is an expression that comes fairly naturally. Here I found our second in command, Captain C. G. Davies. This was my first recollection of this officer, designed later to be our well respected C.O. Oh no! He did not bite me or curse me. Neither did he give me any rations although the hour was well past noon. He told me that the Company had moved to Bazentin-le-Grand. He explained the way I should go, by Mametz Wood and so on.

I cannot say that I enjoyed the trip to find my lost fellow travellers. Too many guns were sending their joyous greetings to Fritz. An unseen heavy field gun firing ten to twenty yards away seems more like twenty millimetres distant, and was certainly twenty miles too near for absolute comfort. I survived the trials and tribulations of that lonely trek, and arrived at Bazentin-le-Grand, or should I say at the spot on the map where the village had once stood. For I saw no sign that a village had ever stood there. My recollection of it is that I left a crowded road, or mud track would be a better description, and turned right up a short sharp incline where I found on the left hand side of the road a number of dug-outs, one of which was Company headquarters.

I reported here, and went on to trenches on the crest, where the Company was billeted. Everyone seemed too fed up to give much notice to me or my wanderings, and I settled down to a much needed feed. I was sent down a trench some thirty yards or so down the left hand side of the road, and here I found the gun team. We seemed to have this trench to ourselves. No one seemed to have any duties and we were simply waiting : for what?

Punch and his superior officers possessed a sense of humour operating in inverse ratio to my own. They knew I had had more than my fair share of sleep the previous night, and I was therefore a fitting subject for an all night guard. The Company's equipment had all been dumped at the bottom of the incline in a field a foot or so below the road level. I was to mount guard over this and see no one won anything. As it was not eatable or wearable I don't think it really mattered. However, duty must be done, and anyhow it is a cushy job. My companion in distress was George Diprose. Dip was a good chap. He inspired confidence, and everything he did pin-pointed a very determined character. Nothing timid about Dip. He knew where he wanted to go, and took the shortest cut, and hang what's in between.

Up and down we walked to keep ourselves awake and warm. Some thirty or forty yards behind our dump was an Australian field battery working overtime in sending their love tokens. After some time the Jerry retaliation commenced, about midnight I should think. Didn't we laugh ! Every shell was a dud. Dip waxed very witty, and I thoroughly enjoyed the puns he made as each dud fell.

But what a peculiar smell : like pineapples. Neither of us had laughed sufficiently to cry. Yet cry we did. Of course, we were not long in rumbling the cause, and had our P.H. helmets on pretty quickly. It was my first experience of gas shells and presumably the same applied to Dip, although he was a much older 'sweat' than I. One sees the humour of these things afterwards. Here are two sentries both fairly well made physically who have been thrown together for the first time in their lives. There they go tripping hand in hand up the road like two schoolgirls of seven,

E

but in place of happy giggles and talk we have gruff obscene growls behind the helmets. Not too clear because of the length of rubber-covered tin gripped by the teeth. The rubber joined outside the helmet, and produced a squeak each time the air was expelled. Result : alternate muffled curses and squeaks.

The two disciples of Ku-Klux-Klan wandered up the road. The outstretched hand of one found the entrance to a dugout. Down the stairs they stumbled until they reached the gas-blanket. Pulling this aside they sat on the step lower down and removed their helmets, the better to wipe their streaming eyes. A rather startled voice asked who was there, and a candle was lit. They explained what had happened and received the officer's permission to stay where they were providing they kept quiet. And there I completed my first turn of sentry duty with the Company, leaving at dawn to find the Company dump still intact and the gas cleared.

I heard afterwards that the Australian battery suffered heavily, and that later the gas shells were mixed with H.E. It is a sorry confession that in the first line duty I had with the Company I deserted my post. The common sense that prevailed was, I think, correct. I cannot imagine anyone raiding a dump of ammunition boxes and the like during a heavy shelling. Even if they had, the ownership would not have altered.

They would still have belonged to the Government whether in the hands of the 142nd or any other Company. So I am unrepentant, and under the same set of circumstances would do the same again, but much quicker. One of the benefits of an elastic conscience.

Bazentin ! The name revives memories of various incidents, although possibly not in the correct sequence of their occurrence, some perhaps relate to our second visit to this 'delightful' area after an interval of two or three weeks.

I remember being on a water-carrying party one day, and coming down to the water point I watched a battalion of Colonial troops, New Zealanders, I believe, march past. What a picture ! Their wonderful physique, marching, and general deportment, sent a thrill of pride through me.

I talked to some of the few survivors a fortnight or so later, and gleaned something of the wholesale slaughter of this battalion. My heart bled for those hollow-cheeked men, and for their comrades, now no more.

In action nearby was a battery of French 75's. Good guns, no doubt, but I preferred our own 18 pounders.

Wandering about one day I beheld one of the strangest sights of my life. A diminutive officer came strutting down the road. closely followed by a huge toad-like monster of metal with the business ends of guns poking out of its sides, a kind of travelling fort. Goggle-eyed I watched this strange monster waddle slowly along. As it grew closer I saw painted on it, H. M. *Landship*, followed by some other name. I think it was Drake. The monster was borne on caterpillars, and at the rear was a comparatively light attachment on two rather large wheels.

In fact the attachment was practically all wheels. What the attachment was for I never discovered, but its lightness was evidence that it could not possibly have been connected with the steering as some supposed. Joining the little crowd dawdling behind it I watched it leave the road. It crawled towards a sloping bank about ten feet high, seeking shelter behind it I suppose. Was it? It simply crawled up, its nose high in the air as though sneering at such a trivial obstacle, and a moment later recovered its normal position, emphasising the fact with a wallop. Amazed and staggered I continued on my way to spread the news of this new and strange instrument of war. This incident was my first introduction to the tanks, or caterpillars, as we called them then, and I still have a vivid mental picture of the dapper five feet nothing officer strutting proudly along in advance of his weird charge.

My first spot of bother since joining the Company came when I received instructions, a few days after arriving at Bazentin, to join what I took to be a carrying party. Decked in fighting order, I was given two, or was it four, boxes of ammunition slung together by a strap. Not the wooden boxes of S.A.A. of course, but tin boxes, each containing a filled machine-gun belt. Whither we were bound I knew not, but I sensed something unpleasant. Believe me I was right. Rain had been falling for some days, and the already muddy earth became more like a quagmire every step we took. In darkness, lit up only by the distant occasional Very lights, we stumbled and staggered for miles. I simply hung as close as I possibly could to the black form in front of me. Corpses became numerous as we approached the line. The stench, increasing in direct ratio to the number of corpses, seemed to have at least the solidity of the corpses by the time we reached the shambles of the old front-line trenches, full to overflowing with bodies which—perhaps only hours or minutes ago—housed lives more valuable to the world than those of their slayers. My tin hat certainly stood me in good stead that night and incidentally saved my life some months later. Every time I slipped and fell, one of the rear boxes would describe a semi-circle and land with a crash on my tin hat, which very fortunately, seemed to fall back to protect my skull. Fed up and far from home? I ask you! I got to the stage eventually where if a handy corpse provided a better foothold than the surrounding quagmire, I used it. I was not alone in that. I suppose there was shelling, but not sufficiently close to cause us discomfort. We all reached that state of physical weariness where we would have welcomed a Blighty one with gratitude. We eventually reached the outskirts of High Wood which had been taken by our Division a day or two previously. We passed through the wood to the far side facing Fritz, and lined up. The infantry, the 24th Battalion under Captain Figg, and the 23rd Battalion under Major Hargreaves, was ready for the level attack, which was to be launched without a preliminary bombardment and the object of which was to man the trenches which Corps hoped had been forsaken by our friends opposite. It was now about 2 a.m., and we crouched in shell holes whilst Lieut. Ivory, who was in charge of the four guns, left us, presumably for a conference. Our No. 1, Lance-Corporal Venis, had been issued with a water-bottle of rum. I don't suggest that on this occasion he won it, but we each had a nip to put much needed life into us, and discussed the impending show. A lone German machine-gun was very active in front of us, and we kept pretty low. Judging by the crack of the gun he was very close. We were all more or less on edge and jumpy, and I expressed my views possibly a little too forcibly on the matters under discussion. I remember I disagreed with Jimmy Simner on some minor point or other and we nearly got to blows. How ridiculous it all sounds now!

A Jerry machine-gun barking from a hundred or so yards away, and two of us were silly enough to expose ourselves unnecessarily because of some trivial argument. The incident does, however, give an indication of the nervous strain we were under, although probably we did not ourselves realise it at the time.

Lieut. Ivory returned, and we learned that the guns were to accompany the Infantry, two on each flank, so as to be able to use enfilade fire in case of counter-attack. The other gun with us on the left was under Lance-Corporal Whitworth with John Batty as No. 2. John was a great chap. Like me he had trouble in pronouncing the King's English. Whereas my trouble was with my r's which more often than not became w's (you know the idea when I refer to coming down a 'wotton woad') his trouble was with his s's. To hear John singing that he would pack up his troubles and 'Thmile, thmile, thmile', was a treat for the gods. John was very even-tempered, very hard to disturb, and if he used army language at all it was very rarely. So solid and dependable that we all liked him. I am not certain of the personnel of John's team. Spence, Windybank, Hughes, and Jock Abbots, I believe, in addition to numbers 1 and 2.

To give everyone taking part in an attack some idea of what he was expected to do by showing him a map, pointing to his starting point, his objective and the route thereto, was, at that time, simply not done. The mere suggestion then as to the wisdom of such a proceeding would have sent many of the old Boer War type into permanent apoplexy.

We were expected to follow as mildly as sheep, minus the bleat. My particular jobs were to carry ammunition and keep close to Venis and the gun, so that the ammunition was available when required, or perhaps 'if' required would be better, and, incidentally, protect myself at all times. I performed my mule's part of the jobs, anyway.

Off we started, a line of moving silence. The slightest rattle of a mess tin on some part of your equipment, and you incurred hoarse whispered curses, with your life's history and doubted legitimacy in a few words. On and on, it seemed miles, but I expect it was a matter of only a few hundred yards. I know little of astronomy, but whenever I could do so I observed at the starting point the direction of some constellation with which I happened to be familiar. I memorised whether it was half left, half right, and so on. This habit stood me in good stead this particular night.

At length it was found that we had lost touch with the Infantry, and we were told to stay where we were whilst Lieut. Ivory and, I believe, Fatty Cresswell re-established contact.

We needed no second bidding. Such nice boys, so well trained and obedient! How long we sat I know not, but later the faint outlines of a small copse, some 150 yards away, could be discerned. A sure sign that day was breaking. Jimmy Simner was, I think, the first to realise the seriousness of our position, and we responded feverishly to his cry of 'Dig in you blighters, dig in'. Human moles! There would be about a dozen of us all told, and we got in three of the largest shell holes we could find fairly close together, and commenced digging with our entrenching tools. I think I have worked hard at odd times in my life, but I have never since expended so much energy in the same time as I did in the fifteen minutes or so following Jimmy's warning cry. All on our knees throwing the dirt to the centre and out of the hole, slogging away as if our lives depended on it—and they did.

When the centre had been raised sufficiently, our gun tackle was deposited there, and we then threw the earth outside only. In our haste we overlooked one point : we were not making sufficient room to sit in comfort, knees taking less space than buttocks; so that having got down something like a yard below ground level, we ceased and sat as nature intended us to sit.

What a mess we had made of it! The man next to me had to face the same way, and to enable him to get round I had to put my knees under my chin. We all had our waterproof sheets on us in the form of a cape. Our team of six were in the same shell hole which we had made in the shape of a horseshoe, and three of the six I never saw for the next fourteen hours although they were so close I talked to them, softly of course, as we had no idea of the proximity of the Germans, but we judged they were fairly close. We assumed correctly too. They were too close for comfort. What a day. Utterly helpless we sat. It rained ceaselessly. I had my first object lesson of the action of water on the local earth. Normally on a level surface the water simply soaks in. This water was of the unfriendly and ignorant sort, evidently unaware that it might find dry earth beneath that already wet. Instead it just inflated the cold and clammy surface until this fell away and found a drier and warmer abode down my neck.

This was repeated throughout the day as successive surfaces became sufficiently swollen. I was at one of the ends of the horseshoe so I had every opportunity of observing the phenomenon over a fairly wide area.

Something had to be done to stop the rot, so making my hands as near the colour of the earth as possible I set about repairing the damage. By careful patting I made the inside of the hole into a clay-like surface, and exerting all the pressure of which I was capable made it slightly slanting. The collapsed earth I threw out bit by bit. My field engineering was not up to standard and there were further falls during the day after each of which the repairing process had to be repeated.

The cold wet day and our confined quarters could be productive of only one thing, severe attacks of cramp. We were all attacked at various times and when it attacked one in both legs at the same time, the pain was excruciating. It was possible to stretch only one leg at a time by persuading the man next to you to squeeze himself closer to the side of the trench; he also assisted the circulation by amateurish massaging of the calf. Interference of the circulation caused by unabated pressure on the buttocks had something to do with the frequent attacks. Throughout the day there was a continual groaning by one or other of us. It became a speculation as to whether one could dodge his normal turn. We all knew we had to stick it, and that to get up and stretch would be fatal in its most literal sense. The rum bottle saved us all. It says much for the sportsmanlike attitude of the team as a whole that the bottle went round the whole of us possibly a dozen times during the day. 'Just a little nip' was the dictum of Venis, and a little nip it was, although most of us would have given a great deal for a good long swig. It sent the blood coursing through the veins, and rum is the only medicine I know which could have served us so well. There was in England, I believe, a section of the community who continually agitated for the withdrawal of the rum ration of the troops. I can only wish that each one of them had to go through the same experience as we did. I am as God-fearing as the average, but on occasions such as these we needed more than faith for protection from the elements. The men in command who resolutely ignored the outcries of the ignorant 'no rum' fanatics well earned the gratitude of the whole Army.

I have already told you that we dug in, in three shell holes. In two there was rum to be had to assist the fight against cramp. What happened in the third where this boon was denied?

Before going on to that though, I had better assure you that we had every evidence during the day that there was still a war on—the usual shelling, far too much of which was fairly close, and machine-gun and rifle fire, but we knew that, apart from a direct hit, we were safe and did not worry. One of our planes came over during the day and we all fished out apologies for handkerchiefs and waved, keeping our hands inside the hole of course. The pilot, however, evidently did not see us. Now to return to the rum question.

Midway through the afternoon I received a terrible shock, mentally and physically, a huge weight hurled itself upon me from out of the grey—there was no blue sky that day. He was one of the two who had dug themselves into an adjacent shell hole. He had simply got up, run the yard or two to our horseshoe, and taken a flying leap amongst us. Quite naturally I was the one to receive the full force. We all re-adjusted ourselves and each managed to squeeze himself up a bit and so make room for Butters. He told us that he and Hughes had suffered from cramp, and that Hughes was in such agony that he forgot where he was and stood up and stretched himself for a matter of a few seconds.

The inevitable happened and he promptly got a bullet in the chest. Butters did his best for him but he died an hour or so later. Stranded in no-man's-land with only a dead pal for company is enough to try the nerves of the strongest and Butters decided to take the risk of the dash to us. A gamble with death for the company of living pals. He made it, and we naturally let him have a good swig out of the bottle. I am not suggesting for a moment that Butters lost his nerve. He was not even wildly excited. He had had a nasty experience but his condition was about as abnormal as our own. The fact that he had not been hit was no proof that he had not been observed. He evidently had and throughout the day a rifle spat continually over our hole. I listened very carefully many times, and decided that the rifle was being fired from the copse. There was a great possibility that the rifle had been fixed in some way to cover our hole, and I decided to avoid the line of fire whenever we decided to move. The longest day of my life drew to a close, and we discussed what we were going to do. My own view was that the attacking infantry had made a left turn, which left us beautifully between two fires.

I am still uncertain of this for reasons you will presently understand. One thing we agreed upon—we were absolutely useless where we were, and we had to get back and report. We all figured that we had to get out of the line of fire by a move to the left (west) some 50 yards or so before we thought of trying to get back in short rushes. I had a pretty good idea of the direction we had to take and hoped for the sky to clear so that I could see the stars. Strangely enough a portion cleared and I was able to confirm that, roughly speaking, I was correct.

Looking anxiously for a break in the cloudy sky, and when it did come, following the break until one recognised some star formation is a fine pastime—I don't think! Another thing we were all agreed upon was that Jerry knew perfectly well that we were there; and that when night fell he would not be long in sending out a strong patrol to mop us up. We were in no fit condition to offer much resistance and the gun might or might not have worked, although Venis had done his best to keep it clean and workable. Our main concern was that if we had to make a stand we should attract the unpleasant attention of the Lewis guns in our rear. It is bad enough to have fire from one direction, but to get it from both back and front is more than any individual can stand. A decision was made that we should try to get in as quickly after dark as possible. What a long-drawn-out twilight it was! As soon as we could we all had a quick peep-over. I looked over towards the copse and saw it very faintly outlined against the sky.

Another five minutes and we would move. Then a whispered 'Ted!' It was Batty from the shell hole some few yards away. I saw a dark form creep out of Batty's hole and—good heavens, he was going the wrong way. It was Sergeant Sargent, whom I do not remember seeing before that night. We shouted softly but he was gone in the blackness. Now we were in a mess. We all crept out and got into shell holes near to Batty's. I was the only one with a rifle (gunners carried revolvers). I made sure it was working, as I fully expected trouble. What were we to do? It was a hopeless proposition to go over and tell Jerry to hand back our Sergeant as we wanted him. It was also hopeless for about ten men to make much of a show against a strong patrol. Batty told us that the Sergeant had decided that it was his job to reach our lines and tell them that we were coming in. Very plucky Sergeant, but why in the name of goodness did he go the wrong way. Very lights did not help us at all. It was use-less to pick out the high ones and to say that that was Jerry's line, and that those low ones represented our line. It simply did not work. Both high and low ones were at every point of the compass. That usually reliable guide failed. We waited, straining our eyes and ears for the slightest movement and sound, and keeping well down. Although there were the continual noises of the Somme battle, there were periods of comparative calm.

What were we to do? Human frames could not stand another day like that just passed. After waiting about twenty times the length of time it should have taken the Sergeant to reach our line and back, we decided that we must move. My own view is that the Sergeant walked straight into the German lines and long before we left the shell-holes he was under a searching cross-exam-ination. It is certain that the Sergeant kept true to his Company. If ever you should read these lines, Sergeant, accept our gratitude for playing the game. What yarn you told your captors I know not, but it was evidently a real white man's lie, otherwise we should have been mopped up pretty smartly.

We must go. It was perfectly hopeless to remain and if dawn meant another attack, as most dawns did—then it was likely we should be mistaken for the foe. Which way were we to go? There were many different opinions. Skirting round shell-holes tended to make one lose all sense of direction. Perhaps the fact that my views were so definite swayed opinion in my favour. Had I had to go alone I should most certainly have taken the same way. Venis decided the matter by saying his team were to follow me. John, with similar ideas to my own, fell in with the decision.

The anxiety for the safety of our Sergeant, followed by our uncertainty as to the correct way to go, made us quite forget the poor lad we were leaving behind. We could do him no good; he had already solved the great mystery; but none of us remembered to take his pay-book and belongings. Looking down now, lad, you will understand, and understanding forgive. Our mode of progress was short rushes. We had come in a north-easterly direction, so we must return south-westerly. Keeping one eye on a vicious Lewis gun directly due south, I travelled west, which, I hoped, would take us parallel to the German line. There was no other hope for it. That Lewis gun was making a hazard of every rush. We progressed possibly two or three hundred yards in this manner. That took us a great deal of time. We had decided that three or four was the maximum number to go at a time, in case we attracted fire. So each twenty yards' rush meant a wait until the next two little parties had joined up in adjacent shell-holes. Some part of the distance was covered by creeping Indian fashion in file.

A crawl for the next two hundred yards and we were bound to strike our line. On and on until a glance revealed Very lights all behind us. How had we managed it?

Had we, by a stroke of good fortune crept through a small break in our line, or had we got through between lines in echelon? It is a mystery to me to this day and one which will never be solved.

Safe! On we plodded, now upright and making the best time we could and we eventually reached the identical corner of High Wood we had left some 24 hours previously. 'Well, Corporal I have lugged these blinking boxes of ammunition miles, and I be darned if I carry them another inch'. Oh no, Corporal, I know you did not hear me. These were my thoughts only.

You were in front, I behind, and bang into a deserted trench went the boxes. On we went until we reached a road, and someone asked the way to Bazentin. The driver of a G.S. wagon directed us, and we plodded on and on, up to the boot tops in mud. It took us a long time to travel the mile or two to Bazentin. 'Is this Bazentin-le-Grand?' enquired one of the straggling party. 'No, this is Bazentin-le-Petit' followed by instructions as to how to reach le-Grand. The last straw breaks the camel's back it is said. The news almost broke our hearts. Numbers One and Two had the heaviest loads with the tripod and gun respectively. The loads were changed amongst us a few times and I did a little carrying. Venis stuck it well considering his light build. John had resolutely managed his tripod without change. To find himself at the wrong Bazentin was too much. Down went the tripod in the mud and down John sat in about six inches of thin batter-like earth resting his weary head on the tripod, vowing that he would not move for the whole of the British and German Armies.

It might have been the discomfort of the mud, or that the rest had revived him somewhat, but John eventually responded to the party's appeals to carry on to le-Grand and staggered to his feet. After refusing aid in the carrying of his tripod he plodded on. We must have looked a wretched crew when we eventually reached Company headquarters, where we were welcomed with open arms. We had been given up for lost and Lieut. Ivory had searched up the line most of the day for us and had only just returned.

Our Alf (the 'old man') was a trump, and rushed about and saw to it that we had much-needed food and a good ration of rum. We needed no rocking to sleep that night.

Behind us lay a very unpleasant experience, but so far as I was concerned it was productive of good and had something to do, I believe, with the decision to retain me in the Company, and I was not sorry to be transferred, thus leaving the P.B.I. (Poor B—— Infantry).

THE SHELF

The one objective that was NOT attained on July 1st, 1916 was Thiepval, on the extreme left of the attack. In September, 1916, General Maxse's division, out on rest up north, was brought down to make a final assault on it. The Division was offered transport, but the General said we would march; and we did. I had just arrived in a draft; a very young boy, and first time out. The taking over of our portion of the line was something I will always remember. The darkness, losing touch, bewilderment, and appalling stench. We arrived very tired, but had to stand-to till morning, so I thought myself very fortunate in finding a comfortable sort of shelf jutting out from the parapet on which to rest my elbows.

At length, when the dawn came, I saw that the comfortable shelf was the knee joint of a German who was half-buried in the parapet.

H.F.E.

IN THE LINE

I was in my first dugout, and looked round curiously. Over the entrance was a notice : 'Suicide Club'. That was what mach-ine-gunners were called.

The floor was an inch deep in water, and from the airshaft immediately above came a drip, drip. The Club was a hole in the second line, eight feet long, ten feet wide, six feet high. The air was foul and cold. Nails driven into the timbers carried an assortment of equipment. The lighting arrangements were one candle in a tin. My teeth chattered.

There was a call for me from outside. Before I could move the section officer appeared at the doorway and gave me a hard look.

Slipping and sliding, I sneaked past him and reached my section in the front line, where the sergeant awaited me, growling, 'Where the hell have *you* been?'

Shivering with cold, and with the rain beating on my face, I went on the gun with another fellow, shrinking, and with my eyes just over the top.

Two hours later I was relieved. The corporal looked at me, and towards the Club with a forbidding expression. I assumed a sitting position on the firestep, and prayed for the morning.

Arthur Empey, writing in 1917

5

With 33rd Battalion Machine Gun Corps

The third stage of the great Somme offensive began on the 14th of September, 1916, and continued until early November of the same year. The 33rd Battalion Machine Gun Corps took part in this historic event, and the following story comes from their History and Memoir.

It will be recalled that the 33rd Division was badly cut-up in the opening stages of the Somme battles of July 1st, 1916, around High Wood, and machine-gun companies suffered high casualties, which made it necessary to withdraw the whole of the Division from the line for re-grouping and to receive reinforcements. This accomplished, the Division moved to the forward area and on November 2nd bivouacked beside Trones Wood. During the Division's absence from the forward area High Wood and Flers Ridge had been captured by the employment of more than ten divisions.

The weather had broken. The roads were a morass of treacly mud through which stuck out the tree stumps and branches which were supposed to form their foundations. Cover of every description had been swept away by shell and fire and every yard of ground was pitted by shell holes.

Desolation was everywhere. On the 3rd November the 19th and 98th Brigades, with the French on the immediate right of the Division, took over the line east of Les-Boeufs and Guinchy, with their supports lying in the old German trench known as Flers Line. From this point could be seen the towers of Bapaume, and it was obvious that the intention was to capture le Transloy and Rocquigny and then to outflank Bapaume itself, which lay about three miles distant. It was equally obvious, however, to those who took over the line, that owing to the state of the ground in the valley between Les-Boeufs and le Transloy, the thick mists that prevented accurate observation, and the large amount of wire which the enemy had already put out, an attack at this time of the year across a quagmire covered with shellholes would be an almost impossible task.

Nevertheless, repeated attacks were carried out on the 3rd and 4th of November by the 33rd Division upon Hazy Trench—which was indeed hazy for it could not be found on the ground but only on the map. Antelope Trench, German Trench, Brimstone Trench and trenches with other evil sounding names; the heavy casualties; the extreme difficulty of getting back wounded across the ground on which it was almost impossible for an armed man to move himself, let alone carry a wounded comrade; the lowering sunless skies and the torrents of rain, will never be forgotten by those who were forced to take part in these hideous operations.

Even the horror of the day spent in shallow, waterlogged trenches under increasing fire was surpassed at night when the full fury of the German guns was let loose.

Men disappeared into the night; one knows not to this date their fate, whether destroyed by shell fire, or swallowed up in the yawning shell holes, stifled with mud and water, gripped and paralysed with cold and wounds. The scream of the shells, the dull boom of the burst, the chatter of machine-guns and the *spat, spat*, of heavy rain drops lashing the surface of the quagmire were incessant.

The only duckboard had sunk beneath the oozing surface of the ground. Boots were torn from the feet of men held fast in the octopus grip of the mud.

Men were seen working without any clothing except shorts and jackets. Exhaustion became a plague. Horses and mules were to die, stuck fast in their tracks. Wagons were abandoned and became the sport of shells.

The number of little wooden crosses increased daily.

Every man was buried where he fell; it was impossible to bear him away.

On November 5th it was decided to have a Guy Fawkes day, and the remains of the Division which had repeatedly attempted the feat only to be bogged down a few yards from our line, and easily shot to pieces like bottles in a fair, were hurled across to take the German trenches surrounding le Transloy.

Success was gained by the 2nd Worcestershires who had concentrated in the French area, and who under Lieut. Bennett (who won the Victoria Cross for his exploit) struggled forward some hundreds of yards to the objective and squatted like ducks in the mud known as Bennett Trench, opposite le Transloy. They were accompanied by two guns of the 100th Machine Gun Company under Sergeant Donalson, who was awarded the Military Medal. Sergeants McLellan and McCullum were reported missing and no trace of them was ever found.

The hostile gun-fire during this period was intense and heavy. Machine Gunners, who fared worse than infantry during that period, had their first experience of carrying intolerably heavy loads across several miles of country, which in peace time they would have said it would be impossible to cross unsupported by drag ropes or without salmon waders.

The difficulties of keeping guns cleaned and in action in this area was seldom appreciated and certainly not understood.

'Land cruisers', as the first tanks had been described, went into action for the first time on September 15th, 1916.

It is a matter of history that only sixty of the original one-hundred-and-fifty made had been shipped to France, that many broke down en route for mechanical reasons and, of the eighteen which went forward with the infantry on that day, only nine survived. They did useful work but the grand element of surprise had been dissipated.

WARLENCOURT

One of the lesser-known battles of the 1914–18 War was the attack by the Durham Brigade of Territorials on the Butte-de-Warlencourt on November 5th, 1916.

The Somme battles had come to an end and preparations were being made for the 5th Army to attack north of the Ancre on November 12th, over ground that was not devastated by heavy shelling. One serious obstacle stood in the way of this new offensive—the Butte-de-Warlencourt—a fortified hill held by the Germans which gave them full observation of the entire Ancre sector. It was imperative that this hill fortress be captured before the main attack took place.

The three infantry battalions assigned the task were the 6th, 8th and 9th Durhams—supported by the 151 Machine Gun Company and 151 Trench Mortar Battery. 151 Brigade had experienced four months of flame, mud and death, on the Somme, but no-one flinched when called upon to advance into the fire of the guns of a whole Germany Army Corps, wrote Major Grierson, C.O. of 151 Machine Gun Company.

Troop Dispositions :

9th D.L.I. (Colonel R. B. Bradford, V.C.) Left Flank. Opposite the Butte.

6th D.L.I. (Colonel Jeffries, D.S.O.) Centre.
8th D.L.I. (Colonel Turnbull, C.M.B.) Right Flank.

The 151 Machine Gun Company had two Vickers guns with each front battalion—six guns in support and four in reserve (16 guns).

Zero hour was 9.10 a.m. The weather was vile-wet-windy and foggy. To soften up the enemy and destroy the barbed wire surrounding the Butte, a preliminary to the attack was a ten-minute bombardment by British artillery—guns of all calibres—then, prompt at 9.10 a.m. on the anniversary of the Gun Powder Plot the infantry and machine-gunners went over the top.

An Australian brigade was to assist on the right flank of the 8th Durhams—but this brigade along with the 8th Durhams was immediately bogged down in no-man's-land.

They found themselves knee deep in thick, gluey mud; many, unable to move, were shot down.

The 6th Durhams fared little better and the machine-gunners hugging guns, tripods and ammunition were left stranded and suffered many casualties.

The 9th Durhams reached its objective—capturing the Butte and all its garrison.

The writer of this story was a member of 151 Machine Gun Company and therefore it is with the guns he is mainly concerned. As previously mentioned, two machine-guns were attached to the 9th Durhams, and when the Butte was captured Corporal T. H. Rutherford, 'B' Section, established his gun on the Bapaume Road, but very soon afterwards he and his team became casualties.

Corporal W. Mewes' gun team, attached to the same Battalion suffered the same fate.

Corporal Watson then went forward with his gun team to replace the one knocked out. Both flanks were now open, and so Sergeant Jimmy Glennall, and Corporal Matt Butler went forward with their guns to help cover the exposed positions, and these three guns played a vital role in repulsing the first German counter-attack which took place at about 11 p.m. that night (November 5th).

Sergeant Leith's team all became casualties during the German counter-attack. Badly wounded himself, Sgt. Leith crawled back to the old front line and refused to leave until his wounded team mates were rescued. Early the following day the Cpl. of the second gun team was killed as he got out of the trench. Private Hay kept the gun in action throughout most of the day (6th November) with only one other gunner to assist him.

Again the Germans counter-attacked and the 151 Infantry Brigade, now decimated, was forced to withdraw to the original frontline, and late at night it was relieved by the 150 Brigade.

A whole German Guards division was rushed up from Bapaume to take part in their counter-attack at midnight on the 5th November—and these élite enemy troops were supported by guns of army corps strength.

There was a plan that the 150th Brigade should renew the attack on the Butte on the 7th of November, but very heavy rain caused its abandonment; so the Butte remained in German hands.

No account of the battle of the Butte would be complete without a mention of Corporal Monty Watson, M.M. and Bar.

Watson, of 'A' section 151 Machine Gun Company, was in command of a gun team supporting the 9th Durhams in a captured German trench, where he fired many belts of ammunition at good targets. The position was most precarious, which made Captain Palmer (in charge of infantry on the spot) decide to climb the Butte and discover what was happening on the German side of the hill. What he saw convinced him that the Germans were about to launch a counter-attack on a big scale.

Arriving back in our lines Captain Palmer immediately ordered his men to return to the original trenches and Corporal Watson was instructed to get his gun back right away to the old gun position.

Watson reached up to take the gun from the trench; turned round and found his solitary gunner, Pte McRoberts, holding a revolver in the ribs of a Prussian Guardsman who had somehow found his way to the rear of the machine-gun post.

Watson knew that McRoberts' revolver was unloaded, for they had no revolver ammuntion left.

Corporal Watson took over and both the gun and the Prussian Guardsman were safely brought back to 151 Machine Gun Company Headquarters, where Major Grierson, D.S.O., Croix de Guerre—C.O. of 151 Machine Gun Company—obtained valuable information from the prisoner.

CORPORAL MONTY WATSON

The Bravery of Corporal Monty Watson, M.M. and Bar, will always be remembered by those who served with him, and the

F

following extract from 'The Tripod' (151 M.G.C. O/C Association Journal) gives his story.

A coal miner from Cockfield, south-west Durham, he joined the 6th Durham Territorial Battalion before the outbreak of World War One, and became a member of the Machine Gun Section towards the end of 1914. Territorials were originally formed for home defence, but when volunteers were called for to replace the severe casualties in the ranks of the British Regular Army units fighting to stop the Boche reaching the Channel ports, the 6th Durhams—like many other Territorial Army units— answered the call, and Watson went out to France as a machine-gunner with his regiment.

Around Christmas 1915 he was transferred to 151 Machine Gun Company, and served throughout the war until May 27th, 1918, when he was seriously wounded during the battle of the Aishe.

Both legs smashed, the guns of his section destroyed, he ordered the few surviving gunners to get back and leave him. The Germans took him prisoner.

One gunner who got back to the British line (very few did) said Monty would never survive, but he did, and came home at the end of the war.

The Germans—according to Watson—patched him up and treated him reasonably well.

This gallant machine-gunner was awarded the Military Medal and Bar, and no man deserved it more.

In 1939, when the evil thing broke out again, Monty despite his disability, became an officer in command of a Home Guard Machine Gun Section.

Corporal Monty Watson, M.M. and Bar, has now answered the final great roll call, but his memory, along with that of thousands of others who fought for what was thought at the time to be a fight of right against might, will always shine out like silver amid the waste and filth of war.

THE DURHAMS' CROSSES

In 1917, the Germans retired to the Hindenburg Line, and the Butte-de-Warlencourt was occupied by British forces.

The 151 Infantry Brigade had left the Somme to take part in the Battle of Arras (April, 1917) and while out resting the 6th and 8th Durhams decided to erect crosses on the Butte in memory of the men who had been killed on November the 5th, 1916.

The 9th Durhams also followed with their cross and there was regimental rivalry for the top position. Colonel R. B. Bradford (9th Durhams) claimed that his battalion had captured the Butte and asked that the other two crosses should be taken off, but General Cameron (151 Brigade) said it was a Brigade attack and all had contributed—so to satisfy all concerned he arranged for a Brigade cross to be erected.

After the war the four crosses were brought back to England. The 6th Durhams' cross is in South Church, Bishop Auckland, the 8th's at Chester-le-Street, and the 9th's at St. Mary's Church, Gateshead. The 151 Brigade cross is in Durham Cathedral.

The cross in Durham Cathedral was, and still is to a lesser extent, a meeting place for ex-members of 151 Brigade, and all four crosses can be seen in these Durham churches where they will always remain as a tribute to the men of Durham who fought and died for their country in the most ghastly soldiers' war of all time.

The above account was also taken from 'The Tripod' with the permission of W. Shuttleworth (Editor) and ex-members of 151 Machine Gun Company.

BRAVE DEEDS AND HUMOUR

In the grim trench warfare of World War One, brave deeds often intermingled with humour.

One such story comes from a machine-gunner who was serving with 151 Company.

During the Somme battle in September 1916, the Infantry (151 Brigade) attack was held up by a German strong point. Lance Corporal Bill Leftley, 'C' Section, 151 Machine Gun Company, crawled across no-man's-land in broad daylight and reached the enemy trench. He discovered that the first traverses were empty, and assumed the Germans had retreated.

Leftley then stood up, slowly walked down the trench, and surprised twenty Germans, who, not realizing that there was just one British soldier to deal with, immediately put up their hands in token of surrender.

Leftley beckoned the party to come to him in single file. He was scared stiff in case the first German should rumble the actual situation and shout a warning to his mates, but all went well.

He brought the twenty Germans back to his machine-gun position, and handed over the prisoners to an Infantry Officer. The attack then progressed according to plan.

Leftley was recommended for the V.C. by Major Grierson (C.O. 151 Machine Gun Company) but the Infantry officer had also been recommended for the same capture.

Eventually an enquiry was established. Leftley said 'The trench is now in our lines. The German prisoners can be taken back to their position and the action re-enacted and my gun team can verify the whole incident'. Of course this was treated as a joke, and the outcome was that Bill Leftley was awarded the Médaille Militaire. The Infantry officer got the M.C.

WITH 126 MACHINE GUN COMPANY
(by one of its gunners)

From Suez to the Somme

It was in late February, 1917, that we arrived at Marseilles. Three feet of snow covered the ground as we unloaded our gear from the troopship which had carried us from the Egyptian port of Alexandria.

Many of us had been on active service in the Suez Canal Zone for a year or more, and some had survived Gallipoli (I among them) but the sudden change from heat to snow was a bit much until we were issued with warmer clothes. After a few days this took place and the Compnay proceeded by rail to Abbeville. In a small village nearby my machine-gun section billeted down in a large loft directly over an inhabited cow shed. What a welcome to France!

The pong from the cows below us was unbearable, and to relieve our fed-upness most of us paid a visit to the one pub in the village and spent all our spare cash.

Very soon, thank goodness, we had more to concern ourselves with than coping with mere evil-smelling cow dung. We were ordered to proceed to the assistance of the 48th Division near Peronne, so we gave the French farmer the soldiers' farewell and set off along a road where only a few moments previously a huge land-mine had blown up, destroying what was left of already badly damaged buildings. Scattered in the road near one building we approached lay hundreds of French gold coins. An order flashed down the ranks—'No looting. Anyone disobeying this order will be court martialled'.

So like Felix the Cat we kept on walking, but I have often wondered who *did* get that little gold-mine.

Eventually we arrived on the outskirts of Fricourt, where we were billeted in the ruins of a farmhouse, using the cellar for our cookhouse.

From this billet we did our first spell of front-line duty in France, taking it in turns to help on the gun teams in the line. We soon experienced trouble in a trench at Fricourt. Fritz found out that we were new to the area and gave us little rest. His 'Minnies' (stick bombs) did a lot of damage to our trenches and kept us busy repairing parapets. We got thoroughly fed up with this, so one evening Battalion Scout, Sergeant Sugden, outlined a plan of action to let Fritz know that we might be new to France, but we were not all that green. 'I want a volunteer to come out with me this evening', said the sergeant. Private Dunmore volunteered and at dusk they set out. It should be mentioned here that Sgt. Sugden could speak German very well. We fixed a machine gun in a suitable spot to cover our chums if they did get into serious difficulties. All was silent as we anxiously waited and watched.

About an hour later the Sergeant and Private Dunmore arrived back in our lines—with six German prisoners plus a Minniewerfen gun. We got the full story from Private Dunmore.

When Sergeant Sugden suddenly appeared in front of the German sentry outside the dug-out which sheltered his mates, the Sergeant (in German) ordered the sentry to put up his hands which he promptly did. 'Now shout down to your mates to come up without their rifles, and the last man bring up your Minnie-gun, I have my men covering you', bluffed Sergeant Sugden. The German sentry did as instructed, and to the Sergeant's amazement the other five Germans trooped up from the dug-out with arms raised in surrender—except the last one who was carrying the gun which had bashed our trenches about. It would do this no more, and for a while we had peace in the trench at Fricourt. Sergeant Sugden and Private Dunmore were each awarded the Military Medal and granted two weeks' leave in recognition of their gallant action.

From Fricourt we moved to St. Omer in the north of France, where we enjoyed a short rest spell.

THE BATTLE OF ARRAS

Arras stands on the River Scarpe, 28 miles from Amiens and 120 miles from Paris.

It was at one time the capital of Artois and noted for its beautiful cathedral, churches, and town hall.

In September, 1914, Arras was entered by the Germans. They were soon forced to retire, but their lines remained quite close to the city.

On April the 23rd, 1917, the British made a great attack called the battle of Arras, but it failed in its objective.

The following extracts from the History and Memoir of 33rd Battalion Machine Gun Company describe the battle.

In this attack the 98th Brigade was ordered to advance southwards down the Hindenburg Line, chiefly with bombs, and join up with the 100th Brigade in the Sensee Valley. While the 100th Brigade itself delivered a frontal attack upon the Hindenburg Line. The whole operation was a particularly difficult one to carry out. The Hindenburg Line consisted of a highly fortified front, honeycombed with concrete machine-gun pill-boxes about every fifty yards along it.

The initial assault of the 98th Brigade was the 1st Middlesex Regiment and the 2nd Argyll and Sutherland Highlanders. The Highlanders attacked across the open on the left, the Middlesex on the right, down the trench system.

At zero hour, 3.55 a.m., the high barriers across both front and support lines were blown up by mines.

Right from the start of the attack by the 98th Brigade, stiff opposition was met, and even before the troops had got down the slope to the Sensee river one Company each of the Argyll's and Middlesex found themselves cut off by the enemy.

Several attempts were made to rescue them, in which the machine-guns of Lieut. Sheriff's section, which had closely followed the advance of the Argyll's, co-operated.

On the front of the 98th Brigade the fighting raged all day. Towards 5 p.m. large bodies of enemy troops were seen going down the road into Fontaine. At 5.30 p.m. a counter-attack developed. Our machine-guns were placed on the opposite side of the hill and had magnificent observation positions.

Sergeant Beard with two guns did great havoc amongst masses of enemy troops before they deployed. This N.C.O. showed great courage and a wonderful example. He was wounded badly during the subsequent Boche bombing attack.

While this was happening the 100th Brigade attacked with the 1st Queen's Regiment leading.

To cover this attack General Pinney (C.O. 33rd Division) ordered that the machine-guns of the 19th and 100th Brigades should be grouped under the command of Major Hutchison.

During the night of the 22nd of April a very remarkable exploit was carried out by the 100th Machine Gun Company. The whole transport drove down the Sensee Valley into no-man's-land, protected only by a small patrol of the Worcestershire Regiment, and deposited 12 guns in their battery positions and many thousands of rounds of ammunition.

The transport returned without mishap, although it had driven within 300 yards of the German lines, and possibly closer to the German Patrols across no-man's-land.

For this exploit Sergeant Keeble and Driver Messenger were both awarded the Military Medal for particular skill and daring. A battery of 12 guns was therefore established within two hundred yards of the Hindenburg Line on high ground east of the Sensee River, so that direct fire could be brought to bear on the enemy in Fontaine-les-Croisilles, and upon those who manned the Hindenburg System.

In addition, an enfilade barrage was arranged to flank the front of the 98th Brigade attack.

This battery was under the command of Lieut. G. Harrison. In addition to this, three other batteries of four guns each were established east of Croisilles. A forward observation post was placed in the bed of the Sensee within 100 yards of Fontaine Village, every battery being connected to it by signal communication. This work was mostly carried out by Cpl. Hodson and Signaller Harrington.

Three tanks were ordered to assist in the attack.

At dawn on the 23rd the attack began and in view of the overnight preparations it was thought that success would be achieved, and during the first hour everything pointed to this. The 98th Brigade took over 300 prisoners, whilst the Queen's penetrated the wire and established themselves well in the Hindenburg Line with very light casualties.

The terrific covering overhead fire of the machine-guns had, it seemed, made all this possible.

As daylight came, however, it was seen that the German machine-gun nests had not been captured, and these guns completely dominated the whole battle area. As the day wore on German artillery shelling became exceptionally fierce.

All communication was destroyed. Light mists hung in the valley which prevented visual communication.

It was during this period that Major Hutchison's groom, L/Cpl. Clegg, was the only connecting link between the forward battalions and Brigade Headquarters.

He rode repeatedly with Driver Jones up and down the Sensee

Valley with despatches through a hail of shrapnel, H.E. and machine-gun fire, thereby winning the Military Medal.

Several machine-gunners including Sergeant Hills, had been sent forward with the Queen's as scouts, to select points for our machine-guns.

It was apparent that the Queen's, for the time being at any rate, were cut off from the rest of the Brigade, it being impossible to move up to the Hindenburg Line without incurring the heaviest possible casualties.

Moreover, both tanks with the 100th Brigade failed to leave their starting point.

By mid-morning the situation of the Queen's was desperate. They had run out of ammunition and it seemed an impossible task to supply them.

Nevertheless, the 16th K.R.R.C., who were in support, with great gallantry attempted this, and despite heavy losses repeatedly made their way up and down the valley carrying bombs and ammunition to the Queen's.

Owing to the tunnel system it was, on the other hand, an easy matter for the Germans to feed their own troops with bombs and grenades. About 11 o'clock a determined counter-attack by the enemy, who were fully aware of the awful plight of the Queen's, drove them and the elements of the 16th K.R.R.C. from the Hindenburg Line; and the 98th Brigade, then losing touch, were themselves driven back from their objective.

As the men came back, the well-posted enemy machine-guns picked them off like rabbits and scarcely a man returned unwounded. The Queen's after the attack mustered only forty-three men. Meanwhile the machine-guns, particularly the forward battery, had rendered very valuable service and were again and again thanked by the Queen's for their help where no one else could render assistance. It is a remarkable fact that although the battery of twelve guns was within 200 yards of the German Line, the bombardment, which was so hideously destructive, fell the whole time about twenty yards behind it. The Machine Gun Company losses in this action although not severe in quantity, were damaging in quality and included Privates McIntyre, M.M., Owden, M.M., Tommy Payne and Billing killed, and Callon, wounded, all five well known, cheery characters of the 100th Company.

After this action at Arras the 33rd Division was withdrawn for a short time to the area of Bienvillers-Pommera, to refit and receive drafts for further operations.

WITH 3RD MACHINE GUN SQUADRON

(Cavalry)

The Cavalry units of the Machine Gun Corps, although not so much in the limelight as their Infantry comrades, were, nevertheless, always waiting and ready for a chance to show their mettle.

Picked men from the Cavalry Regiments served in the Machine Gun Corps, and one of these—a Military Medallist of the 12th Lancers—writes of his experience.

After service in France from the outbreak of the war I was sent home for a time to recuperate from a nasty bout of dysentery, but rejoined my Regiment in mid-1916. After service at Combles and various other places in the front line up to January 1917, all cavalry machine-gunners were sent back to Camiers Machine Gun School to go through a course on the Vickers gun.

At the end of the course I was posted to the 3rd Mounted Machine Gun Corp Squadron at Honval.

The battle of Arras was about to begin, and we were earmarked for this action. Battle plans were outlined to us. The Infantry would cut a gap in the Hindenburg Line, and then the cavalry would go through the gap. On paper it all looked so simple.

We waited. War is for long periods just waiting, not knowing what the morrow holds in store.

The discipline in the 12th Lancers Regiment had always been exceptionally strict, but at times some orders seemed silly. For instance, most of us took the wire out of our service caps to make them more comfortable to wear. Our C.O. would have none of it, and ordered the Armourer Sergeant to put the wires back again. After this order the lads sang :

> 'You can't go through the gap
> Without a wire in your hat.
> Do you want to lose the War?'

It made little difference, for we never got a chance to go through the gap. The planned gap never happened, and we trekked back to Honval. Then we did a turn in the trenches around Montigny Farm, going up the line as far as we could mounted, with our machine-guns on the pack-horses, and completing the rest of the journey on foot.

While in the forward positions at Montigny Farm we had a sort of arrangement with the Germans about collecting water from the small stream that ran between our lines.

We did not interfere with each other, and on occasions even waved a greeting. This friendly arrangement went on for two or more weeks, but was knocked on the head when a certain Yeomanry Regiment took over from us and fired their light machineguns at the Germans.

We discovered this only when taking over again from the Yeomanry. Then the place was really hot, and we could not get our water in safety. Waving a greeting was no use, all we got was a burst of machine-gun fire.

One thing was evident to me, those Germans did not hate us all that much, any more than we did them, and on more than one occasion I thought of the peaceful moments alongside that small stream at Montigny Farm, when enemies became friends for a short time during the hell of war.

The Brass-Hats knew nothing of our little armistice and the war dragged on and on.

That summer we moved to Tincourt, where we did a lot of front line duty, intermingled with anti-aircraft duty around Cote. Many 'dog-fights' (air battles) took place.

While at Tincourt Sir Harry Lauder came to us, to be escorted to Roisele to visit the grave of his son. An officer and I escorted him. I well remember how very upset he was.

About this time we were issued with a clinometer, for battery firing, and we took four guns up the line and fired them at battery targets just behind the enemy lines, firing through wet sacks and by map reference.

A Marvellous Rest Spell

We moved to billets in the villages of Salou, Sallouelle, and Pont-de-Metz. In the last week of September I was granted 14 days' leave, and when I came back, rejoined my Squadron near Cambrai, and went into the line in Bourlon Wood, where we were subjected to heavy shell fire. Eventually we were relieved by an infantry battalion, and the Squadron moved back to a place called Molliens-Vidame.

I am afraid we were bad boys here. Close to our billet was a nice little estaminet. We would get in there after reveille and order coffee which Madame was kind enough to make for us. Then one educated Alec asked to have rum in his coffee. Madame obliged again. The idea escalated. Everyone wanted rum and coffee and it did not stop at one coffee for some of the lads. Madame was very liberal with the rum.

Exercise time came almost directly we got back to billets, and some of the lads could hardly get into the saddle. This went on for a few days until one morning Lt. Arbuthnot (our section officer) took the exercise, and that finished it. Lt. A. was a good sporty type, but the horses had not altogether liked the handling they had experienced when their riders were half slewed. Madame was instructed not to let us have any rum in our coffee.

While Madame of the estaminet continued to make our rest period a real joy, the same could not be said of an old French farmer who owned a small farm higher up the road. He had it in for us.

British soldiers had stolen a lot of his potatoes, and he blamed his loss on to us. Our lads did not relish being told they were the culprits, because actually we were not involved, and so it was decided to give the farmer something really to moan about. An idea put forward was to steal one of his pigs and have it for dinner, but I'm afraid I scotched that idea, so it was planned to go for his three geese at the first opportunity. Next day the order came to clean up billets and be ready to move at 09.00 hours the following morning, which meant moving fast if the geese operation was to be carried out. That night several of our lads did move fast, and the geese were caught, plucked, and dressed. Three men had one goose each, fastened in the nose bag of his horse and fixed to his saddle, when we paraded next morning.

The Squadron was ready to march off when the gendarmes appeared and spoke to our C.O. He gave permission for the Squadron to be searched. G.S. wagons, and limbers were thoroughly examined but nothing was found, and so the order was given 'walk march', much to our relief.

We trekked to Ham and on to La Fere forest, where the Squadron pegged down. Our section was billeted in a nice quiet little glade under the trees.

While we groomed down and fed our horses, Bruton, our section cook, got a fire going and the dixies on and, of course, the geese cooking. It was then that Lt. Arbuthnot thought it was his duty to see that we were being looked after. I accompanied him. He went over to Bruton and asked, 'What have you got cooking, that smells so nice?' 'Bully-beef and spuds, sir, flavoured with herbs', Bruton said, standing smartly to attention.

My officer continued to sniff. 'Would you like to try some, sir?' Bruton enquired. 'I certainly would Bruton, I am a bit peckish'. He ate with relish, remarking, 'With a stew like that, Bruton, flavoured to taste like goose, you could one day be head Chef of the Savoy Hotel', and as an afterthought, 'I would like to know where you got the herbs'. 'Out of the woods, sir', Bruton replied. A knowing smile from our officer as he said, 'Tell the men to make haste and eat their dinner before the C.O. comes along, and thank you very much, Bruton, I thoroughly enjoyed it'.

Officers in the 3rd M.G.C. Squadron at this time included Captain Wilson (C.O.): Lieutenant Swan, county cricketer: Lieutenant Day, a member of the music publishers Frances, Day and Hunter; Billy Bennett, who after the war became a well-known comedian and radio personality; and Lieutenant Arbuthnot (my section officer), a relative of well-known Service personalities.

SIR DOUGLAS HAIG

A member of the 50th Machine Gun Company, 17th Division, pays this tribute :

Before entering the battle area of Arras, Sir Douglas Haig spoke to us in a place we called Barbed Wire Square.

After the address, Sir Douglas Haig accompanied his troops part of the way towards the battle line.

At a given spot—within shelling distance—he sat on his charger and as we passed him, took the salute.

I well remember how magnificent a figure he looked, and what concern he had shown over the details of our guns and equipment during the preliminary talk.

I think that the troops' respect for him was advanced by this act.

My luck did not hold out long this time. I had served right through the Somme battles of the previous year without mishap, but during an action in the early stages of the Arras battle around the small town of Monchy, I was wounded and did not rejoin my Unit until late 1917.

The 10th Machine Gun Company, by their C.O.

This Company had experienced much service on the Somme and around Ypres before being detailed to take part in the battle of Arras. During the early weeks of 1917, the weather was very severe and we suffered a good deal until March, when, with approaching spring, we were withdrawn in preparation for the Vimy-Arras offensive.

On Easter Monday (April the 9th) we went forward north of Arras and had our first taste of victorious advance for several miles with few casualties.

It was too good to last, and on April the 11th the 10th Brigade caught it badly, the 10th M.G. Company among the rest, in front of Fampoux.

We continued for some months to take part in the Arras battle. In June 1917 two developments of M.G. organisation occurred; the introduction of divisional M.G. Officers, and the arrival of a fourth Machine Gun Company to each Division.

I was appointed D.M.G.O., rather to my dismay, since it meant leaving my old M.G. Company. I think I must have been the most incompetent D.M.G.O. (Divisional Machine Gun Officer) in France—but it was not for long.

At the same time a Service Company from Grantham came to join 4th Division, and was a source of interest to old sweats. It was No. 234 Company, and was promptly dubbed 9–10 Jack.

Arras remained untaken until in September 1918 the advance of the Allies drove the enemy from the neighbourhood. In 1932 a British war memorial was erected there.

BATTLE OF MESSINES RIDGE

Messines is a village of Belgium. It is in Flanders, six miles from Ypres, and gives its name to a ridge of hills conspicuous during the Great War of 1914–18.

On November the 1st, 1914, the Germans entered Messines and held it and the ridge until June the 7th, 1917, when British forces recaptured the ridge.

A machine-gunner who took part in this historic event recalls one of the most outstanding and momentous victories of the war on the Western Front :

For almost two years the sappers of the Royal Engineers had been tunnelling underneath the ridge, which is about seven to eight miles in width. Scores of miles of galleries were dug out to reach the ultimate sap-heads in which were stored the explosives —consisting mainly of many tons of ammonal.

On different turns of duty in the line, I well remember seeing the sappers coming out of the tunnels, looking very begrimed and plastered with mud and water, and feeling sorry that they had to work in such appalling conditions.

I was glad to be just a machine-gunner and above ground. The date of the big 'blow-up' was June the 7th, 1917. Zero hour was fixed for 3.10 a.m.

My Machine Gun Section (74th Company, 25th Division) was situated at a place called Fort-Pinkney—a man-made earthwork about fifteen feet high. We had two guns there, well camouflaged with trees and bushes.

The weather was ideal, and birds were chirping, this being a quiet part of the line.

As zero hour approached, my heart thumped. Our guns were checked by clinometer for overhead fire. Then in a flash it all happened.

The earth shook and all hell was let loose, as nineteen mines were exploded. The entire horizon was heaving with destruction.

No words can adequately describe the horrors of that cataclysm. Vast masses of earth and mangled bodies were hurled skywards, and surviving masses of the enemy ran about dazed and demented by the most awful upheaval in the history of warfare. For a moment or two I was struck dumb by what I was witnessing. Then I heard the voice of my section officer shouting, 'Fire, dammit, Fire'.

My thumbs pressed on the trigger of my gun and the bullets spurted out, and there I sat doing—quite mechanically—what I had been trained to do—traversing-fire.

The field guns in close proximity were belching out shells, and the air in our gun-emplacement was almost choking us.

The colossal scale of the operations took the Germans completely by surprise, and enabled our infantry to take their objectives with few casualties.

We advanced to the brow of the Ridge according to plan, without opposition, and lay by in the huge craters—some being deep enough and wide enough to hold a fair-sized church. Vegetation for as far as the eye could see was blasted, and the Ridge was one mass of holes—large and small—with dug-outs, mazes of trenches, barbed wire, and battle-field debris strewn on every side for miles.

Subsequently we advanced to Warneford Farm, situated on the Ridge itself. In the meantime the Anzacs took over the forward positions of the attack.

Passing through our position an Anzac officer got hit by shrapnel in the muscle of the arm. After receiving first-aid, he came and lay down beside us.

He took off his haversack and told us to have the contents— food which was lavish by our standards.

Next day, June the 8th, we went back to the reserve positions, and regretfully saw the officer in the same place but with his legs shattered in death.

After a short spell in reserve positions the whole of our 25th Division marched back to rest billets, and on a beautiful Sunday morning (I forget the exact date) a Divisional Church Parade was held in a large valley.

I well remember the hymn, 'Oh God, our help in ages past', being heartily sung, which seemed to fill me with a feeling of thankfulness I was still alive, and at the same time a sadness to know that man's inhumanity to man continued.

After the parade the G.O.C. presented each man who had taken part in the Messines battle with a book-marker, specially designed in silk with 'MESSINES' printed in outstanding letters.

*　　*　　*

The Messines operation of June the 7th and 8th, 1917, was directed by Lord Plumer, and 7,000 German prisoners were taken.

The Ridge and other gains were lost in April 1918, during the final German offensive, but they came into British hands again during the Allies' advance in September, 1918.

At the Messines battle of June, 1917, a total of two-hundred and eighty machine-guns were directed on German front and second line trenches—100,000 bullets per minute, with terrible consequences to the Germans. The British machine-gun fire was organised by Colonel Applin and the barrage fire covered a four mile frontage.

THE DUNES DISASTER

(An N.C.O. tells his story)

On a day in early July, 1917, 126 Machine Gun Company arrived at La-Panne near Dunkirk. It was the end of a twenty-four mile march and I had marched under great strain owing to a carbuncle on the back of my neck. The weight of my equipment had caused the carbuncle to burst and upon arrival at our destination I was about all in.

My section officer noticed and immediately ordered me to report to the field hospital at Dunkirk, where I was detained. I was in hospital when the Germans launched their attack, on the morning of July the 10th, against the British 1st Division defending the line amid the sand and swamps of the Belgian coast near Nieuport.

The field hospital became a target for German Botha-pilots who dropped bombs on and around the hospital, killing several and wounding others. This decided me to get out while the going was good. After an argument with the Medical Officer, I was allowed to leave, and I rejoined my gun team just as they were about to proceed to the battle line. As an N.C.O. I was detailed to go on ahead of the Section to explore the possibilities of suitable targets, position, range, etc., I was still far from fit and this led Sergeant Campbell to intervene : 'All right, Bill, you stay with the lads, I'll take over from you,' and away he went with John, the No. 1 on my gun team. It all happened so fast that I had no chance to say 'thanks'—before he and his mate were out of sight in the early morning half-light.

We eventually followed on. Arriving at the entrance to a pill-box kind of dug-out, a gruesome sight met us. Fred Campbell and his companion lay there—both dead.

For a moment or two I was paralysed with shock and grief. We had joined up together in the Oldham Territorials before 1914 and soldiered together right through the war to date. Sergeant Fred Campbell had taken my place and he need not have done so. 'Pity if I can't help an old pal under the weather,' he had said, when I protested about his replacing me.

As I helped wrap Sergeant and Gunner in their blankets for removal for burial, dancing through my mind was the knowledge that he did it for me. I remembered the scriptures, which said— 'Greater love hath no man than that he lay down his life for his friend.' But this knowledge gave me little comfort as I continued to do my job in an automatic kind of way. An infantryman of the 2nd K.R.R. Corps gave us his version of what happened. 'A big shell came right down the coast line and exploded dead in front of the loophole in the trench, at the very moment when Sergeant Campbell and John arrived on the spot. It was a shot in a million,' concluded our informer.

My grief—although deep down inside me—became over-shadowed by events taking place all round us.

The heroic but helpless stand of the British 1st Division amid the sands and swamps of the Belgian coast near Nieuport, constitutes one of the most outstanding episodes of the 1914–18 war. No Britisher can read without a pang of pity, how valiantly but vainly they held out against overwhelming odds amid a whirlwind of liquid fire, and shot and shell, from six a.m. till nine at night on July the 10th, 1917.

The only retreat was across two bridges over the Yser, both of which were destroyed by shell-fire early in the fight, leaving whole battalions stranded, and without any help from land, air or sea. The Germans brought an overpowering artillery fire to bear in advance of the limited area, and after shattering the British front-line defences, lifted their barrage of fire behind the front line, cutting off reserves and retreat. It was estimated that the Germans had the fire power from 168 artillery guns of various calibres.

The tornado was kept up at short intervals all day, shells landing on trenches built on sand at the rate of about four a minute. All telephone and wireless communications were cut, runners (messengers) were knocked out and rifles and machine-guns became clogged with sand as we waited for the coming attack.

At seven o'clock in the evening a whole German Division attacked in three waves in outflanking formation, the aim being to cut off our men completely.

Parties of marines, Flammenwerfer, smoke and petrol bombs preceded the first waves of German assault troops.

Our trenches were hopelessly blocked. Half blinded by smoke and sand, with weapons out of action, our men held out until eight o'clock, fighting the German infantry with bombs and clubbed rifles. C Company of the 1st Northamptonshire Regiment resisted valiantly until nearly all of them were casualties, and survivors were surrounded and captured.

A few men, about a dozen in all, managed to swim the river Yser with bullets hissing all about them. Two riflemen of the 2nd Battalion K.R.R.C. also swam the river with ropes which they fastened to a pontoon in mid-stream, and assisted a party of twenty-two to escape. No other escapes were, however, possible. The enemy rushed up machine-guns, with which they swept the north-west bank of the Yser.

Among the prisoners taken by the Germans was Colonel Tollemache, C.O. 1st Northants Regiment.

Twenty Officers and 570 other ranks of the 1st Northamptonshire Regiment were killed, wounded or captured during the battle of the Dunes on July the 10th 1917, and other battalions

G

in this battle-scarred Division suffered the same fate. Machine Gun casualties were very high.

DAILY ROUTINE ON THE SOMME (1917)

(By a gunner of 62 Machine Gun Company)

I was mostly on the Somme during my spell in France, but to tell you the truth I didn't know where I was at first, only that I was in a reserve trench and under fire.

Our machine-guns were in specially prepared sites dug in the side of the trench, and poking their noses just over the top of the parapet. To fire the gun one had to stand on a raised fire-step.

Ration Fatigue

Ration fatigue was a night operation of importance and entailed many hazards. I had been in the line only a few days when I was detailed for my first R.F. We had to meet the transport at a point some distance from the trenches.

Rations were brought up from the H.Q. dump on pack-mules, these animals being able to get much nearer to the trenches than motor vehicles, and with less noise.

The rations—delivered to us in sand-bags—consisted of bread, meat that had been cooked, rashers of bacon (uncooked), cheese and tins of 'McConnachie' (a miniature dinner which could be warmed up), dry tea and sugar and tins of milk.

The cheese—not properly wrapped—came in contact with the rough sides of the sandbags and consequently became impregnated with fibres, but that was a minor trouble.

Loaded up like mules, we were returning when a harassing enemy artillery fire developed and whizz-bangs lobbed near us. My chums (old soldiers) quickly flung themselves to the ground, but I—being a novice—was much slower off the mark, and by the time I had picked myself up the rest of the ration party was up and off again. When I caught up with them I was told by the N.C.O. in charge that I should have dropped flat when they did. I had much to learn about this foul game.

Upon arrival back in our trenches—near a place called Bullecourt—rations were dished out to each gun team. Being, as usual, very hungry I began to eat my bread and cheese, thinking it was for late supper, but I was quickly informed that rations issued were for the next day and maybe for a few more days ahead, therefore I ought to have resisted eating that night. 'It's not the bloody Ritz here, you know', my section sergeant, an old soldier, informed me. I was learning!

At night-time two men did sentry duty on the guns—two hours on and four off being the routine. Men off duty slept in a dug-out situated at the back of the trench gun-emplacement. This particular dug-out was of the type portrayed by Bruce Bairns-father in his famous cartoon of 'Old Bill and the better 'ole', there being hardly enough room for two tallish chaps to stretch out to full length.

The dug-out was lit up by a couple of candles and issued with rations. Sacking was erected at the entrance to the dug-out to prevent any light showing and to stop gas from entering. One would think that sleep was impossible under such conditions, with guns often roaring throughout the night, but I was always so weary at the end of my spell that I usually slept well. When I first went into the trenches, I noticed men catching lice from their clothes, and secretly hoped I would not get like them. Mere wish-ful thinking on my part, for it was not long before I was also 'chatty'. I well remember a most pleasant feature of my first spell in the line which occurred on some days just before daylight—called 'stand-to' time—when the singing of skylarks high above us seemed to send down a message of peace to the hell on earth below them.

Rest Period

After several weeks of duty in the front line we prepared to proceed to rest billets, and with warm weather it was a nice change. On this occasion the whole of the 62nd Division gradu-ally moved out as the relief took over.

The changeover took place at night. We left our tripods in position, only removing the guns. The incoming machine-gun companies brought their own guns.

Such an operation called for much skill in organisation. During the process of moving, Very lights were continually sent up. This was not done for our convenience, but to enable sentries to watch out for enemy patrol movements in no-man's-land. Everyone knew his allotted task, and got on with it silently and swiftly.

By midnight we had left the trenches well behind, and after marching some eight miles arrived at our billets—a nice dry barn. 'Be careful with the matches', shouted the C.S.M., as we hastily took off our equipment and enjoyed a smoke.

While on rest, reveille was not too early, and after breakfast a general clean-up was the order of the day. Hair had to be cut, and boots dubbined.

The most important duty was the thorough cleaning of our guns, and ammunition was taken from the belts round by round, cleaned and replaced ready for use. Transport limbers were washed and greased.

A few parades were held but nothing was overdone, as we had to build up energy for our return to 'Hell'.

While on rest, we received some pay—sous and francs included —which looked a lot of trash to me, but it was all spendable, said the pay-clerk. To prove it, most of us paid a nightly visit to a nearby estaminet. The cafe was open for troops until 8 p.m. At this hour the proprietor would call out 'huit heures' and the Orderly Corporal would appear on the scene to see this order carried out.

Another luxury we enjoyed was fresh eggs and butter obtained from friendly village folk near our billets; also French bread, long and narrow affairs but very wholesome, and a welcome change from stodgy ration bread.

Return to Trenches

Rest spell ended and preparations were made for a return to the trenches. Gun limbers laden and troops refreshed, we moved off along leafy lanes. On this glorious afternoon of a July day the peaceful surroundings, only disturbed by the steady tramp of marching men and the resounding hoofbeats of the mules pulling our gun and equipment limbers, made war seem unreal and stupid.

We had to march nearly 12 miles before we reached the trenches, and after covering about half of this distance a halt was made. An infantry battalion on the way to the front passed by us. A section of one Company sang as they marched—

> At the halt of the left form platoon,
> At the halt of the left form platoon,
> If the odd numbers don't mark time two paces
> How the hell can the rest form platoon?

Most of the singers were men of Britain's conscript army, and were on their way to the trenches for the first time, but their courage was evident.

'Good old machine-gunners' shouted an N.C.O. as he brushed past me. 'Good luck' several of us called back.

I knew that they would need it. Infantry lads had dubbed us 'suicide squads' but from what I had seen of the infantrymen I was certain that they were mere cannon-fodder in many instances. I continued to follow them with my eyes until they had disappeared from sight. Silence again embraced the lane where we rested. It was as though a ghost army had passed by. Mules chewed up anything they fancied within reach in the hedge-rows; officers and men talked quietly : all so reminiscent of training days around the lanes of Grantham, England. Nostalgia was, however, suddenly shattered when a sharp command rang out—'Fall-in'—and we continued on our way to another round of trench routine, which sapped one's vitality and polluted the mind.

As soon as the order 'No smoking' was given, one sensed the nearness to the sector of the line we were to occupy. It was almost dark when we eventually reached the entrance to the communication trenches, and began to unload our limbers. Very lights distinctly outlined the shape of the front, which was bulged and dented. At some points the line curled behind us. These bends were called salients.

The thunder of the guns vibrated through the air and echoed across the valleys. The whole aspect now seemed morbid. Limbers unloaded, each gun team took over its own guns and equipment and began the long trek through communication trenches to alloted positions in the front-line.

Ammunition, water and rations all had to be manhandled, which entailed several journeys before finally taking over from the out-going gun-teams. 'This time we are several miles from our old positions,' said my section officer.

Actually I could not have cared less where we were, for by the time we had finished fatigues up and down those long C trenches my shoulders and limbs felt pulverised.

'You'll get used to it, if you live long enough,' cracked my old soldier section sergeant.

I remember seeing the Transport Section making a bee-line for Company headquarters, situated some distance from the line, and wondered if I could get a transfer to their crowd.

It must be safer and more palatable I thought, although I knew that if Jerry did spot them he would most certainly introduce them to his 5.9 shells—which were very unpleasant things.

Another drawback in the Transport Section : those temperamental mules who were not too fussy about giving you a kick in the stomach if they did not take to you. No ! upon reflection I decided to stay a gunner.

Another spell of front-line duty commenced.

At 'stand-to' time we trained our guns on specific points. After 'stand-down' (daylight) the bacon was soon frizzling in the lid of a dixie over the heat of a Tommy's cooker (a small receptacle filled with cotton wool soaked in methylated spirit). Three prongs stood up from the flame, on which the lid was placed containing the rasher. On occasions we ran out of methylated spirit, and then we improvised. Candles were cut up and mixed with cotton wool as a substitute for the meths. It worked, but took half an hour longer to boil water to make tea. Water supplies often came to us in old petrol tins—not always thoroughly cleaned out—with the result that our tea invariably tasted of petrol, but no-one bothered much providing Fritz left us in peace to enjoy our breakfast. During quiet spells this was usually the case. It seemed that both sides had a sort of undeclared agreement and settled down to breakfast simultaneously.

Some days, shelling would persist, interwoven with machine-gun fire. Men not on gun-duty could relax in a dug-out situated behind our gun-emplacement. This dug-out was a different proposition from the one I had experienced on my first spell of front-line duty. Royal Engineers had built it. A real haven of rest compared to the previous hole in the ground. Another booster to morale was the arrival of what was termed 'Comforts for the Troops' which included socks, scarves, gloves, and other garments knitted by kind people and relatives back home.

Socks were especially welcome, and we did some swapping around which enlivened tedious rest spells in the dug-outs.

In the line, water was always very scarce, but even so, Lieut. Wright, my section officer, insisted that the men under his command shaved whenever possible, which meant every day when things were quiet. To conform to this order we used to fill an old tin or a dixie-lid with water, dip in our shaving brushes, shave, and then run the soapy brush over face and neck, drying off with something resembling a towel.

The only other chance to get a decent wash was to crawl out after dark to a water-filled shell hole in no-man's land and fill one's tin-hat with water, taking care to scoop and not dig down. Sometimes we did this.

I cannot say I relished front-line trench routine, and was always thankful when the time arrived again for a rest spell. In billets time seemed too short, and up there all too long.

MEMORIES OF A FRONT-LINE RUNNER

(62 Machine Gun Company)

Continued heavy shelling by the enemy often severed telephone communications between the front line and Battalion and Brigade Headquarters.

At such times vital messages were carried by runners. One who served with the 62nd Machine Gun Company relates his experiences.

My company was in the line around Bullecourt-Sector during the summer months of 1917.

It was an area of devastation. The countryside was pitted with shell holes, and only the stumps of once beautiful trees remained.

Our machine-guns were set up amid the ruins on the outskirts of Bullecourt. It had been the scene of a big battle and when we took over there, bodies of dead soldiers still lay unburied. There was much strafing by day and night. Gunners not on duty rested in an old cellar of a house at the far end of the village. We had to share our rest billet with a team of trench-mortar men who had their gun fixed above us in the ruined house.

Periodically, throughout the day and night they fired their mortar-bombs, which resembled small footballs on long sticks. The noise of the gun discharge was terrific, and every time the gun fired pieces of rubble and masonry came down into the cellar. It was certainly no place in which to sleep, but as no other billet was available for us we had to make the best of it in between telling the T.M. Battery what we thought of them and their blasted gun. Actually they were a brave lot of lads who never got the recognition deserved for their valiant service in the line.

About this time I was appointed runner for No. 62 Machine Gun Company. This new job meant my being away from the guns in the line, but I was always liable to be re-called to help on the guns if circumstances warranted this. For identification purposes I was issued with a red armlet.

During my spell of messenger duties I travelled long distances in the trenches by day, and overland at night.

Almost every day I had to pass along a deep trench which had been dug through the graves of soldiers.

Protruding from the sides of the trench were portions of stockinged feet, and various parts of the human body. Although this spot was disinfected regularly by the pioneer squad, the stench was unbearable, and this was summertime and very hot weather.

In many parts a simple cross appeared, marked 'To an unknown soldier'. After passing through this long deep trench I came to a shallow system of trenches—more like earthworks. Here was a notice—'Beware of sniper', and during daylight I almost crawled through this section of trench.

Most of the trenches were dug in a zig-zag pattern called traverse which lessened the effects of shell fire. A certain amount of humour existed among the troops, and one way of expressing this was by naming trenches and dug-outs from place names in England. One dug-out I passed was named The Dorchester, another The Regent and a bend in the trench was named Windy-Corner. There was Piccadilly Circus, Hell's Drive, and so on. These names helped me considerably as a means of direction. When entering a new sector it was sometimes very difficult to find my way round. Being a country lad I was accustomed to making mental notes of landmarks, such as a certain tree stump or clump of trees, and when I travelled overland at night time, I found this method of observation most helpful.

At night time I always travelled over the top—unless of course I encountered artillery shelling, and then I quickly dived into the nearest trench for cover.

Very often during these night expeditions I was halted by a sentry, and his challenge of 'Halt who goes there' called for a quick response from me of 'Friend'. Then came another order 'Advance and be recognised and give the countersign' (a certain codeword known to all Sentries and of course myself) and this was quickly given by me. Any slip-up on my part might well have been a fatal one. The rifle and bayonet carried by the sentry was a nasty bit of kit to lark about with. Satisfied I was on legitimate business after a close inspection of my arm band, I was directed to 'Pass friend, all's well' and most sentries I met usually added, 'Best of luck chum'. At times I certainly needed it.

ON THE WESTERN FRONT WITH
47 MACHINE GUN COMPANY

(By a Worcestershire lad)

When war was declared on August 4th, 1914, I was barely sixteen years of age. Many young men in our village joined Kitchener's Army, and Territorials of the County Regiment went to France in 1915 to reinforce the decimated regular army units.

During the first year of the war I tried to satisfy my eagerness to help by writing to my older friends 'out there', usually enclosing two or three packets of Woodbines—which were at that time a mere penny per packet of five cigarettes.

I read and followed up in the daily and local newspapers reports of battles. In 1916 I tried several times to enlist, but directly it was discovered I was working on my father's market garden I was told to forget about enlisting.

My job had suddenly become of vital importance. German

U-Boats were sinking Allied merchant ships faster than it was possible to replace them. Every ounce of food must be got out of the land at home. Britain must not be starved into submission; and it was not until after the British Navy began to get on top of the U-Boat menace and strict rationing was introduced in Britain in 1916, that the threat of starvation was averted. 'Thank God for the British Navy,' said everyone fighting for the allied cause.

On January 18th, 1917, my frustration ended and I was allowed to enlist. After three months' recruit training at Chiseldon several of us were interviewed for No. 5 Training Battalion Machine Gun Corps, and posted to Belton Park, Grantham, Lincs. where we underwent intensive training on the Vickers machine-gun over a period of a further three months. On August 9th, 1917, Tom Wilson (a local pal of mine) and I, having been put on a draft for No. 47 Machine Gun Company (serving somewhere in France) disembarked from a crowded troop ship at Boulogne around 10.30 a.m. August 10th, 1917.

We marched through the town and up the hill to St. Martin's camp. Many French women lined the pavements of the streets we passed through. Some of the women shouted bawdy remarks at us, but there were others who remained silent, and the look on their faces seemed to say, 'Poor devils! they little know what they are in for, and very soon now'.

We arrived at the camp just in time to see the troop ship which had brought us over the Channel beginning her return journey to England. A twinge of home-sickness entered my stomach as I watched the last link with dear old Blighty gliding away into seemingly empty space.

Next day we entrained for the machine-gun base at Camiers, where we underwent certain efficiency tests on the gun, and also went through the gas-hut to test the worthiness of our gas-helmets.

The following day we marched to Étaples, 17 miles from the port of Boulogne. During the march we passed a large military cemetery which was absolutely covered with bright red poppies : a spectacle I have never forgotten.

The 'Base-Wallahs' having satisfied themselves that we were ready to take our places in the front line loaded us on a train for Poperinghe, a small Belgian town six miles west of Ypres. It was here that the Church Institute, known as 'Toc H' was established in 1915. 'Toc H' still lives. I always seemed to have a lot of luck during my war service and it began upon arrival at Poperinghe.

'Where are you lot for?' asked the Railway Transport Officer. '16th Division', replied the officer in charge of our draft. 'Your luck's in, they were relieved from the line a day or so ago', said the R.T.O.

The officer told us to stand at ease, and while we were so doing an enemy plane circled high overhead, looking like a moth in the searchlight beams.

Ack-Ack guns nearby opened fire and I got my first taste of shrapnel as a bit tinkled down on my steel helmet. Further instructions arrived and instead of marching up to Ypres, we went the other way towards Wattan St. Jean. The Ypres Salient was clearly visible. Very lights and continuous exploding shells made the area look like the half circle of a rising sun.

From Poperinghe to St. Jean was not far, but even so our officer—as green as we were—got lost in the inky blackness of the night, and it took us from 9.30 p.m. to 4.00 a.m. to reach the R.E. dump in the square at Wattan St. Jean.

After over six hours of marching with full pack, it was a great relief to take the weight off our back and rest our feet. At Wattan we got a substantial meal of bread and meat, washed down by tea. A few hours' sleep followed and this revived our flagging energy.

Next day we journeyed by lorry and train to Bapaume where we got a cup of cocoa and a biscuit at the Y.M.C.A. hut, after which we marched to Gomiecourt—one of the places flattened during the Somme battles of 1916—and there, camping on the outskirts of the ruins was 47th Machine Gun Company. I was detailed to share a bivouac with an old soldier of the Company. As soon as I had settled in I began to write a letter to the folks at home. Out of my north eye I saw my companion take off his shirt and begin to search the garment most diligently. There was an occasional crack. I looked up from my task and asked 'What are you doing then?' 'Haven't you got any?' enquired my new chum. 'Got any what?' I asked. 'Bloody lice,' came the reply. 'I hope not,' I said. 'Bloody lucky you are then,' I was told. I continued my writing and the occasional crack continued without any apparent animosity.

Rest period for No. 47 Machine Gun Company ended, and on Saturday afternoon, August 22nd, 1917, we marched overland via Ervillers and St. Leger into the trenches on a ridge above Croisilles. It was my first time in the front-line trenches, which were very deep and well revetted. I was detailed to join a gun-team under Sergeant Coots and anchored down in a captured German pill-box, not very roomy but very substantial.

I was also detailed for my first Sentry duty from 8 p.m. to 10 p.m. An easy spell 'as you was a newcomer', said my Sergeant. It rained like hell the whole of the two hours. The rain penetrated my greatcoat and the waterproof sheet around my shoulders and ran down my legs into my boots.

I could not help casting my mind back to past Saturday nights back home with the lads at Evesham, before the world went mad. A few minutes after 10 p.m. my relief took over. 'Nothing to report,' I said, and gave a sickly grin.

The water in my boots made a peculiar squeaking noise as I walked along the duck-boards and crept into our dug-out. Sergeant Coots looked up as I entered. He said nothing, but gave me a rather friendly smile, as though he understood. He watched me trying to dry out, and then gave me one or two good tips. Sergeant Coots had experienced the Ypres Salient.

After a week or more in Sergeant Coots' team I was transferred to L/Cpl. Duggie Stuart's team, which occupied a more congenial position in a railway cutting extending from the right of Croisilles to Ecoust—immediately behind Bullecourt.

Apart from various discomforts this part of the line was, at the time, very quiet. A rest-cure indeed to the battle weary 16th Division. However, it was while on this supposed rest-cure that I experienced my first gas-shelling and saw death strike, and it happened so suddenly.

From the entrance of our dug-out I stood idly watching a party of Royal Engineers removing some gas-cylinders embedded on the bank of the railway cutting nearest to us.

Suddenly Jerry sent over a shell which landed right among the R.E's and one of them was no more—remnants of his body being blown on top of our dug-out.

After this incident we got instructions to dig another dug-out in a part of the railway cutting less vulnerable to enemy shell-fire. After a few days and nights hard work, we completed a dug-out much larger and more comfortable than the previous one, and we moved in. We named our new abode 'The Nest'.

Hair cut, sir?

One day when things were exceptionally quiet, Cpl. Stuart asked, 'Can anyone cut hair?' No one rushed, so he repeated the question. 'I'll have a go,' I said, and after the edge of the scissors had been rubbed with emery paper (both obtained from our machine-gun spare parts box), I set about the task. Sometimes the scissors cut and sometimes they merely went through the motions without any visible results.

Occasionally the scissors got jammed and I had to do a sort of wrestling act to disentangle cutting instruments from hair, which brought remarks from the sufferer such as 'Oh! Bloody Hell!' However, I eventually did a passable job on the locks of my team-mates, but by that time I had blisters on thumb and finger of my right hand. Rest period from the front line came round and while we were in billets, our Company Sergeant Major—who had eyes everywhere—asked Cpl. Stuart, 'Who cut your hair, Corporal?' I was sent for and instructed to take over as Company barber. Big clippers (one spring broken), small neck clippers, and scissors were handed over to me by the C.S.M., with the words 'It's all yours'.

I soon discovered that the big clippers were useless so I persevered with the neck clippers and scissors. Everything went well with the soft hair types, but when I struck a good crop of long strong hair, shoulders would start crouching as my bluntish cutting instruments dragged, and there would be an oath or two from the sufferer. When this happened I would apologise and say, 'Keep still. I'll soon have them out.'

At the conclusion of each hair cut I showed off by making a clicking noise with the scissors (they were practically useless for anything else) and loudly exclaimed 'Who's next?' to the waiting queue. The C.S.M. who suffered first stood by to see that everyone did get a hair cut, and from time to time encouraged me with the remark : 'Keep at it, boy, you're doing fine.'

Although most of the sufferers moaned, ordinary ranks gave me a tip of half a franc, and officers I dealt with usually gave me two francs. Even the C.O. allowed me to operate on his hair, which being on the thin side, turned out to be quite a picnic. When I gave him an old mirror to view my work, he remarked, 'Splendid, I don't see what the blazes they are all grumbling about.' By the time we were due to return to the line, practically everyone in the Company had experienced the horrors of my barbering efforts, which led our C.S.M. to remark to me, 'Well, lad, they look more like soldiers now.'

'What have you done with all the money you have robbed us of?' shouted a gunner marching in front of our team, as he tramped along the road towards the front line. 'Who's your next of kin?' was another good leg-pull. I certainly had a few francs tucked away in my belt, and secretly planned a binge with my pals when we struck the right place.

THE THIRD BATTLE OF YPRES, 1917

The third battle of Ypres began in June, 1917 and did not end until November of that year. The battle formed part of the Allied offensive in Flanders. Although mud seriously impeded the tanks, the Allies succeeded in capturing the whole range of heights between Armentières and Passchendaele without, however, dislodging the Germans from the coast.

In this momentous battle men of the Machine Gun Corps played a vital role—as the following extracts from the History and Memoir of the 33rd Battalion Machine Gun Corps show :

The third battle of Ypres had already begun, and so obsessed now was the higher command by the Machine Gun Barrage, that the Machine Gun Companies of every available Division were crowded into line to support the offensive.

Accordingly half the 19th and 248th M.G.C. companies were despatched by train from Watou to Dickebusch, where they camped, to construct barrage positions and carry ammunition to the neighbourhood of Stirling Castle, a fortnight before the operation was undertaken.

A week later Major Hutchinson, with the remaining half of these two companies, joined the advance party, and these two companies under his command were attached for operations with the 23rd Division. The whole scheme involved many hundreds of guns co-ordinated by Lieut-Colonel Bidder, the 10th Corps M.G.C. officer.

The Division with the 98th and 100th Machine Gun Companies followed into the Dickebusch Area on the 18th of September, but by this time the 19th and 248th Companies with the Divisional M.G. Officer co-operating with the 23rd Division, had moved forward to their barrage positions to take part in the first big assault on the line of hills which runs through Inverness Copse, Polygon Wood and thence to Passchendaele and West-rooskeke.

On the morning of September the 20th, 1917, the assault was made. Batteries supporting the 23rd Division lay in the middle of the Boche barrage fire-line.

No sooner had the attack begun when two complete gun teams of the 248th Company were killed, and Captain J. R. Bellerby, and several other men were severely wounded.

The first and second phase of the attack included the capture of Inverness Copse and Dunbarton Lakes—important German strong-points.

For the next phase of the operations it was necessary to move forward the barrage position to the edge of Inverness Copse. This was an exceedingly arduous task, but it was carried out to time under the most able direction of Captain Falkner, in spite of heavy enemy shell fire. The machine-guns were thus able to cover the third phase of the attack, which included the capture of the Tower Hamlets Ridge. During this operation Captain Falkner was severely wounded. For this action, which occupied both the 20th and 21st of September, the following awards were made in the 19th Machine Gun Company :

Captain Falkner was awarded the Military Cross.

Sergeant Gillespie was awarded the Distinguished Conduct medal, and Private Dellenty the Military Medal.

In the 248th Machine Gun Company, Sergeant Dean (who had been transferred to the 100th Company) was awarded a bar to his D.C.M. and Sergeant Goode the Military Medal.

On the morning of the 22nd of September both these Companies were relieved, and returned to Dickebusch.

Already orders had been issued for a second attack upon the great Belgium Ridge to include the capture of Polygon Wood, the Reutelbeke and Polderhoek Chateau on the 33rd Divisional front. Very little time was available for reconnaissance and for dumping ammunition in the forward area—in the case of one Company as far as Northampton Farm, two miles across broken and boggy land. Supporting the 33rd Divisional attack, their 98th Brigade was to go on the right and 100th Brigade on the left. The 19th, 248th, and 207th (Independent) Machine Gun Companies were selected as barrage groups. The 19th Brigade was ordered in support.

By midnight on the 24th-25th of September, both the 98th and 100th Brigades were concentrated for the attack. In the 98th Brigade were the 2nd Argyll and Sutherland Highlanders, 1st Middlesex and 4th Kings; and in the 100th Brigade the 9th H.L.I. and the 1st Queens were the leading battalions. The 98th and 100th Machine Gun Companies were concentrated to support their own Brigades.

The 207th Machine Gun Company, under Captain Gelsthorpe, was ordered to be in position by 1 a.m. on the morning of the 25th, about 150 yards behind our front posts, close to Northampton Farm—composed of two batteries of eight guns each;

the 19th Machine Gun Company was ordered to be in position by 3 a.m. just west of Inverness Copse—composed of two batteries of eight guns each; the 248th Machine Gun Company was ordered to be in position by dawn on the 25th of September opposite Bodmin Copse—composed of two batteries of eight guns each.

The attack of the Second Army, including the 33rd Division, was ordered for dawn on the 26th instant. At about 3.30 on the morning of the 25th, the enemy opened a bombardment of hitherto unparalleled intensity upon our Front.

The S.O.S. Signal was seen at every point, and our machine-guns of the 19th and 207th Companies, which were in position, opened fire. So intense was the bombardment and in such great depth that it reached our rear communications, and it was impossible to get transport of the 248th Company up the roads. An attempt was made by Lieut. Franklin and Sergeant Tyson, but the Company suffered such severe casualties in vehicles, animals, and personnel, that it was determined to await a lull before proceeding. Lieut. Franklin, C.O. of 248th Company, himself went forward and reported to Major Hutchinson.

Meanwhile, at dawn, following up their bombardment, the enemy counter-attacked in massed formation upon our lines, no fewer than five Divisions being used in this attack upon the 33rd Divisional front. We had already suffered severe casualties from the German bombardment, Inverness Copse, in particular, in which were concentrated two Battalions—having been swept aside as though with a scythe.

The post of the Queen's was driven in and two Companies either slaughtered or captured.

The Glasgow Highlanders, fighting with great courage, were driven back, as were the 2nd Worcesters and the 4th King's.

The 1st Middlesex and the 93rd held their ground, two Companies of the latter Regiment being completely cut off from the rest of their Battalion, with the enemy in between them and their friends.

It was during this attack that most valuable services were rendered by Lieut. Huskisson, Sergeant Heanley, Corporal Bates, Corporal Hudson, and Private Samuels, of the 100th Machine Gun Company, in support of the 2nd Worcestershires and the 4th King's. Two gun teams were cut off and attacked with Flammenwerfer. The teams fought to the last, being either shot dead or hideously burnt, wounded or captured. Private Rogers, M.M., who was taken prisoner and released at the end of the war, wrote confirming the heavy casualties inflicted upon the enemy. Lieut. Adams and Sergeant Harris of the 98th Machine Gun Company, on the flank of the Division co-operating with the Australians in Polygon Wood also did fine work.

The 207th Machine Gun Company, which, as already noted, was close behind our front line grouped in batteries, opened fire with sixteen guns at almost point blank range into massive hordes of the enemy concentrated behind Polderhock Chateau Ridge. As soon as their bodies were seen down to the knee topping the lines, Captain Gelsthorpe's batteries opened a murderous fire into their ranks.

Low-flying enemy aeroplanes soon, however, detected him and both by machine-gunning and directing artillery fire upon the 207th Machine Gun Company, the enemy inflicted very severe casualties on the gunners. Captain Gelsthorpe realised that his position was untenable and withdrew his guns (excepting four which had been totally destroyed), in perfect order to a new position east of Stirling Castle, dug-in, relaid his lines and personally reported what he had done.

During the whole period Captain Gelsthorpe and his two remaining officers, one of whom was wounded, and his whole Company, such as were left of them, displayed the most conspicuous gallantry and devotion to duty and inflicted heavy losses on the enemy. No less gallant work was done by the 19th Machine Gun Company, which, although more fortunate in its position, answered twenty-one S.O.S. calls, being the whole time exposed to the heaviest shell fire. Every prisoner taken reported the annihilating effect of the machine-gun barrage, and the hideous losses inflicted both on the attacking and supporting troops. Lieut. Stokes was killed while gallantly directing the fire of his guns.

In the 207th Machine Gun Company, Captain Gelsthorpe was awarded the D.S.O. and two officers the Military Cross. Two D.C.M.'s and five Military Medals were also awarded to this Company.

In the 19th Machine Gun Company, Lieut. Harrison was awarded the Military Cross, Sergeant Bull the D.C.M. and Sergeant Rose and Lance-Corporal Clark the Military Medal.

In the 98th Machine Gun Company Lieut. Adams was awarded the Military Cross, Corporal Dean, L/Corporal Boast, and Private Campbell the Military Medal, and in the 100th Machine Gun Company, Sergeant Heanley was awarded the D.C.M.; and Corporal Gates, Corporal Hudson, L/Corporal Samuels, D.C.M., Private Joyce and Private Barrass were awarded the Military Medal.

During this action, so heavy was the German counter-battery bombardment, that despite the fact that we had undoubtedly a preponderance of artillery—guns of all calibres being locked almost wheel to wheel along the whole front, and in many lines —it could be felt to grow weaker and weaker.

Except for a lull of about twenty minutes the intensity of the bombardment never lessened during the whole of the 25th and the night of the 25th-26th.

At 9 p.m. orders were received from the higher command, that although Division had by this time suffered about 5,000 casualties, the original attack would be carried out according to plan on the morning of the 26th.

During the night of the 25th-26th, 700,000 rounds of ammunition were got up by the pack train of the D.A.C. to replenish the dumps at our Machine Gun battery positions, and such reliefs of gunners as were possible were carried out.

Captain Lewthwaite arrived to take over command of the 19th Machine Gun Company, replacing the wounded Captain Falkner. Possibly no more severe trial of machine-gunners was ever made. Everything was ready by zero hour on the 26th. The attack swept along the whole of the 33rd Divisional front with extreme bitterness. Very few prisoners were taken. Enormous numbers of the enemy were found dead, and the 93rd and Middlesex, who were cut off, were found to have maintained their original positions of the 25th intact, having endured not only the enemy attack, but our own bombardment.

Captured enemy documents showed what efforts the enemy made on the 25th September, 1917, against the front held by the 33rd Division between Ypres–Menin Road and the southern edge of the Polygon Wood.

The difficulties experienced by our troops were enormous. Not a square yard of ground existed which was not pockmarked with craters, resembling rather some hideous disease than a once beautiful wooded countryside.

Although it had been in action for only two days, the Division had incurred over 6,000 casualties, and had been through what was probably its worst ordeal in battle.

It was withdrawn to the Bailleul-Ravensburg area to rest for a few days, and then was put into a comparatively quiet, though uncomfortable, part of the line east of the Messines Ridge to reorganise. Our so-called rest period ended on November the 16th when we relieved the 4th Canadian Division in the Ypres Salient.

The winter experience of the 33rd Division, which had gone

from worse to worse, undoubtedly culminated in unpleasantness and horror during its tours of the Passchendaele Salient. To reach the machine-gun positions it was necessary to traverse a single duck-board for two and a half hours, and then plunge into a slough of filthy shell holes amongst which hundreds of unburied dead grinned from miles of tangled wire and stunted trees. The gun teams carrying complete rations for the period were lost to sight in the sea of mud for four days without relief; violent harassing fire, requiring thousands of rounds which had to be carried daily to the guns, was demanded, and it was impossible to get limbers within two miles of the guns. The Salient was only 1,000 yards across and extended to a depth of about 3,000 yards, and the whole area was overlooked by the enemy and swept by shell fire and gas of all descriptions, continuously, particularly the single duck-board, both during the day and during the night.

Some idea of what the machine-gunners underwent, both psysically and mentally, may be imagined. The casualties sustained from shell fire, gas and exposure, were very considerable.

FROM GRANTHAM TO PASSCHENDAELE

Passchendaele, a low ridge in Belgium about seven and a half miles north-east of Ypres, was the scene of bitter fighting.

In June, 1917, the Second Army under Sir Herbert Plumer, advanced and stormed the Messines-Wytschaete Ridges, but it was not until November 6th that the Passchendaele Ridge was carried, and the Third battle of Ypres concluded.

Machine Gunner No. 66518 had every reason to remember this date, for on November the 5th, 1917, he received a wound which necessitated amputation of his left leg above the knee. A grim souvenir, but, as he cheerfully comments, he did survive the battle and many of his chums did not do so.

My part in the war began when I was called up in late 1916, and after a spell of training with the Yorks. and Lancs. Regiment, I volunteered for the Suicide Club (M.G.C.), eventually being sent to Harrowby Camp, just outside Grantham. I was promoted to the rank of Lance-Corporal (unpaid) and very soon qualified as an instructor on the Vickers machine-gun. From Harrowby I was sent to Belton Park, Grantham. Snow and frost gave the hutted camp the appearance of an Arctic outpost.

Guard duties always bored me, and on one of these I got reported for going to the latrine, which was a hut, two feet square.

Cavalry machine-gun team coming into action, Querrieu, July 1916.
(By kind permission of the Imperial War Museum.)

Officer and gunner moving a machine-gun into the front line.
(By kind permission of the Imperial War Museum.)

Battle of the Somme. Lewis gun in action near Ovillers, July 1916.
(By kind permission of the Imperial War Museum.)

Battle of the Ancre. Men of the North Staffordshire Regiment
with German machine-guns captured at Beaucourt sur Ancre,
14th. November 1916.

A winter night, Western front, 1917.
(By kind permission of the Imperial War Museum.)

Machine Gun Corps anti-aircraft post near Zillebeke, 21st. September 1917.
(By kind permission of the Imperial War Museum.)

Machine-gunners in action on the Somme, dealing with a gas attack.
(By kind permission of the Imperial War Museum.)

Lancashire Fusiliers cleaning their Lewis gun in a front-line trench opposite Messines, January 1917. Note the gas alarm and wind vane.
(By kind permission of the Imperial War Museum.)

No.1 Section, 257 Machine Gun Company enjoying a halt on the way up to Kut, February 1917.

Indian troops entering Baghdad, March 11th. 1917.
(By kind permission of the Imperial War Museum.)

1/8th. Battalion Gurkha troops resting in captured Turkish trench at Tekrit, Mesopotamia, 5th. November 1917.
(By kind permission of the Imperial War Museum.)

Machine-gun post in the open, Mesopotamia.
(By kind permission of the Imperial War Museum.)

Machine-gun as an "Archie", Salonica front.

French machine-gun team in support line, relieving British machine-gunners.
(By kind permission of the Imperial War Museum.)

General Horne inspecting the 24th.
Motor Machine Gun Battalion at
Dieval 12th. June 1918.
*(By kind permission of the
Imperial War Museum.)*

*"The Boy David" by Derwent
Wood R.A.,* The Machine Gun
Corps Memorial, Hyde Park
Corner, London.

In order to enter I was obliged to discard my equipment and I lodged my rifle by the outside of the hut. The whole lot slid gracefully into the snow. Going his rounds the orderly officer spotted my kit, with the result that I was put on a charge. Terrible crime to leave my guard-post said the camp C.O., and L/Cpl. 66518 became Private 66518.

In the Spring of 1917, playing at soldiers ended when I was put on a draft to join No. 205 Machine Gun Company serving somewhere in France. I was not sorry to leave the desolation of Belton Park, but I little knew that very soon I would encounter a desolation that would make Belton Park appear like Buckingham Palace in comparison.

Arriving at Camiers—the Machine Gun Base in France near Étaples—our draft was sent up the line to join No. 205 M.G.C. attached to the 5th Division. We found them in a rest camp at Roclincourt near Vimy Ridge, midway between the towns of Lens and Arras. In passing—for the information of the reader—Vimy Ridge played an exceptionally important part in the Great War. In early 1915 the French successfully opposed the Germans at Vimy : In 1916 a Canadian force, by dint of sheer bravery, took possession of the Ridge.* This possession was extremely valuable during the stemming of the German onslaught in March 1918.

Number 205 Machine Gun Company did a spell of duty round Vimy and it was here that I received my initial battle-training. Then we went into the line opposite 'Oppy Wood', a name acquired, so I was told, some time earlier when Germans and British were continually hopping in and out of the place. Leaving Oppy Wood, our Company moved on to Ypres. The Third Battle of Ypres had begun when we arrived. There was mud waist-deep around support and front-line trenches. As we tried to cope I remembered the ideal trench I had seen somewhere near the base. It was dug to a depth of 10 feet with five rows of sandbags neatly dovetailed on the top of the trench. A real show piece, and as dry as a bone that had been well licked by a dog.

It was said that King George V, accompanied by high-ranking army officers, had inspected this show trench, and had been most impressed. When I saw it, so was I. Only a large shell making a direct hit could shatter such a trench, I thought, and it would certainly give adequate protection from shrapnel.

What a joke it all seemed when one became acquainted with reality—holes in the ground surrounded by evil smelling muddy water which filled up the huge shell craters around Ypres. Ac-

* There is a Canadian Monument at Vimy Ridge.

cording to men I talked to who had, by the grace of God, survived a year or more in and out of Ypres Salient, there never had
been any ideal trenches. 'Brass-Hats' very rarely went anywhere
near the front line in the Salient. They hadn't a clue what conditions were really like from experience. Theory and practice
were always miles apart on most of the battlefronts of the war
that was supposed to end wars, so far as the Western Front was
concerned.

At night time, we tried to dig emplacements for our machine-
guns, but after two feet the sides slid into the mud and water.
As we dug, quite often Jack-Johnson's (German five-nine shells)
were dropping all round us, leaving us exposed in the open
ground.

On the night of November the 5th, 1917, a phosphorus shell
exploded among the machine-gun team I was serving with. In
the dark it was a gruesome sight. My wound was a Blighty one.

RATION FATIGUE IN THE SALIENT

As already mentioned, getting rations and other vital supplies
to front-line troops in the Ypres Salient was a terrible job. Recollections of this will for ever remain in the memory of a Yorkshire
man who served with 98th Machine Gun Company transport,
and experienced the ordeal of many ration fatigues in the swampy
blood-stained Salient of Ypres (Wipers to the troops).

Men due for a ration fatigue column were usually detailed the
previous day, by the transport section sergeant. 'Ration fatigue
tomorrow night at eight pip-emma, Rendezvous. Company Lines,
half timber, two mules or horses, and pack for same, Right?'
'Right sergeant.' A hard, risky and disagreeable job lay
ahead.

Animals were fed and watered in good time; various packs
looked over; water jars filled up; post bags collected; and other
seemingly small but nevertheless important jobs completed. This
was promptly followed by a meal of some sort and a couple of
hours' sleep. Promptly at 8 p.m. the column lined up ready to
proceed, and after a quick check by the Quarter Master Sergeant
the order was given, 'Walk march!' and we were on our way.

Very soon the darkness of night blotted out all except those
immediately in front or behind, but we knew that the rest of the
column was still there when from time to time the rattle of something making contact with a pack, or a wagon jolting over rough
ground reached our ears.

Our journey was uneventful until we reached the Cloth Hall Square at Ypres. All transport going up the line had to cross this square, and Jerry knew it, but he was too methodical in sending over his shells, which came at regular intervals. A Provost Marshal stationed at the corner of the entrance to the Square would portion off the waiting transport, then when each little section reached the edge of the queue for crossing, he would shout, 'Nah, when the next bloody Jack-Johnson (big shell) drops, you go over the square like bats out of hell. See?' 'Yes, sir'. 'Right! Wait till it drops, then go.'

Whee! Crash! and away we went, hell for leather.

Even the mules realised the need for haste, and stretch out they did. At the far end of the Square we were sorted out, and re-directed. Although still quite a distance from the line, strings of Very lights became visible, and gave the area a sort of Fairyland appearance.

Suddenly a challenge rang out, 'Halt, who are you?' Identification followed, and a corporal gave us further instructions. 'Carry on for about fifty yards and you will see a ruined house, where solid earth ends and the duck-boards begin. At this point unharness your animals from the limbers, put your packs on the mules, and load them up with rations, water, letterbags, etc., and don't forget the rum ration—some poor blighter up there may be sitting in water, and it's bloody cold. Keep on the duck-boards until you meet a guide; he will direct you to the dump. Rendezvous at this point when you return. Right?' 'Right, Corporal.'

So we set off up the duck-boards. With a nervous mule trying to push you off and you pushing him back again, you knew that if either did leave the duck-boards, there would be a good chance of being sucked down in that vicious, bubbling, evil-smelling river of mud.

As we got nearer to the line Very lights transformed night into day. We were supposed to halt until the lights dimmed again, but trying to carry out such orders with a snorting nervous mule loaded up to the withers, was well-nigh impossible. At last a voice from the wilderness of mud enquired, 'Are you 98 Company rations?' 'Yes.' 'Follow me' said the voice. Eventually the ration dump was reached, and supplies swiftly unloaded.

The nightmare outward journey ended for us at this point, but the return journey had to be faced. I well remember seeing the once beautiful Ypres Cathedral battered into a mass of rubble. Broken statues, priceless stained glass, and shattered wood carvings lay mixed up with the stones of the Cathedral. The streets and squares were piled up with the remains of buildings. All the former inhabitants had fled. It was a city of the dead.

Somehow, soldiers existed in holes along the roadside. When the Third battle of Ypres ended in early November, 1917, 98th Machine Gun Company was moved to billets in a quieter part of the front, where we were able to stand on firmer ground. It made a nice change.

REMEMBER BELGIUM
by A. White (ex-142 M.G.C.)

Ay, we recall thy ghastly grime,
The oft-cursed battered duckboard trail,
The greedy sea of mud and slime
From Menin road to Passchendaele.

Remember thee! Ay do not fear,
Would to Heaven we could forget,
Despite the years the memory's clear;
Thy bloody salient haunts us yet.

THE MENIN ROAD

The Menin road—in November, 1917—was a hip-deep mass of slimy mud, wrote a Gunner of the 56th Machine Gun Company.

During the hours of darkness, Very lights shone as eyes for execution. Our gun teams were dotted along the road, and were continually in action.

One night (I forget the exact date) I was detailed to guide a gun team to relieve another, although I had never before been in that district.

If you keep still when the Very lights go up you may avoid the executioners, was the generally accepted belief of the Brass–Hats. A fallacy! But we endeavoured to carry out this procedure, for it gave us courage to continue.

Eventually we arrived at our destination and took over from the gun team, who quickly beat it towards their rest billets. They had hardly got clear away when Very lights from Jerry's observation posts picked us up, and in a trice our carefully nursed, valuable gun position was flattened.

Through receding concussion, I heard a voice telling me to

collect the effects from the pockets of three of my guided team, who would need them no more.

The time came for our relief. The alive and able prayed for darkness to cover our return along the Menin Road.

No one must halt. No one must lose touch. Keep to the duck-boards. These were the orders, which we endeavoured to carry out, but there was always a nagging thought at the back of one's mind of the possibility of sinking for evermore in that deep slimy mud on either side of the duck-boards.

After what seemed an eternity we reached rest billets—an old farmhouse barn, but heaven to the weary. No bombardment noises were audible.

Our peaceful rest spell was all too short. We were hurriedly rushed off to a section of the front line which was in distress, again along the Menin Road.

In our gun-team was the pleasant son of a priest who, being anti-rum, refused his rum ration and also broke the rum jar to deny the half-frozen their right to avoid becoming frozen. None would admit to being ill, for none could be replaced.

A German prisoner—smoking my cigarettes—related in good, clear English, how the Australian howitzers always found their machine gun positions. He was glad he was taken prisoner or he would have been dead. 'Your soldiers were climbing over piles of dead. You are all mad', he concluded.

A newly-arrived, very young but courageous and gentlemanly officer from Sandhurst paraded us outside a mortuary sort of trench. He frowned at our face hair, and dirty caked uniforms, unaware that we wanted to conceal the busy foe—lice.

Almost immediately a powerful destroying enemy shell slew a number of our section on an observer's message, and a very distressed officer knew that Sandhurst was not the name of this trench.

There were now fewer men for longer sentry duties, and one had to fight off another enemy—sleep!

Braziers for coke fires in well-camouflaged dug-outs brought survival after exposed sentry duty, but made a last sleep likely if feverish action to shut out cold also shut in the fumes.

> Chill blows the wind by the broken mill
> Where the white-ribbed trenches cross the hill
> And the myriad rain-filled shellholes stare
> Like sightless eyes in the star-light's glare
> and the whining shells sing, 'KILL!'

CAMBRAI

During the Great War of 1914–18, two battles were called after Cambrai, city of France. It stands on the River Schelde, 37 miles from Lille, and is an important railway junction.

On November 20th, 1917, the British 3rd Army, under Sir Julian Byng and helped by a strong force of tanks, broke through the German lines near Cambrai and took many prisoners and guns. The advance lasted until November 27th, when the battle ended. This action was known as the first battle of Cambrai.

The vital part played by Machine Gun Companies during this was spotlighted by an officer who served with the 3rd Battalion M.G.C.

> On the first day of the attack we fired a barrage of 100 guns from a position on the left of Bullecourt, and when the S.O.S. went up in the afternoon our infantry told us they just sat in their trench and heard the bullets whistling over. (100 guns each firing 500 rounds per minute.) A Captain Allan, who later became adjutant of the 3rd Battalion M.G.C. was in charge of the barrage-fire.

The second battle of Cambrai, fought between September the 27th and October the 5th, 1918, was an assault on the Hindenburg Line and part of the great offensive that ended the war. These facts are mentioned in order that the reader may not be confused.

Machine-gunners of many Companies took part in the first battle of Cambrai, and one of these, who served with 62nd Company has related his experiences.

> It was early in November when we moved into the support lines not far from Bullecourt. Our gun teams had been made up to strength while in rest billets, and some of the new men were fresh out from Grantham, England. We were told that the attack was to be along an eight mile frontage. Our C.O., being aware that eight miles might just as well have been eight hundred so far as the ordinary soldier was concerned, simply called on us to do our best in the battle area we covered.
>
> On the evening of the 19th we entered a wood and followed white tapes for direction, until we arrived at the foot of a large incline. Here we plunged ourselves into holes already made and dug fresh ones, just in case.

Tanks in Action

During the night and in the early hours of the morning, the tanks could be heard rumbling into their battle formations. Three hundred of them, spread out over an eight mile frontage. It was the largest number of tanks assembled on the Western Front up to this date.

Zero hour was fixed for 6.30 a.m., November 20th, 1917. At 6 a.m. we got an issue of rum, and some had others' shares. Much fog hung around but promptly at 6.30 a.m. the attack started. The tanks, having broken through the German front-line in our sector, made it possible for us to leave the cover of our trenches and advance over open ground.

It was the first time we had experienced this kind of warfare, and it was soon discovered that machine-guns and tripods were cumbersome things to carry. A small detachment of the West-Yorks Regiment were detailed as ammunition, water and cartridge-belt box carriers to our gun teams.

A certain L/Corporal—who was a little drunk from too much rum—shouted 'Give 'em hell' every time he flopped down near us. As we advanced a German plane flew low over our gun team and sprayed us with machine-gun bullets, but by some miracle no one was hit. The fog lifted and German artillery guns got the range of several of our tanks—putting them out of action.

We approached the Hindenburg Line. German snipers operating from the cover of an upturned captured tank, held us up for a while, but a barrage of British 18 pounder shells silenced the snipers.

Continuing to push on, we encountered much barbed-wire, and although it was battered down a good deal, it was still a tremendous obstacle to overcome. I collected plenty of holes in my trousers to prove this.

As darkness approached the weather turned foul and much fog persisted, which caused a lull in the battle.

We spent the night regrouping. Next morning the advance continued and by the evening of November 21st we reached a large concrete dug-out said to have been a German staff billet. The bottom of the dug-out was lined with a wooden floor, and there were several beds installed. A real luxury set-up. At this point we were not far from Bourlon Wood, the limit of the planned advance. Orders came through that we were to remain where we were and fix up our machine-guns in readiness to help repel any enemy counter-attack.

That night, gun crews, when relieved from sentry duties, were able to sleep in the captured luxurious dug-out. It was an experience I have always remembered.

We spent four days and nights in and around Bourlon Wood, and in that short space of time I packed in quite a lot of events. It all started on the morning of the 22nd. During the advance, communications between us and H.Q. had been severed, and I was detailed to take a message to the advanced infantry at a spot near Bourlon Wood, which proved a perilous journey. I had to pass through a deserted and ruined village in the valley, the area being pounded by enemy shell fire. How I survived I do not know, but after emerging safely I crossed a road, entered a communication trench and delivered my message.

On my return journey I picked up a considerable amount of rations in a sandbag, which some unfortunate devil had discarded. There were tins of jam, bread, cheese, tea and sugar. Upon arrival back at our machine-gun post, I was declared a great asset. Since the evening of the 19th we had existed on what was known as iron rations (bully-beef and rock-hard biscuits), so my find was as though we had been invited out to lunch at some smart café.

The lull in the fighting was most marked around our area, and so I decided to do a little exploring on my own, hoping to come across more abandoned rations.

This was made easy for me because I was still earmarked for 'runner' duties, and excused gun-sentry, so directly it was twilight on the evening of November 23rd, I wandered off. I decided to explore a section of the valley where I saw a couple of our tanks, apparently out of action and deserted. I entered one of these, which seemed only slightly damaged. Not a soul was about. It was as though the war was something I had dreamt about, and this is what I was soon doing. It was now dark outside, and the utter stillness inside the tank brought on a strange mental reaction. Quite suddenly I slumped to the floor and fell asleep.

When I awakened I peered out of my hide-out. It was almost daylight. I had slept throughout the night. It seemed for a moment or so that I was the only living person around, as I climbed up the incline from the dip in the ground which had sheltered the tank and me.

Reaching the top of the hill I saw puffs of white smoke (exploding shells) dancing along the Hindenburg Line, a mile or so away. I stood for a moment to take it all in. It seemed as though some magic wand were being used to form the picture I beheld. A ghastly picture after the peace of the inside of that tank in the valley. Eventually I reported back to my gun-team. My Section

Officer was waiting for me. 'Where the blazes do you think you have been?' he growled. I told him. 'It was quite unintentional, sir,' I pleaded. He calmed down a little before enquiring 'Did you find any more grub?' 'No, sir,' I had to confess.

After a lecture pointing out that I had committed a serious offence, but bearing in mind that I had on a previous occasion done some useful work, I was let off with a caution. 'Don't let it happen again', he said.

I have never forgotten that glorious sleep in an abandoned tank during the battle of Cambrai in November, 1917, but it ruddy nearly got me court-martialled.

On the morning of November 25th, 1917, the Germans launched a counter-attack, and I was once more a gunner with 62nd Machine Gun Company. The attack began in broad daylight, and looking across the valley on the opposite slope about half a mile away, I saw long lines of field-grey figures steadily advancing. German artillery, supporting their infantry, sent over many gas shells, mixed up with shrapnel and H.E.'s. We quickly donned gas masks, sighted our machine-guns and opened fire on the grey figures, who rapidly withdrew to a distance our guns were unable to reach, and eventually disappeared from sight in the valley below.

The 62nd and 51st Divisions held on all that day to the furthermost advanced positions reached in the initial attacks, but eventually the German counter-attack outflanked the British positions, and forced a withdrawal. It was another nightmare experience.

By November the 28th we were back to where we had started. Many lessons were learnt at Cambrai regarding the use of tanks in open warfare, but the price paid in human lives was ghastly.

THE YOUNGEST MACHINE GUNNER OF ALL!

An officer of 137 Machine Gun Company tells this story :

I shall always remember him. We were resting from front-line duty near the town of Armentieres when he came out of the darkness lit only by the flicker of gun fire and the distant Very lights, and stood watching No. 4 Section eating a meal round a brazier in the remains of a barn.

When he ventured a little nearer he appeared to be seven or eight years old, with a white, thin, face and big dark eyes which never left the group of soldiers. Even when we called out 'Allay toot sweet!' he did not move but just stood staring. After a while one of our chaps gave him a piece of biscuit with a slice of bully-beef and he devoured it ravenously. It was impossible to tell if he was French or Belgian as he answered no questions and apparently had no name.

Children were not encouraged to hang about as they were often hungry AND light-fingered, but this one stubbornly refused to go away even when he was threatened with a belting, and after a few days he was accepted, fed, and cared for, in fact he became the Company mascot and was called 'Dumbo'.

No parents came to claim him. He never said a word, but was eager to sweep up, polish things and make himself generally useful. When the Company moved he was smuggled in a limbered wagon, and after a month or two he was one of the Company. If any senior officer saw him they turned a blind eye. Dumbo's attitude towards the Machine Gunners was one of awed hero-worship. When one of our chaps came back from leave bringing him a small khaki cap, his delight knew no bounds, and when he was ceremoniously presented with a highly polished M.G.C. badge he wept tears of sheer delight, and never was there a prouder member of the old Suicide Club.

He obviously regarded himself now as one of those God-like heroes who used those terrible weapons against those dreadful Germans, and his walk assumed a swagger which 4 Section found highly amusing.

One day he suffered a humiliation which he could not endure : he was caught in the kitchen of our billet helping himself to something or other, and the farmer's wife walloped his backside with a large wooden spoon. He stood the pain without a whimper but the indignity was more than he could stand. That he, a British Machine Gunner, should be treated thus called for vengeance indeed, but 4 Section, who had thought the incident funny, only realized the depth of his feeling when he was caught, with an expression of grim determination on his face, taking a rifle from the limber. That meant more impacts on his little bottom, from a belt this time !

But Dumbo was not one to let the matter rest, and a day or two later when we got back after a long day's tactical exercise, we found the farmer's wife in a raging fury. Someone had sneaked into the cellar and turned on the taps of three huge cider casks which were now empty and the cellar ankle deep in cider ! She had no doubts about the perpetrator of this outrage ! She would tell the Mayor of the village ! She would go straight to our General ! She would cause international complications ! She would personally skin our little mascot as soon as she could find him, and so on. Even when we got the best liar in the Section (and it had some good ones!) to swear to her that Dumbo had been out all day with the Section, she still claimed tremendous damages and blamed him for the trouble.

Ultimately we had a whip round, which did not amount to the value of the cider (though all officers helped) so the cook contributed two dixies, some cutlery, a broken carving knife and three tins of plum-and-apple jam.

Later, of course, these were claimed for and replaced as having been 'lost by enemy action'.

So the lady, though not appeased, was at least silenced, and our great fear that the affair would leak to the General and that our mascot would be ruthlessly taken away was averted.

Maybe it would have been better if he had been, because a few months later, after being in the line all over the place, we were rushed up to Neuville St. Vaast to support the French. The roads were inches deep in mud with invisible shell holes here and there. It sometimes happened that men hit by shrapnel fell into the mud and were immediately flattened out by the endless stream of heavy vehicles, guns and tanks and never seen again.

Poor Dumbo, clinging on to a limber which was going all out, was suddenly thrown out and run over by the following vehicle. A gunner picked him up but he was dead.

He was put in a shell hole on the verge, a spade was produced, mud was thrown over him. In two minutes our mascot was gone for ever and the Section was pressing forward at top speed. Anyone seeing No. 4 Section going into battle that day might well have thought them a windy lot. When your face is covered with mud, tears make a tell-tale track down your cheeks. Dumbo had meant more than they thought. Away from their wives, children and sweethearts for what seemed an eternity, they had found Dumbo something to love, something which kept alive the human emotions in spite of the evil, soul-destroying job it was their duty to do.

Dumbo had only a short life yet he had known the pride, the joy, the ecstasy of being the youngest member of the Machine Gun Corps.

Here is another story of the same Company by one of their officers.

They had never been so utterly exhausted. Three times they had been promised relief and had to go forward to support another attack. Now, at last, they were away from the front line and were to rest in a farm house a few miles back, but many of the Company were having the utmost difficulty in getting there. Men were collapsing by the wayside, others sleeping as they marched in the ranks. They had reached the state where they did not care whether they lived or died, all they could do was to crawl slowly away from the scenes of battle, utterly weary and spent.

At last they reached the farm house which was of the usual sort, described as a 'rectangular block of buildings with a triangular shell in the middle'. The men took off their equipment and sat all round the yard with their backs against the walls. They looked the picture of exhaustion and misery. While tea was brewing in the kitchen, suddenly was heard the last sound which could possibly have been expected.

If it had been the roar of a shell arriving it would not have surprised anybody, but a peal of laughter was astounding! Through the shattered window could be seen what was causing it. In the middle of the yard lay the remains of a motor car. It had no wheels and bore shrapnel marks all over it. One machine-gunner was sitting at the wheel and another was about to get in. Apparently they were going to Blackpool for the weekend, and were telling each other what they were going to do when they got there. No holds barred, no details suppressed, and lurid reference to previous trips and to sundry female characters of doubtful virtue. Each episode was greeted by peals of laughter. The two men doing the clowning were not the best machine-gunners in the company but they had that wonderful something which prompted them, weary as they were, to entertain and revive their comrades, to divert their minds from the shock and horror of the last few days and to restore their shaken morale. Men like that were worth their weight in gold.

THREE DAYS IN A SALIENT

An officer who served with 142 Machine Gun Company 'C' Section recalls an experience directly after the first battle of Cambrai. He writes :

My first sight of the Salient which we were eventually to defend, was a black dense wood on the skyline surrounded by bursting shells, and very ominous it appeared.

We were coming from near Arras and Oppy Wood, which had been comparatively quiet, to the place from which all the news had emanated in the last few days. General Byng had broken the famous Hindenburg Line, and the tanks had over-run the barbed wire defences and had been within an ace of preparing the way for a breakthrough at Cambrai in November, 1917. Why the tanks had been held up was a matter for the experts to wrangle about afterwards—our immediate concern was to hold the ground already won, and a very nasty job it was. Jerry was making frantic efforts to recapture the wood, which projected into his line and overlooked part of his trenches.

It was a day or two later that our Company received orders to take over in the wood, and a certain officer was sent in advance to make arrangements for guiding us in.

What eventually became of this officer, I don't know, for after waiting hours, Captain Davies, our C.O. at that time, decided to go on without guides and carry out the relief.

While waiting for the missing officer by the roadside, Sergeants Mackintosh and Sermon and I shared a tin of bully in a little shelter—this was the last we saw of Sergeant Sermon, who was severely wounded a little later, and eventually died. He was a fine fellow who had been with the Company for a long time and was liked and admired by his comrades. He had previously been awarded the M.M. and Bar.

While we were still waiting we saw a battalion of London Irish, staggering along in single file after having been relieved by our infantry—not a very cheering sight.

Eventually, after receiving some help from a padre as to direction, we plodded along the Cambrai–Bapaume road towards Bourlon. We made a halt at a sugar factory where a case of army socks was discovered and issued to all and sundry. In those days how we prized certain things—a tin of condensed milk, something to eat, or a clean pair of socks; these were much more prized than anything costly.

Nearby was a fearsome sight—all the debris of war—for the cavalry had been in action and parts of horses and human corpses were strewn about and under a pale moon looked eerie in the extreme. Eventually we found ourselves, after traversing the wood, in a sunken road near the village of Bourlon. This was to be our home for the next three days and after getting the guns into position our thoughts turned to food and something hot to drink.

It was Jerry's custom at this time to send over salvoes intermittently (about half a dozen shells in a bunch) and we were lucky to get through without casualties.

Mr. Smith's section was not so fortunate, and it was here that Sergeant Sermon was mortally wounded.

During a lull in the shelling Sergeant Mackintosh and I had a look round. To our front were several hastily dug trenches with bodies lying about, and we discovered many cunningly concealed observation posts.

We had to scurry back to our road as the shelling was starting again, and it was continuous for 23 hours of the 24—shelling from left, right, and front, and enemy aeroplanes with the ominous black cross flying very low over our heads. During the night Mac and I heard a curious noise near us, not unlike a cat mewing. On investigation we found one of the shelters to be embedded in a mass of earth from the side of the sunken road, and one of our gun teams was imprisoned in it. The curious sound was from the men crying for help.

Working like Trojans we released two or three men who were badly shaken, but Corporal Barker and Private Sawyer were dead when we eventually reached them.

They had put up a good fight and had lost their lives as nobly as if they had been killed face to face with the enemy. We left a simple wooden cross made from firewood with their names inscribed thereon.

While digging our comrades out we were shelled continuously and Sergeant Mac and two other men on either side of me were hit by splinters, fortunately not seriously.

It was very cold at night, so much so, that I was afraid the water in the guns might freeze, in spite of the anti-freezing mixture of a glycerine solution which had been issued. So, as a precaution each gun in turn was dismounted and the team kept the gun warm by contact with their bodies. Although we were deluged by shells we were fairly safe from machine-gun bullets; the contour of the ground we were holding prevented Jerry from dosing us with indirect fire, and as his trenches were lower than ours this favoured us, and on the fringe of the wood we could look down on the Germans. A situation I imagine he did not like at all—hence his strenuous efforts to dislodge us.

At length we had orders to evacuate this death trap, and seldom have orders been carried out with greater alacrity; all belts of ammo were to be emptied and carried away. Perhaps it was as well that we had no inspection either before or after, and anyhow there were plenty of belts in our own lines.

Back we scrambled through the branches of once mighty trees that were blocking our path, back the way we had come, which was unrecognisable because of the fallen trees.

How we retreated through the dark, and ultimately reached Company Headquarters, I have only a hazy recollection, but by the wonderful sense of direction of our guide we reached our place in the Hindenburg Line and rejoined our comrades. On our way back I remember passing two companies of my old battalion, the C.S.R. (Civil Service Rifles).

They were quietly preparing a defence position to delay Jerry when he discovered that we had flown from Bourlon Wood. I am glad to remember that these C.S.R.'s put up a splendid fight though many were captured, including their Commanding Officer, Major Warne.

It was during these operations too that Colonel Seagrave of the 15th Battalion, gained the D.S.O. by gallantly filling a breach in our line by getting the H.Q. staff, transport and cooks together. Had he not done this Jerry may have surrounded the wood and killed or captured all its occupants.

Father Christmas

At Anzim-Saint-Vaast we were at rest in the Old Mill House on the last day before we were due to return to the line at Oppy. I had been without a sub-section officer for some months, and was intensely relieved when notified at breakfast that one had arrived. My relief was somewhat damped after breakfast when I beheld my 'spare part'.

He was in the late thirties, wore pince-nez (which fell off every alternate minute), had a large and very rotund paunch, a very well wired cap (instead of the beloved soft ones) with a clip to keep the front up—which clip was continually failing to function, and he was one of those people who carried everything an officer should carry slung around his neck on separate straps. When I say that these included compass, glasses, map case, water bottle, haversack, gas mask, lanyard, and raincoat amongst others, it will be appreciated that standing he looked like a well furnished Christmas Tree, and when he stooped, as he frequently did to pick up his glasses which periodically fell off, it was about a five minutes' job to re-sling his etceteras in their appropriate places. Mr. T. was however not really a bad sort; subsequently I discovered that he had a most violent passion for 'pork and beans' and would barter all his (and sometimes my) rations for tins of this somewhat windy fruit. He used to fill the dug-out with tins and wind. He had one rather aggravating habit, and that was a punctilious salute for me on every solitary occasion we ever met: in the line or out, even in bed.

On this, his first day, he attached himself to me like a leech for the kit inspection which always took place prior to a return to the line.

Having manfully tolerated falling over everything for about ten minutes I had one of those heaven-sent inspirations which come to all on rare occasions. I sent him off to inspect the limbers and see that they were properly packed.

In those days we had on the limbers a contraption known as a 'flash protector', commonly called the stove pipe. This consisted of about 20 inches of tubular piping about 4 inches in diameter with a slot at each end like an organ pipe. Theoretically you put the affair over the front of the gun at night and its flash was not visible to bother brother Boche. Actually in practice it filled with unexploded gasses and about every twelfth round ignited in a flash which could be seen for about two miles.

Suddenly in the midst of the inspection Mr. T. appeared with a stove pipe under his arm, clicked his heels and saluted—'Excuse me, sir, this periscope has lost its mirrors. Shall we take it up with us?'

Anon.

When 142 Machine Gun Company were at Ypres in 1917 it was decided to convert a ruined estaminet into a strong-point. Lieut. Chambers (known as Jerry), something of an engineer, was put in charge of the operations, so the 21st section spent most of their reserve rest in doing navvy work, much to their disgust.

The following words were written just as the work was finished.

BARKING CREEK

Barking Creek, Barking Creek,
Where the hell is Barking Creek?
See that smoke wreath in the air,
See those ruins over there,
Those few bricks and sandbags near,
That was Barking Creek.

Barking Creek, Barking Creek,
Who the hell built Barking Creek?
Chambers started on the plot,
Baxter helped—but not a lot,
Also Ferguson a Scot,
White discouraged in language terse,
Talked of hell and things much worse,
THEY built Barking Creek.

Barking Creek, Barking Creek,
Why the hell called Barking Creek?

'Cause the place smelt like a river,
And the smells made strong men quiver,
Smelled like London's greatest sewer,
Hence called Barking Creek.

Barking Creek, Barking Creek,
What the hell *is* Barking Creek?
Before the war it was a mansion,
Since the war a halt for rations,
Then became a salvage station.
A dreary place to pass at night
When Fritz's bullets were in flight,
Was our Barking Creek.

Barking Creek, Barking Creek,
What is this damned ruddy Creek?
Patience, and I'll soon be done,
We drained the hole and laid a gun
All complete with number One
With just a modicum of rum
To ease the troubles of everyone
Inside Barking Creek.

Barking Creek, Barking Creek,
What became of Barking Creek?
The team a roaring fire made
With paper, sticks and charcoal laid,
Though broad daylight, were we afraid?
Not in Barking Creek.

Barking Creek, Barking Creek,
What destroyed this Barking Creek?
Smoke began to rise like hell,
Fritz dropped in an eight inch shell,
Exit charcoal, fire and smell,
Exit gun and team as well,
Exit BARKING CREEK.

H. J. Baxter

VAT '16 (MEMORIES OF)

By Capt. H.N.E. (Ex 48th Machine Gun Company)

The baths at Nieppe were in a brewery adjoining the River
Lys. We removed tunic and trousers and tied them with our

identity disc cords to be put through a delousing machine. We then proceeded to the washhouse across the road in full view of a foregathering of village maidens.

Inside, we were split into dozens, each group being allotted to a vat, where we remained immersed up to the neck for five glorious minutes. At 5 mins 15 sec a cold hose was turned on to rout out the laggards. A clean shirt, pants, and socks were handed out, and in these we returned to the first building. If anyone was then unable to find his deloused trousers, he wandered around like a lost sheep until given a pair yards too big, which he had to wear until he could arrange to rip them beyond repair on the next wiring-party.

6

The Final German Offensive

(March 21st, 1918)

ALL QUIET ON THE WESTERN FRONT! British newspapers often
printed such headlines during the winter months of 1917. Actually, it was far from quiet for those 'out there' although no major
offensives took place.

During the so-called quiet winter months of 1917 the Germans
prepared to make their final effort to reach Paris and win the war,
and by March, 1918 had massed 6,500 guns, of which 2,500 were
of the heavy type—along a front of some fifty miles—between the
Sensee river and the Oise.

A few hours before dawn on March 21st, 1918 the German
guns opened fire on the British lines. A machine-gunner of 9th
Divisional Company describes the scene :

> So intense was the bombardment that the earth around us
> trembled.
>
> It was a dark night, but the tongues of flame from the guns—
> 2,500 British guns replied to the German bombardment—lit up
> the night sky to daylight brightness.
>
> Mixed up with the high explosive shells crashing on our tren-
> ches, were the less noisy, but deadly, gas shells. Trenches collapsed,
> infantry in front-line positions, groping about in their gas-masks,
> were stunned by the sudden terrific onslaught.
>
> There had never been an artillery bombardment like it, and in
> all probability there has never been one since on such a scale.
>
> Machine-gun posts were blown sky-high—along with human
> limbs. Men were coughing and vomiting from the effects of gas,
> and men were blinded.
>
> The whole earth around us turned into an inferno—akin to
> the 'Three Divisions' described in Dante's description of
> hell.

An extract from the 3rd Machine Gun Battalion magazine (written up on the Rhine in early 1919) further spotlights the March offensive.

On February 23rd, 1918, the four companies of the Division were incorporated as the 3rd Battalion Machine Gun Corps. The division was on the Arras sector with a frontage of 5,000 yards. The machine-guns remained there without relief until April 1st.

Unending fatigue-parties carried up rolls of wire and iron stakes night after night. Nearly every day a prisoner was taken who emphasised the menace of attack within 48 hours.

Our hopes and fears that it was a gigantic bluff were shattered on the morning of March 21st.

Furious bombardments covered the entire system at 2.50 a.m. and 3.20 a.m.; each succeeded by utter stillness. Dawn broke unusually misty. At 5.00 a.m. everything the enemy possessed opened up with a reverberating crash. The attack developed on our right and the enemy gradually established himself on that flank, where our machine-guns could see columns of the enemy transport on the march—out of range.

The unremitting fighting went on until the afternoon of March 22nd; at dusk the enemy was on both sides of us. We posted bombers to left and right while the guns were withdrawn over the top, not a moment too soon. Late that night Monchy was abandoned and orders were issued for a withdrawal to the Corps line. On the 23rd the enemy came over the crest of Henin Hill and our machine-guns did great execution. The battle raged all day long. The enemy were determined to break through and take Arras, and we were determined to fight back, step by step. Very few of the guns got back. Some fought to the death, some fought rearguard actions. Not one withdrew till driven out by the enemy, and then only far enough to come into action again. By 4 p.m. the Division was back to the Army line which ran through Neuville Vitasse, sadly weakened, but unbroken.

> 'Spurning the grey-clad hosts,
> Heroes they held their posts,
> Throwing the charge aside,
> Steadfast they fought and died.'

Written material relating to the British Fifth Army during the German assaults of March, 1918, as far as the ordinary soldier was concerned, is few and far between owing to the terrifically confused nature of the circumstances which existed at that time —particularly insofar as they affected front-line machine-gunners.

The late Major E. H. Veitgh, M.C., Staff Captain of 151 Brigade—did, however, manage to compile some material of the part his Brigade experienced—and these notes were passed on to Mr. W. Shuttleworth—(ex-151 Machine Gun Company) who has presented them for publication in this book :

On February 20th, 1918, 151 Brigade, including 151 Machine Gun Company, moved out of the line at Passchendaele to the neighbourhood of St. Omer. On March 8th the Brigade entrained at Arques and the following day, March 9th, arrived at Longeau, near Amiens. In the siding stood the special train of Sir D. Haig and Staff, a sign that the German offensive was at hand and had been localised. The third and fifth armies were to bear the brunt.

On the evening of March 20th warning was received by 151 Brigade that the German offensive was expected to begin the next day and all units 'stood to', ready to move at 4 hours' notice. Eleven Divisions held the line, with three Infantry divisions in reserve, and also three Cavalry Divisions—total 17 against 40 German. When the order to move came, less than one hour was allowed for the Brigade to march to Guillaucourt (one hour's march away) and entrain for Brie at 10 p.m. Then followed a forced march along strange roads in drifting ground mist, with only the light of a new moon. Now and then two or three walking wounded and loaded limbers passed. It was the first sign of retreat.

No transport was allowed to cross the Somme with 151 Brigade and so the 'green line' was occupied by 151 Brigade from Boucly-Villevesque, a distance of eight miles.

When no transport was permitted to cross the Somme it meant the Vickers Machine Guns had been left west of the Somme, for the O.C. (Captain D. Ralston, 151 M.G. Company) had received no orders. However, the C.O. decided to ignore orders and on the early morning of March 22nd brought most of his guns forward. The fighting became closer and the Germans occupied Roisel and the streams of men from the 24th and 66th Divisions were allowed to retire through the 50th Div. ranks in order to reorganise behind the green line—originally the reserve line and now the front line.

At 4 a.m. large formations of the Germans became visible. Artillery support was asked for; when it came the barrage fell on the green line. Telephone lines broke down and nothing could be done. Utter confusion resulted.

About 5 a.m. the Germans attacked the whole of the 50th Division front. Severe fighting followed and the 50th were gradually forced back.

Indeed the 19th Corps position was so precarious that the 50th Division was ordered to withdraw west of the Somme.

Mention must be made of Sergeant Monty Watson, M.M. and Bar. He was ordered to help cover the retreat to the west bank of the Somme. After the infantry had crossed, the bridge was to be blown up. One span had actually been blown when there appeared Sergeant Watson's machine-gun team ('A' Section 151 Company) on the east bank—stranded. Watson threw his gun into the river and he and his team waded and swam to the west bank. This happened at 3.15 p.m. on March 24th.

Later the same day remnants of 151 Brigade were relieved and marched back to Foucaucourt (151 Machine Gun Company had occupied these trenches in 1917).

The 50th Division was now in reserve to the 8th Division. There was to be no rest. It was ordered to reinforce the 24th Brigade. About this time some Cavalry Machine Guns reinforced the Brigade but gradually remnants of 151 Brigade Machine Gun Company were forced back to Caix where some old French trenches were occupied between Caix and Guillaucourt and the three Brigades of 50th Division were organised as three Battalions—so reduced in strength had they become.

Between Caix–Harbonnieres and Quesnel there was a ridge and four machine-guns of 151 Company covered the northern banks of the Luce, supported by remnants of the 5th Durhams. When the enemy appeared the Vickers Guns got their chance and right well they took it.

'This looks like the end' said one gunnery officer.

The survivors of 151 Infantry Brigade were formed into a composite Battalion and included cooks, storemen, buglers, clerks etc. A defensive line running north from Demuin, past Marcel-leave and Hamel to Sailly-le-Sec was formed—this line held and Amiens was saved. The 50th Division was now merely a composite Brigade. On April 1st the remnants of the 50th Division were relieved by the 14th Division, and 151 Machine Gun Company (what was left of it) marched back to Longeau. On April 2nd it entrained at Pont-de-Metz for Rue, arriving there on April 3rd. At Rue, a French bell-ringer paraded the town streets informing the inhabitants that these were the British soldiers who had been defending their homes against the Germans. The British were to be treated kindly.

The stay was brief. No rest. On the 4th the Brigade embussed for Bethune. On April 9th Germans attacked on this front and the 50th Division and its Machine Gun Companies went into action on April 10th.

The situation changed rapidly from hour to hour. The diaries of the various units are mostly blank, for all hands were full and there was no thought of keeping official records. It is therefore impossible to do anything like justice to those men whose numerous brave deeds when fighting a long rearguard action against terrible odds, were just taken in their stride. The Rev. R. Callin, one of the 50th Division Padres, summed up the position :

> Apart from heavy casualties, the worst feature was the incredible fatigue and lack of sleep. Men simply could not keep awake and the slightest chance of a short rest found them sound asleep, on a heap of stones—in a ditch—a field—a sloping bank.
> Cold and hunger were forgotten in nature's clamour for sleep. Physically the men had come to the very end of their tether—only sheer will-power kept them going. Nevertheless what that will-power could do the enemy learned to their cost.

The experience of the 50th Division was also the experience of every Unit engaged in the vital defence of the passages to the Channel ports during the German offensive of March to July, 1918.

LEFT ON THE SHELF

At Ploegsteert on April 9th, 1918 the enemy crossed the Lys in force, broke through, and put all the guns of 25th Division out of action. We were hastily organised to fill the breach as infantrymen, digging ourselves in pairs into a small trench. During a lull a small ration of bread and 'pozzy' reached us. We were hungry, but there was no guarantee when we'd get more. My comrade and I tossed up : should we eat the lot, or save some? The latter alternative won, and we cut a small shelf in the trench as a larder. Shortly afterwards we were forced to retire and had to leave our carefully-preserved reserve of food behind. Never again would we risk our ration-issue on the toss of a coin !

AS SEEN BY A SIGNALLER

I was posted to 17th Battalion, 9 D Company, in late 1917. We had our Company Headquarters in a very good dug-out, built by the Germans in the old Hindenburg Line, in front of Canal-de-Nord (which was dry at the time), and roughly 15 kilometres in front of Cambrai.

We were almost at the tip of a very advanced salient—the tip of which was defended by the 63rd Naval Division.

Our Company Headquarters would usually be based about three kilometres behind the front line, and we had lines to forward positions which ran in some places into no-man's-land.

Also we had lines to Battalion, Brigade, and Divisional Headquarters. We had a small exchange, and operated a Don 3, with a Fullerphone superimposed on the same line—described as a metallic return—having a positive and negative wire. The object of the Fullerphone was to scramble the message.

During the months of January and February 1918 things were quiet enough, just the occasional shell and whizz-bangs, but otherwise uneventful.

Our rations seldom varied—about three to a loaf, bully-beef, and Tickler's jam, which we used to hate. When we got a Machonachie, which consisted of meat and vegetables, we thought it was a banquet. Life was not too bad for us signallers until March 21st, 1918, and then it happened.

I was in an advanced post with the Second-in-Command of our Company when the German bombardment started. Very soon one end of our small dug-out was knocked in and we lost communication with our Company Headquarters. I went out to mend the line, and made about 18 joins (reef knots) until I got to a single track break line, but was still unable to obtain comunication.

After trying visual signalling with discs or semaphore without success, my Captain decided to make a dash for it when at about 9 a.m. the Germans stormed forward.

Aided by fog they quickly over-ran our front-line positions, and in a very short time from the beginning of the German attack many units became isolated. The bravery of the men who fought against the terrible odds was never fully known as they died at their posts.

Battalion Commanders, Brigade and Divisional Headquarters knew little of what was actually happening in the forward areas apart from an occasional report brought by some brave runner who had been fortunate to get through. While at Grantham Machine Gun Depot I had been taught—as all signallers were—to fire a machine-gun, but there was no chance to stand and fight just then, with the German guns firing from the back of us in the Salient.

Someone brought a message instructing us to make for Le-Transloy, a fixed rallying-point for our Brigade.

A small number of us marched across the desolated Somme battlefields and made for Bapaume. Arriving there we were instructed to march on to the town of Albert.

On the way my co-signaller John Pratt and I dropped down from sheer exhaustion and went to sleep. When we awakened we found ourselves with a strange lot of chaps. Battalions—what were left of them—were all mixed up in small groups, often with only an N.C.O. in command.

We eventually reached Albert. The main street was crowded like Petticoat Lane on a Sunday morning. Relays of German planes dropped flares and bombs incessantly.

My friend and I slipped out of the town and slept in a hay-cart. I noticed that the famous Virgin and Child statue on the Church of Notre Dame lay in an almost horizontal position. The town had suffered much shelling from the Germans in 1914—but the town had not been captured.

The Germans were not far away when we resumed the search for our Machine Gun Company, eventually finding the few survivors at a place called Boullens where, I think for the only time on active service, I had a bath.

The bath consisted of a shower with tepid water and we went under the shower by numbers. The Sergeant in charge blew a whistle to denote next in—and after about two minutes he blew the whistle again which meant out you come—*now*.

We were given a change of underclothes, which some reckoned were chattier (more lousy) than the ones we had given in.

Historical footnote

On March 27th, 1918, the Germans captured Albert. It was recovered in the following August during the Allies' final advance.

METERAN (April 1918)

The Great German offensive continued into April 1918. The situation, particularly in the South, was most obscure. It was known that the enemy had captured both Merville and Estaires, some seven miles from Meteran.

It was supposed, though not known, that his advance had been arrested in this area. As a measure of safety, full military precautions were ordered and in conjunction with troops of the 19th

Infantry Brigade, outposts were at once put out covering the approaches east and south of Meteran.

At 10.30 on the morning of April 12th Lieutenant Colonel Hutchison (C.O. 33rd Battalion Machine Gun Corps) received orders from the General Staff to have a reconnaissance made in the vicinity. At 10.45 a.m. three cyclist patrols from the Scouts (machine-gun section) were ordered to proceed and, having located the enemy, to report to 33rd Battalion Headquarters, established at a farmhouse about one mile south of Meteran. Each patrol consisted of an N.C.O. and four men.

The Commanding Officer, with Lieut. McLaren (Intelligence Officer) proceeding in advance, reconnoitred due south of Meteran.

Here large numbers of both wounded and unwounded men were found to be in full retreat northwards and westwards.

Rearguards of the 31st Division, particularly from one Battalion, were found to be in precipitate retreat without officers.

The enemy was observed about 600 yards distant in groups pushing forward under covering fire. On more than two occasions they were seen deliberately to shoot down at short range women flying from their flaming homesteads.

The infantry were rallied and lined up on a 500 yards front facing south, south of the village, full use being made of buildings and ditches as cover.

Lt. Col. Hutchison placed 2nd Lieut. McLaren in command, and disposed the rest of the patrol (under Scout Sergeant St. Ledger, M.M., and Corporal Bawn) to rally the infantry and organise the locality for defence, he himself cycling for assistance. In twenty minutes he had reached Divisional Headquarters in Meteran, having dumped his cycle and commandeered a Ford ambulance and reported direct to G.O.C., suggesting that machine-guns should be rushed up to fill the breach and infantry sent as soon as possible.

A motor lorry, part of an A.S.C. (Army Service Corps) column, was asked for. The officer in charge of the Column refused to give it, although the urgency of the case was explained to him and it was empty. Lt. Colonel Hutchison therefore put the Motor Transport Officer quietly to sleep with a right hook, commandeered the lorry, and took it to the 33rd Battalion Machine Gun Headquarters.

It was driven by Driver Sharples of the A.S.C., who thoroughly entered into this rather dramatic joke. In a few minutes it was loaded with eight guns and material and crowded with gun-teams. Orders were given to establish Headquarters at the Moulin-de-Hoegenmacker, and Signallers were sent forward. Two hundred yards south of the Mill, the lorry was halted by Lt. McLaren and the Scouts who, having fought in close combat with the enemy with rifles, had been forced to retire to Windmill Ridge. The infantry, in complete disorder and often led by their officers, were retiring on Meteran.

Between 10.30 and 11.30 a.m. the advance of the enemy was carried out with astonishing rapidity.

Elements of the Division which had been rallied by the Machine Gun Scouts under Lt. McLaren, evaporated west and north before the enemy advance, which was checked only by the resolution of the Scouts. Sergeant St. Ledger, Corporal Bawn, and Private Busby in particular, all showing extraordinary heroism, ordered the defence with astonishing coolness and initiative, ably supported by the Scouts and a few stout-hearted stragglers.

The excursion of the motor lorry came to an abrupt end when it was halted by the last of our advance guards under the Intelligence Officer. It came immediately under machine-gun and rifle fire.

The order 'Action Front' was given, and in a very few minutes eight machine-guns were disposed on the northern slopes of the Windmill Hill crest, covering, in particular, the southern and south-eastern approaches to Meteran and the Meteran Becque.

The lorry returned to its base to collect half of 'C' Company under Major Judson.

This incident was probably the most thrilling in which the machine-gunners of the 33rd Battalion ever took part. The rapidity of the action; the extraordinary situation; the perfect discipline and drill; the setting of untouched farmhouses, copses and quietly grazing cattle; the fleeing civilians and retiring infantry behind; the magnificent targets obtained; and the complete grip of the situation by, and determination of, Machine Gun Commanders; all these combined to make it unforgettable.

This action, and the subsequent operations of the 33rd Battalion Machine Gun Corps, undoubtedly will take the highest place for all time in the history of the M.G.C. and are an epic of the tenacity and grit of the British soldier with his back to the wall fighting against great odds.

The following record is made of the action :

IX CORPS SPECIAL ORDER No. 2
33rd BATTALION MACHINE GUN CORPS
12th–19th April, 1918

On the night of the 11th–12th April, the enemy had captured both Merville and Estaires, some seven miles south of Meteran, but the situation was somewhat obscure and machine-guns, in conjunction with the 19th Infantry Brigade, took up an outpost line covering the approaches east and south of Meteran.

By 10.30 a.m. on the 12th April the enemy had advanced very rapidly both from the east and from the south, and had it not been for the excellent use made of an abandoned motor lorry which quickly brought up eight more guns and teams, Meteran would undoubtedly have fallen into the enemy's hands.

By skilful handling of his machine-guns Lieut. Colonel Hutchison was able to hold off the enemy and fill up the gaps that occurred in our line, so that by nightfall on April 12th the line, though thinly held, was continuous.

On the 13th a heavy hostile attack was successfully dealt with, during which the enemy suffered enormous losses.

In one instance 200 horsemen were decimated by the fire of one machine-gun section under 2nd Lt. Watts. In spite of the hard fighting of the two previous days, night harassing fire was maintained during the night of the 13th–14th. The 14th was probably the most critical day of these operations.

At dawn the enemy launched heavy attacks against our positions and our line was penetrated in many places. The enemy exploited these gains to the full advantage by pushing forward his light machine-guns. On this occasion very valuable service was rendered by Major W. C. Andrew (second in command) who handled his machine-guns very skilfully, and by filling gaps and forming defensive flanks, prevented the enemy from penetrating our line in depth.

The maintenance of our line was undoubtedly due to the splendid devotion to duty and initiative displayed by the machine-gunners, whose losses were very severe.

This line was held by machine-guns in face of great odds until ordered to withdraw on the evening of the 14th instant, this withdrawal being carried out in the most creditable manner without further loss either to personnel or material, showing the excellent state of training and efficiency within the Battalion.

On the 16th April the enemy again made a determined attack after heavy bombardments against our positions south-east of Meteran, during which Machine Gunners did great execution.

It was during this attack that the enemy gained a footing in Meteran where he was held and the line handed over in this position on the night of the 18–19th April.

Throughout the operations the action of the 33rd Battalion Machine Gun Corps very materially assisted in preventing the enemy from capturing the Meteran position and exploiting the gains made by him during the first day's fighting

(Signed) W. Maxwell Scott,
(Brigadier-General)
General Staff, IXth Corps.

RIDGE WOOD

By early May 1918 it became clear that the great German offensive had been broken, its way barred on both the road to Paris and the road to the port of Calais.

But although the main force of the onslaught was broken, the German troops were still being flung into the attack in enormous numbers, and many tremendous battles continued.

One such battle took place along the line running through Ridge Wood and Scottish Wood in the Dickebusch Sector.

Machine Gunners who took part in this action wrote down their experiences for inclusion in the history of the 33rd Battalion Machine Gun Corps, now reproduced for this book as follows :

On the 8th May the Germans delivered a very violent attack against the 98th and 19th Brigades on this front. These Brigades were supported by D and B Machine Gun Companies amongst the front posts, with C Company in close support and A Company in reserve.

The Argyll and Sutherland Highlanders, in particular, fought with the greatest heroism, but were driven back out of Ridge Wood into the western side of Scottish Wood, whilst the enemy succeeded in driving a wedge between the Cameronians and the former regiment. Into the breach Lieut. Liddiard and Sergeant Goode and Corporal McKirdy thrust forward their Machine Gun Sections, and by their combined fire, not only inflicted heavy casualties on the enemy, but effectively checked their advance. Lieut. Liddiard was seriously wounded during the day, but would not permit himself to be borne from the field by the stretcher-party until he had given orders for the conduct of his section.

The Cameronians, in particular, had suffered heavy casualties as had also the French on the right of the 33rd Division.

A second attack was delivered at about 2 p.m. but broke down before our lines. To meet this attack, two machine gun sections of C Company had been brought up to Halebaast Corner on the Dickebusch Road and were most effectively handled by Lieut. Stentiford, M.C., L/Cpl. Storr and Private McLean, with Private Ayres acting as runner.

Whilst this attack was developing the 33rd Divisional Commander had already decided to make an immediate counter-attack, recapture Ridge Wood and restore the gap in the line between the Argylls and the Cameronians.

The 5th Scottish Rifles were moved from the extreme right of the Divisional front round the back of Dickebusch Lake, where they were well screened from observation by the trees surrounding the lake and then were deployed by Lt. Colonel Spens, D.S.O.; and a most energetic counter-attack, carried out with outstanding valour and enterprise, re-won the whole of the lost ground.

During this operation the machine-guns of D and C Companies in particular, again rendered most valuable assistance with their fire and found excellent targets.

For this action the following awards were made to machine-gunners; Captain Stentiford, Bar to M.C.; Sergeant Goode, M.M., D.C.M.; Corporal McKirdy, D.C.M.; Sergeant Hendrie, M.M., Bar to M.M.; L/Cpl. Storr, M.M.; Privates Allen, Willett, Hicks, Ayres and Gilbert, M.M.

On the 11th May the Division was relieved by the 44th Regiment d'Infanterie, the machine-guns being relieved under the direction of Le Capitaine Medino, a most intelligent and brave officer who was last seen by us disappearing into a cloud of smoke through a very heavy barrage : clad in a long blue overcoat which flowed behind him like a dressing gown and bareheaded, wearing both his medals, the Legion d'Honneur and the Croix de Guerre, swinging on his overcoat.

We remember him distinctly eating porridge for the first time with his knife and fork, the porridge itself being seasoned with whisky to make it a thoroughly Scottish dish !

LIKE A BAD DREAM

From the D.M.G.O. to the 36th (Ulster) Division :

In the early part of the year 1918 we went due south into the line just taken over from the French. The trenches were in front of St. Quentin.

I remember our dismay. As is well known, French defensive schemes—even when dispositions on the ground matched the paper ones at divisional H.Q.—did not usually fit British organisation.

In this case we found complete chaos. There was a wide gap between theory and practice; there were few properly constructed defences, and practically everything had to be done from scratch. Trenches and works had to be dug, ammunition reserves to be built up and, as we were soon made aware, there was not much time in which to do it all.

We set about it and, soon after taking over our new Machine Gun Service Company arrived from Grantham, and we formed ourselves into the 36th Machine Gun Battalion.

While we were sorting ourselves out the German blow fell on March 21st, 1918. The battalion lost heavily in personnel and material, and finished up somewhere not very far in front of Amiens.

That period was then, and has ever since remained in my mind, like a very bad dream, at the end of which we moved what we had left up to Ypres where we were supposed to reorganise and recuperate. This idea was rather interfered with by the fact that we found ourselves involved on the flank of the second German stroke, the drive towards Hazebrouck.

At this period heads in the 36th Division began to roll, including that of the G.O.C. Rather later, when the tide had turned, having incurred the ire of the new General, I was packed off to 47th Machine Gun Company where I took over D Company, which I had known the year before as 255 Company at Belton Park (Grantham).

I found the Company in action at Bouchavesnes on the Somme, where we spent a few hectic days. I was exceptionally lucky not to be blown sky-high.

Those days I shared with Colin Matson of the Dublins and an old comrade of the 10th Brigade M.G. Company.

Later, the 47th Division moved to Aubers Ridge. This had been a battlefield since early 1915, when the disaster of May 9th of that year left an indelible scar on the landscape.

After service around Aubers Ridge the 47th Division had the

K

honour of making a ceremonial march through Lille when that City was recaptured. The population were completely off their heads with excitement, joy, relief, and I know not what.

I remember it as a wonderful day but my company was slightly sobered by the knowledge that we were going directly from our triumphal march to take over a section of the front.

THE MACHINE GUN CORPS BAND

It has been said that the band of the Machine Gun Corps had the shortest life of any Regimental band known to have existed. Be that so or otherwise—its history was unique.

Its formation actually took place while the heavy fighting was in progress on the Western Front—and much credit was due to Colonel Hutchison (O.C. 33rd Battalion Machine Gun Corps) for bringing this about. The band came to this Battalion under the most mysterious circumstances—wrote Col. Hutchison.

The 18th Battalion Manchester Regiment, to which the band originally belonged, was disbanded in February 1918. The band was then loaned to 30th Battalion Machine Gun Corps.

After heavy fighting and losses of March and April 1918, it was decided to disband the 30th Division. The 30th Division was at that time co-operating with the 33rd Division. Although the band was under orders to proceed to another Unit they were now trained gunners; and taking into account the supply of man-power for the Machine Gun Corps and the fact that the bands-men themselves wanted to remain together as one Unit with the M.G.C. and that possession is nine points of the law—a wire was sent to D.A.C. 3rd Echelon, asking for permission to transfer 'forty specialists', including Major McPherson, M.C., D.C.M.; and ten expert machine-gunners of his old Company to the 33rd Batt. M.G.C. The request was granted, and the instruments were collected from Watou. They were found to be worn out and mostly damaged. It was decided on the spot to re-equip the band completely. Lieut. Dean was sent urgently to London to purchase new instruments, stands, slings, and cases, and a vast repertoire of music; and in a fortnight's time the band of forty-two perform-ers now reinforced by other musical machine-gunners found with-in the old battalion, was a fait-accompli. Over £600 was spent on re-equipping the Band.

The stealing of the band has been described as the biggest ramp of the war! At any rate, as a conjuring trick, that is the art of producing something instantaneously without being detected, it probably rivals any other similar trick performed during the war. In any case it made the band happy, it made the C.O. happy, and it made the Battalion happy; and its unrivalled performances added to the happiness of nearly every Unit in the 33rd Division and many outside it.

The musicians themselves, under Bandmaster P. Ogden, originally were members of the 18th (Pals) Battalion Manchester Regiment, and had previously seen very heavy fighting on the Somme in 1916 and in March 1918. Most of them had over two years' service in France and many had been wounded.

The drums were painted by Private Arthurs and their design was most striking and original.

Many a time when men of the M.G.C. and others were fortunate enough to get a rest from the line, and hear a concert given by the M.G.C. band, they blessed the musicians who for a short while enabled their audience to forget the horrors of the trenches.

Historical Footnote

On the 5th August, 1918, the King and Queen of the Belgians attended a concert by the Machine Gun Corps Band, and also autographed their programme.

MEMORIES OF A 9th DIVISION MACHINE GUNNER

In the Autumn of 1917 Italy, one of Britain's allies in World War One, was talking of making a separate peace with Germany. The Italians had just about had enough, and so—to bolster up their morale—it was decided to send the British 9th Division— serving in France—to the Italian Front.

A machine-gunner of the 9th Division, who well remembers the trip from France to Italy, describes this and subsequent experiences :

We had to show the flag, so we marched through Italy and finally arrived at our destination, taking up positions on Mount Grappa by the banks of the River Piave.

It was the end of two weeks' marching and everyone was pretty weary. However, no time was wasted in letting the enemy know we had arrived and directly we had settled in, our machine-guns fired a barrage into the enemy lines, which at this time were held by the Bavarians on the opposite side of the river. Each gun had hardly got through a belt or two of ammunition when, to our great astonishment, the order came—'Cease Fire'. We learned afterwards that an Italian General had played merry hell because he said we were destroying his town. From then onwards we did not fire a shot, and after Flanders it was like being in heaven.

Every morning, just as daylight approached, we went to the river bank and greeted the Bavarians with a 'Guten-Tag' and this went on for about a month. Then the Bavarians were replaced by the Prussians. It was the end of the peace period. Again we resorted to the Hymn of Hate at 'Stand-to' times.

Nevertheless we still thought ourselves fortunate to be on this part of the Italian Front—away from the hell of France and Flanders and I secretly hoped to spend the rest of the war alongside the River Piave, which did help to keep one clean. But my hopes were suddenly dashed to pieces in March 1918, when the 9th Division were ordered back to France.

Although it had taken us over a fortnight to get to Italy, the whole of our Division was transported back to France in three nights and two days.

Directly we arrived back on French soil we were rushed to the firing line. The German offensive was sweeping everything before it. I was allocated to 'C' Company. For several weeks it was absolutely chaos, and during this time we took a terrible beating.

Our machine-guns were continually fighting, either in no-man's-land, or between the first and second lines.

On one occasion we were called upon to give covering fire to a Canadian regiment which was going to attempt a counter-attack.

After nearly two months of retreating and fighting rearguard actions, our machine-gun teams were sadly depleted and the losses in the ranks of the infantry were ghastly.

On the night of July 3rd, 1918, our Machine Gun Sections took up positions in front of Meteran Becque. Much heavy fighting had already taken place around this area and was still going on. The Meteran position was a vital one and now an effort was to be made to push the Germans further away from the British lines. In six days from the time of our arrival at the Becque we had succeeded in digging gun emplacements in no-man's-land by working during the night and hiding up in the Becque during the day-time, having taken care to leave our gun-pits well camouflaged. By July 9th I had four guns in position. We waited three days for zero hour—fixed for 05.15 hours, July 12th.

Our targets were a Cross Road and a farm named Bogle Farm.

We manned our guns during the night of July 11th with each gun team reduced in personnel and waited for zero hour.

The period of waiting was nerve-racking. Promptly at the fixed time the attack began. Our machine-guns fired a barrage to support the attacking infantry and this lasted for nearly 40 minutes before Jerry's artillery located us.

Then a shell caught No. 2 team—manned by L/Cpl. Gillanders—with a direct hit. After that our positions became impossible and we were forced to withdraw to the cover of the Becque to avoid annihilation. We remained in the Becque all that day. The Infantry attack had been held up and eventually fizzled out. We were back to square one, less many brave lads who remained behind for good.

The following night when getting out of the Becque I put my hand on the rear bank to ease myself up, and as I did so something moved. Upon investigating I discovered it was a tarpaulin covering a huge dump of trench mortar shells. I shuddered to think what would have happened to us if Jerry's artillery guns had increased their range by about 18 feet. How lucky some of us were.

7

The Final Act on the Western Front

By the end of July, 1918—the great German offensive—aimed to win the war—had collapsed, and on August 8th, 1918, the British and French Armies, in conjunction with their Allies and the American Force under General Pershing, commenced an all-out attack on the retreating German forces, who were falling back on the Hindenburg and Siegfried Lines.

It was the beginning of the end of the most terrible war of all time, but before the end did arrive much heavy fighting took place and many more thousands of valuable lives were sacrificed on the altars of the gods of war.

Men of the Machine Gun Corps played a vital role in these final battles just as they had done on previous occasions throughout the war.

A machine-gunner who served with the 58th Division writes :

During the early part of the night of August 7th, 1918, our machine-gun section left the cover of trenches and moved forward over the open ground for a mile or so until we reached a ridge, where we halted and worked feverishly throughout the remainder of the night digging gun emplacements behind the crest of the ridge. Entrenching tools and bare hands were used to scoop the earth into a protection from enemy shell fire. Next morning August 8th the advance got under way from the Albert-Amiens-Monididier front with the French on our right flank. We had been firing bursts throughout the night and, as anticipated, when daylight came German artillery gunners pinpointed our positions. Shells killed three of No. 1 Section gun team. A little later on our Section Officer received a shrapnel wound in the chest. Stretcher-bearers got him away.

Before moving on again we buried our fallen comrades in shallow graves and marked the spots with simple crosses made from ammo boxes. Names and Regimental Numbers were inscribed in rough scribble on the crosses. Such simple grave markings helped those who had the thankless task of removing the bodies to military cemeteries.

Just before leaving our ridge-positions, a lone German prisoner approached. He spoke to me in perfect English and said he did not want the war, and that he had once worked in London.

We advanced over sloping fields and came to a trench heaped with German dead. There was also a number of our own wounded and dead infantrymen. In this trench I found a pair of German field glasses which I have to this day.

After the advance had been in progress several days my chum and I ran out of cigarettes. We came across a dead German and decided to search his pockets. 'Never rob the dead' was a sort of standing order in the British army, but upon finding a packet of cigarettes in a pocket of this unfortunate German we decided to ignore orders and enjoy a smoke.

I well remember these things as though it all happened only yesterday, instead of over fifty years ago.

A Section Commander of 76 Machine Gun Company (3rd M.G. Batt.) who experienced the Allied Final Offensive wrote the following report :

At 4 a.m. August 23rd, 1918, my section of 'C' Company moved forward and established positions towards Gomiecourt. The Gordons pushed forward to a sunken road. We engaged an enemy field-gun with good results, but not before it had put one of our guns out of action.

About a hundred prisoners being conducted by two Gordons turned on their escort and killed them. Our machine-guns immediately opened up on the prisoners and did great execution.

After about three hours a party of the enemy issued from a dug-out in the sunken road and took about 20 Gordons prisoner and with them two of our men. We could not fire on them, our own troops were in the way. The enemy and the prisoners went along the railway-line towards Achiet-le-Grand.

In the evening I walked along the sunken road and found eleven abandoned enemy machine-guns. The dug-outs near the railway were full of enemy wounded, the results of our fire.

BY ONE OF THE CAPTURED PRISONERS

Just before reaching the railway cutting we saw the two Germans carrying our gun fall over. They were killed, and our gun destroyed. We went with the Gordons into the sunken road and fought in this position for three hours.

About 7 a.m. on August 24th—a large party of the enemy emerged from a dug-out and rushed us.

I shot one officer through the head; then we two were taken prisoner with about 12 Gordons.

We were taken along the railway. A Hun officer beat one of the Gordons with a stick and said he was going to shoot us machine-gunners as we had inflicted heavy casualties on his men.

At that moment a German Colonel appeared who was very nice to us and ordered us to take our wounded to Achiet under escort. He said we were brave fellows.

At 11 a.m. our barrage fire opened up on Achiet and the Huns took refuge in a deep dug-out—leaving us at the top of the stairs! We waved for our fellows to come on and they took prisoner all the Boche in the dug-out.

We told the K.R.R's of 37 Division about the officer who had beaten the Gordon prisoner, and they bayoneted him.

As the reader will have gathered there existed much bitterness between some sections of the German and British front-line soldiers.

The following copy of a letter written by Lieut. Colonel Hutchison, D.S.O., M.C., and published in the private History and Memoir of the 33rd Battalion Machine Gun Corps—compiled in 1919—gives some of the reasons for such bitterness from the British angle.

July 15th, 1918

CIVILISATION VERSUS THE HUN

During the minor operation on the 14th July, 1918, in which we co-operated, twenty-nine prisoners of the 5th and 8th Companies 166 Infantry Regiment, of the 31st Division were captured.

Most of the prisoners came from the Rhineland Province, in which is situated Cologne, one of the most beautiful cities in the world.

Upon these prisoners, almost without exception, were found the most revolting photographic picture postcards depicting British dead.

In some cases these pictures showed our dead stripped and mutilated, being grinned upon by German soldiery.

In one case, the photograph showed a dead Highlander with his kilt up to his chest, the whole of the lower limbs exposed naked and a German helmet placed over his privates, whilst a small crowd of German soldiery stood facing the camera grinning.

The postcard was taken from one of these prisoners. There were several copies of this distributed among them.

It is the least revolting which I saw. It will be observed that none of these men showed signs of any shell wound; they none of them showed limbs missing or death agony; they were in regular lines and were stripped. One man had his hands tied behind his back; one man, whose face was clearly seen, had only recently died.

One man had his left hand in his pocket. From these indications it appears more than probable that these men were taken prisoners, were ordered to strip, and then brutally murdered in cold blood.

It is most improbable that a cart driven by a cleanly dressed soldier would have been present on the battlefield, unscarred by shell holes, to carry, as a mock hearse, men so freshly dead.

No white man, few savages, can look on this photograph without feelings of disgust, rage, and horror. Yet the Germans carry these photographs amongst those of their families, in order that they may gloat again and again over their victims.

I hope that no man of this Battalion will forget this in his dealings with Germans both during this war and after.

I hope that the men of this Battalion who see this will tell their friends and relations at home what they have seen.

I hope that every man will do his best to ensure that those men and women of all classes who fawn upon German beasts in our prison camps, upon the farms or uninterned, are themselves faced with the full vengeance which we can mete out to those who so murder and mutilate our comrades whom we love.

(Signed) G. S. Hutchison,
Lieut-Colonel,
Commanding 33rd Battalion Machine Gun Corps

GERMAN RETREAT BECOMING A ROUT

An N.C.O. of 126 Machine Gun Company gives this account :

By the end of August, 1918, the German Army was in full retreat everywhere along the whole battle front and we were soon on our way to Cambrai.

Squads of Germans were continually surrendering to our infantry and many were in a panic as they shouted 'No shoot'. Nevertheless, it was often necessary to mount our guns to give covering fire to the advancing infantrymen in our sector.

In the early days of September we reached the outskirts of Cambrai, where we spent a night in a captured German dugout.

The assault on the Hindenburg Line between Cambrai and St. Quentin (part of the offensive that ended the war) was gathering momentum and directly it was daylight on the morning of September 12th we left the outskirts of Cambrai and marched across open country, bypassing the city.

Pack mules carried our gear—but after a while we struck so many communication trenches it became necessary to get rid of the mules. Headquarters then sent us a tank—complete with driver—to carry our gear. We were almost at the Hindenburg Line when our tank-driver was shot in the face and killed.

We dismantled our gear again and finished up carrying guns, tripods and other equipment into a trench full of Germans who were waiting to surrender.

We saw the machine-gun that we assumed had killed our driver. The gun was ditched against the parapet, but all we could do was to give the prisoners a nasty look as our infantrymen hustled them out of the dug-out.

Infantry bombing squads began to work their way along a maze of enemy dug-outs, which were palaces compared to most of those we had occupied in the British Lines. I remember one German dug-out in particular : it had forty steps leading down to a veritable home from home, with bread and bottles of wine on tables. There was also a piano, the top of which was covered with picture postcards of places in Germany where, apparently the occupants of the dug-out came from.

'They must have had quite an enjoyable time when off duty,' remarked my section officer. We were not able to sample any of the German luxuries for it became necessary to help our infantry comb the many deep shelters, having a gun ready in case of serious resistance.

Some occupants of these shelters seemed most reluctant to come up and surrender when our infantry chaps shouted down to them, but after a Mills-bomb had been chucked into the shelter they soon changed their minds. Many young boys were among the men.

Reaching a trench which we took to be a dead-end, we discovered our mistake when about twenty Germans suddenly appeared in our rear and one German opened fire on us. We shipped our machine-gun round and covered them. They immediately offered to surrender—shouting almost in unison—'No shoot, we got children at home, war fini'.

We withheld our fire and the Germans (mostly artillerymen), after giving us small souvenirs as a sort of thanks for sparing them, quietly joined their mates in a main trench, waiting to be marched off to a prisoners' reception depot.

In the next bay to us an infantry N.C.O. was shouting orders to his men over something or other. I recognised the voice and slipped round to confirm my belief. We were neighbours from Oldham. For a few moments we talked of home—as refreshing as rain in a desert—but our talk was ended abruptly as a German tailed mortar-bomb came whizzing over from a section of the German line not far distant and my Oldham neighbour received orders to help sort out other problems.

Our machine-gun section got instructions to move into a valley behind us and take shelter in a captured trench.

As we moved it simply rained bullets. I had one through my haversack and water bottle before finally reaching cover. Luckily for us the Germans were firing too much to our right.

In front of us was a German redoubt of machine-guns. It had to be silenced before we made any further advance.

We waited until after dark before doing anything about it, then in conjunction with infantry scouts, took out a gun and got a closer look at the German strongpoint—which turned out to be several tanks protected with concrete shields and well camouflaged. A miniature fortress.

The tanks were British—captured from our lads during the 1916 offensive, we were told later on.

Next day, preparations were made to subdue this little German fortress which we knew was going to be no picnic.

On the last day of September I believe it was, the assault took place. Field guns of the Royal Horse Artillery first bombarded the enemy redoubts and 126 Machine Gun Company put down a heavy machine-gun barrage in support of the infantry who rushed in and captured the whole outfit, with few casualties. It was now quite apparent that the Germans would much rather surrender than fight.

At this point 126 Machine Gun Company was relieved by

gunners of the 48th Division, who pushed on further into the Hindenburg Line.

Buckingham Palace

His Majesty KING GEORGE The Fifth, is graciously pleased to confer upon,

TOWNER, Lieutenant Edgar Thomas M.C.
2nd Battalion Australian Machine Gun Corps.

The award of the VICTORIA CROSS for most conspicuous bravery, initiative, and devotion to duty on the 1st of September, 1918, in the attack on Mont St Quentin, near Peronne, when in charge of four Vickers guns. During the early stages of the advance he located and captured, single-handed, an enemy machine gun which was causing heavy casualties, and by turning it on the enemy inflicted severe losses.

Subsequently, by the skilful and tactical handling of his guns, he cut off and captured twenty-five of the enemy.

Later, by fearless reconnaissance under heavy fire, and by the energy, foresight, and promptitude with which he brought fire to bear on various groups of the enemy, he gave valuable support to the infantry advance.

Again, when short of ammunition, he secured an enemy machine gun, which he mounted and fired in full view of the enemy, causing them to retire further, and enabling our infantry to continue the advance. Under intense fire, although wounded, he maintained the fire of this gun at a very critical period.

Throughout the night he kept a close watch by personal reconnaissance on the enemy movements, and was evacuated exhausted thirty hours after being wounded.

The valour and resourcefulness of Lieutenant Towner undoubtedly saved a very critical situation, and contributed largely to the success of this attack.

The London Gazette, December 14th, 1918.

MEMORIES OF BOHAIN

On a day in mid-October, 1918, we received orders to proceed along the railway track verge towards the French town of Bohain. It was, for me, a day I have never forgotten.

The Germans had retreated beyond the town, but no-one seemed to know where the next contact with the enemy was likely to be.

We were marching up the valley following the railway track when, upon rounding a bend I first saw Bohain.

It looked in fairly good shape, having escaped the heavy shelling experienced by many other places in this area.

Beyond the town was a steep hill, similar to the Chevin, Otley, Yorkshire, where—as schoolchildren—my brother and I spent many happy days, and as I surveyed the picture before me I thought of my brother, who had been killed on the Somme in 1916. We had been close companions since childhood and had worked together in the rope-trade until the outbreak of war in 1914, and, as I remembered, a hatred of war was intermingled with sadness.

The C.O. called a halt, and went into a conclave with officers and N.C.O.'s. While this was taking place we sprawled alongside the rough verge of the railway track, and waited for further instructions. We had no infantry support and everywhere around us was quiet—an uncanny quiet. 'I have a feeling we are being watched' I said to Ginger—my No. 1 on the gun. He simply grinned in acknowledgement.

The sergeant rejoined us from the conclave.

'We are going to dig in,' he said. Officers marked out positions to be taken up by their Section-guns.

Alternate guns—one each side of the railway track, four guns in all were spread out.

We began to dig in full view of the summit of the hill, which seemed, I thought, a bit rash for no-one knew for certain that Jerry was not spying from the top of the hill. We completed the digging of gun emplacements, checked various components, spare parts, ammo, got the range-finder to work, re-checked everything just to make sure and finally reported 'All O.K. Sergeant'.

We then relaxed and waited—for what? Nobody really knew. I had experienced this sort of thing on previous occasions and taken little notice, but this time I had a premonition that something unpleasant was not far away, which led me to remark to my sergeant, 'It may seem like the Garden of Eden just now, but what's coming?'

'Have a nap,' he replied, which I did.

When I awoke it was dusk. Our cook brought us some tea and I was standing at the side of the track when the shelling started.

I was suddenly knocked off my feet and lay looking rather stupidly at my right foot, from which a large piece of shrapnel was sticking. My sergeant came along, and said, 'You lucky so-and-so'. Stretcher-bearers collected me, and in due course

I was put on a hospital train en route for Rouen Military Hospital.

It was the end of the war for me. I was, as my sergeant remarked, lucky.

(By a 6th Division machine-gunner)

THE FINAL ADVANCE

It was the second time out for my friend Charles Mazzone and me when we arrived in France with a draft for 46 Machine Gun Company. On the evening of October 12th, 1918, we reported to Company Headquarters—situated at Joncourt. The place was absolutely shattered.

Next morning the Company Quartermaster gave us the following information, 'You will now be going up the road to join your sections, do not touch any German bodies you may see lying around or you may get your fingers blown off; some German dead are booby-trapped.'

I pondered on his advice, but became more concerned when I saw a large number of British dead collected together in the square at Joncourt awaiting identification prior to burial. The grim spectacle somewhat turned my stomach over. We reached the Company later that day and were detailed to join No. 2 gun-team, No. 1 Section—under L/Cpl. Dixon who informed me that there had been quite a 'do' a couple of days ago. I told him I had seen for myself the outcome of that 'do' in the square at Joncourt.

On the afternoon of October 14th the whole of the 46th Machine Gun Company moved to a position overlooking Fresnoy-le-Grand, where sections were split up again. My friend Mazzone was sent with another gun-team to the village of Mericourt—a short distance away on our left flank.

After unloading our transport limbers we got orders to dig-in. It was quite easy digging compared to some and there was no shell-fire to hinder our labours.

A tank came rumbling along. It made a hell of a noise, but did not draw any enemy fire. That evening we moved freely around our newly-dug gun emplacements. Not a German was in sight. Fresnoy-le-Grand was quite visible, although tucked away in the fold of the low ground below us.

As I looked through field-glasses the place seemed devoid of life—not a movement of any kind could be detected; but, knowing Fritz, nothing could be taken for granted and as night approached we manned our machine-guns and kept a sharp observation.

During my turn of sentry duty around 4 a.m. I observed a dark object lying only about eight yards from our position, hidden partly by a scoop in the ground and, upon investigation, discovered the dark object was a dead German lad of no more than sixteen years of age. At daylight I helped bring him in, and although he was an enemy a pang of sadness surged within me that this had to be.

Later that same morning we packed up and followed our transport limbers through Fresnoy-le-Grand without enemy opposition and continued along the road towards the town of Bohain.

We skirted the town and took up a position about 800 yards in front of a wood. From this point we had a grand-stand view of the surrounding countryside. Clearly visible on our right flank was a battery of French 75's. A small farmstead a short distance in front of the guns made a natural screen for them. In the open country between the left corner of the farmstead and the right of the wood was the tank we had seen pass us the previous evening. We later discovered it had been knocked out and abandoned.

It was believed that the wood in front of us, which we named Bohain Wood, had been evacuated by the enemy, but our scouts discovered otherwise. At 6 a.m. next morning, October 15th, British 18-pounders and French 75's strafed the German positions, after which Infantrymen doubled along the road and entered the wood; but after a few moments they came out again and lay along the sides of the green bank adjoining the wood. The enemy rearguards were difficult to budge.

We got orders to support the infantry lads with an overhead machine-gun barrage, and this effort, allied to a further bombardment by the 75's and 18 pounders, had the desired effect. The infantry went in again and this time they continued to advance unmolested.

At this juncture of the advance our machine-gun company was pulled out of the line and marched back to Bohain for a rest spell. We slept in the cellars of an abandoned house.

Our pleasant rest spell ended somewhat abruptly at 1 a.m. on October 30th, when we were ordered to follow on after our transport limbers, which had already got moving.

Upon reaching a fork in the road—new territory to us—Lt. Brookes, my section officer, took the wrong turning. This was not discovered until we had marched some half-mile and learnt from a scout that a German rearguard force occupied the far end of the road we were marching along. We retraced our steps at the double. This time we took the correct turning and caught up with our transport after some two miles of marching.

We received orders to unload our limbers and take up a position in an orchard, where once-lovely apple trees lay uprooted as a result of a previous shelling by both British and German guns.

Jerry started shelling us. It became so hot that we raced for shelter behind the fallen trees in the orchard.

Shrapnel knocked out two of our gunners. We had already taken away our guns and tripods, ammo and other items, but the limbers remained exposed and lying beside them were our two chums. Sergeant J. decided to return to where the wounded gunners lay. 'You lot stay here', he ordered, and we watched him go out. At the very instant he reached the side of our chums Jerry opened up again. It was as though he could see what was going on.

L/Cpl. Dixon and another chap left the cover of the trees and helped get in the wounded gunners.

Then Sergeant J. went out again to the gun-limbers and was returning when a dud enemy shell landed near him, tipping him over on one hand, cart-wheel fashion.

The Sergeant staggered to his feet. We got him in, but he was so badly shaken that for a few moments he was unable to speak. He had had an amazing escape.

Had the shell been a live one Sergeant J. would have been blown to bits.

THE LAST BATTLE

The battle of the Sambre was the last major engagement of the Great War. It began on November 1st, 1918, and was carried out by three British Armies. In ten days they advanced 25 miles, taking Valenciennes, Landrecies, Maubeuge and finally Mons, and 19,000 prisoners. The battle ended with the Armistice on November 11th, 1918.

Many Machine Gun Companies took part in the Sambre battle, which included the 19th, 100th, 98th, and 248th—known as the 33rd Battalion Machine Gun Corps. The following extract from the history and memoire of this élite M.G.C. Unit tells of their part in the last big engagement of the war on the Western Front :

On November 5th, 1918, the 33rd Division was fighting an advance guard action, moving towards the village of Berlaimont on the banks of the River Sambre. Having captured the village it became necessary to cross the River Sambre to follow up the retiring enemy. The Germans had destroyed all bridges and were strongly entrenched on the opposite bank of the river, thereby making further advance impossible until the river crossings were re-established, or bridges re-built.

The Division was being led by the 1st Battalion Middlesex Regiment, under Lt. Colonel D. C. Owen, D.S.O., with whom was co-operating the 33rd Machine Gun Corps Battalion. The advance through the Foret de Mormal during the early part of November 4th had been very rapid. The Machine Gun Corps in this action proved that their system of transport was so efficient that, notwithstanding the fact that the infantry had advanced almost as quickly as the men could march, when the front line was actually checked and held up near the river bank, the mach-ine-guns came into action immediately. It is doubtful whether under the old system of fighting—the machine-guns with the Infantry Battalion—this could have been achieved.

The ground sloped sharply down for about a mile to the river bank, in full view of the enemy entrenched in the opposite bank. Had the advance continued we must have lost heavily. Instead of which, a section of machine-guns was brought into action in the front line itself, and engaged the enemy trenches at a range of 1,800 yards. Under cover of this fire, our patrols were able to work their way down to the river bank and reconnoitre thoroughly with a view to rebuilding the bridges.

Had not these machine-guns been up with the advance line, considerable time and probably many more lives would have been wasted in performing the necessary reconnaissance.

Subsequently two machine-guns worked their way down to the river bank itself and engaged the enemy trenches on the op-posite bank. All the machine-gunners were in action on the enemy trenches early; and they kept up such an accurate fire that the Infantry were able to choose their spot for building the bridge, and even to dump a large portion of the material near the spot. At dusk the enemy had become so demoralized by our machine-gun fire and sniping, assisted by a certain amount of artillery, that we were able to push our first bridge across the river, which was unfordable, and establish a crossing.

It is interesting to note that this bridge was built by 'B' Com-pany, 1st Middlesex Regiment, entirely by untrained men under the supervision of a Sapper officer, and that all the material used was found in Berlaimont village by the officers and men of the 1st Middlesex. This was indeed a very creditable performance.

The whole 98th Brigade crossed by this one bridge and established a footing on the opposite side, capturing many prisoners, guns, etc.

The 1st Middlesex were the first over the river, while the Brigades on the left and right were held up. The success of the action was very greatly due to the co-operation between the infantry and the Machine Gun Corps. It was not an action which came off by chance. The Machine Gunners were the whole time in closest liaison with Lieut-Colonel Owen, and the dispositions of the guns were made in accordance with his requirements.

During the whole operation casualties were practically nil. The 33rd Battalion Machine Gun Corps worked splendidly throughout these operations, thoroughly upholding the traditions of the British Army. Their Commanding Officer should be a very proud man, said Captain F. C. Booth, V.C., D.C.M., of the 'Die-Hards', in his written report of the battle.

Both the village of Berlaimont and the passage of the Sambre river having been captured by the valour of the Middlesex Regiment, with Major Dean's machine-gun company co-operating, the 98th Brigade swept on through Aulnoye, a small manufacturing town which had suffered considerably at the enemy's hands, towards Petit Maubeuge, where considerable opposition was encountered. The rapidity of the advance had left pockets of the enemy undetected by our patrols and caused us several casualties.

At this time the 38th Division relieved the 19th Brigade, and on November 9th, 1918, the whole of the 33rd Division was withdrawn from the battle area. Its machine-gun companies—with the exception of 'A' Company under Major Stentiford, M.C., who remained behind to cover the concentration of the 38th Division for a further advance next day—were billeted in the town of Aulnoye.

THE END

It was strongly rumoured that the enemy had sent over plenipotentiaries to Marshal Foch pleading for an armistice. This was officially confirmed on the 10th November—stating that Marshal Foch had agreed to an armistice under conditions very severe to the enemy, and that he must accept by 11 a.m. on the 11th, or continue fighting.

The excitement, both among the British soldiers and the civil-

ian population, was intense. It was immediately decided by this
Battalion to open an immense one franc sweepstake on the result;
and a deserted shop was taken over for this purpose. Subscrip-
tions poured in, both from our own men, and those of our neighbours, the Welsh Division; shortly before 11 o'clock on the 11th
it was announced that the enemy had accepted the terms, and
over 1,500 francs were paid out as a result of the sweepstake to
Private Diamond of 'A' Company, M.G.C.

With characteristic promptness it was, again, immediately decided to celebrate the event in an equally characteristic and original manner. At 11 a.m.—the hour of the Armistice—the Machine
Gun Corps band turned out in the streets of Aulnoye in full war
paint, and, preceded by a peal of bells, marched through the
streets of the town playing soul-stirring marches, and ending in
the square with 'La Marseillaise' and the National Anthem.

An enormous crowd of soldiers and civilians thronged the
streets and hung from the windows, cheering and waving flags,
whilst the Mayor of the town presented a bouquet of flowers to
the Bandmaster and hung a garland of roses round the neck of
the Commanding Officer.

At 7 o'clock the same evening, a torchlight procession, forty
torches on five foot poles having been provided at a moment's
notice by our energetic Pioneers, was organised through the
town, ending at the old German Officers' Club in the Square, in
front of which an enormous bonfire had been built and a stage
set for an impromptu concert erected. The progress of the band,
through even greater crowds than during the morning, was preceded by volleys of Very lights of every known colour being
fired into the air. The bonfire burned so fiercely that the A.P.M.
turned out from his comfortable billet at night to see if the town
was on fire, whilst other Staff Officers imagined that a huge
German dump had gone up!

For several days the Battalion lay at Aulnoye; and finally
marched back to Malincourt over the line of its old advance and
battlefields, where it rested for about three weeks in a very comfortable deserted village. Sports of all kinds were arranged, whilst
the C.O., in his inimitable manner, lectured on the horrors of
demobilization.

HOW OTHER MACHINE GUNNERS SAW THE END

We reached the town of Bapaume in late October, and took
refuge in some old buildings—intending to stay the night. In the
early evening our single-gun team was left on its own. The sud-

den solitude of the place made me a little anxious, so I decided to do some scouting around.

I took two of my lads with me. We spotted a car which looked abandoned and in good condition. I crept round the corner of the deserted ruins of the main street (Bapaume had been badly knocked about) closely followed by my two chums.

It was now semi-dark. Entering another ruined building I got a shock. Suddenly a cold hand caught my face. My heart seemed to turn over and for a moment I stood rooted to the spot. My two companions—having heard my gasp of terror—quickly took cover.

I eventually brought my revolver up to challenge—when I realised it was the hand of a dead German, who was entombed in the ruins. How long he had been there I never stopped to find out, and we decided not to bother any further about the car but instead rejoined the rest of my gun-team.

Next day we continued to advance and eventually arrived at St. Catherine—a pleasant French town and it was while we were there that the Armistice was announced.

Flags and bunting decorated the streets, and we were greeted with gladness, and fruit and drink.

(An N.C.O. of 41 Machine Gun Company)

In early November, 1918, 126 Machine Gun Company reached the Foret de Mormal—an immense and thickly planted forest of dense undergrowth, extending from west to east for over seven miles. As a result of an attack made by the 38th Division on November 3rd, strong enemy positions had been captured as far as the village of Locquignol, about three miles inside the wood.

We found enormous shell craters everywhere, and in the forest rows and rows of enemy dead were piled behind the fallen tree trunks and in slit trenches. The fierce onslaught made by the infantry of the 38th Division was very apparent. Many of the German dead had been bayoneted.

By November 7th the Foret de Mormal was cleared of the enemy and carnage and death sprayed the roads out of that wood.

On the evening of November 10th we reached a small village and our gun-team had a good night's kip on the floor of an abandoned school.

Next morning, November 11th, we had assembled ready to move off when the order arrived 'stand-fast'. This order was soon followed by an announcement from our C.O., 'The war is over', he said. In the early part of the afternoon a large batch of German prisoners came along the road which passed by the school. They were laughing and singing. A little French boy stood by me to see the prisoners. The boy had a branch of a tree in his hands, and when the German sergeant—at the head of the column—reached the spot where we stood, the French lad rushed at the German and hit him with the tree branch. A great roar of laughter went up from the prisoners directly behind the sergeant.

A few moments later I looked into the school playground where about 30 of our lads—killed the previous day—lay awaiting burial. The sight rather sickened me, and as I turned to walk away I saw the French boy standing by my side. He looked up at me but said nothing. I understood.

(A gunner of 126 Machine Gun Company)

I well remember the final stages of the War on the Western Front in the Sector where I served. It was something one cannot ever forget.

It began when we relieved the Aussies at Willers Bretonneux, after they had made a wonderful advance. Our Division 'went over' at Thiepval Ridge. We were on emergency rations for several days and I remember the great welcome we received from the first liberated village folk, who had been under German rule for the whole of the war. These humble French peasants offered us the only food they had and never stopped cheering us.

I remember that we went through Inchy, and on to Bachant, arriving there on November 10th, 1918.

In the early hours of the following morning, November 11th, the message went out from Haig's General Headquarters.

AN ARMISTICE HAS BEEN SIGNED—HOSTILITIES WILL CEASE AT 11.00 HOURS TODAY NOVEMBER 11TH, 1918.

When the message reached me I could not believe it. I thought I must be dreaming, but after a check the great news was confirmed and I relayed the message to everyone I could reach.

The fighting went on until a few moments before 11 a.m. and then a strange silence descended over the battlefield.

There was something unforgettable about that silence.

That night it was difficult to sleep.

Not long after the Armistice our 17th Division was inspected by the then Prince of Wales, but this did not create much interest. The lads in our mob were far more interested in looking for any spare grub knocking around in the farms around us, and very soon a sort of reaction set in. Everyone wanted to get home.

(A signaller with 17th Battalion—9D Machine Gun Company)

During the morning of November 6th, 1918, the Royal Engineers built a pontoon bridge across the River Sambre, and later that day 46 Machine Gun Company crossed over.

Upon entering the first village after the crossing we saw signs that our Cavalry had been in action.

A horse lay dead with half its rump shot away. What had happened to its rider was anyone's guess.

That evening we occupied a disused house in the village and prepared to kip down for the night. Our field kitchen had been left at the entrance to the village and volunteers were called for to fetch a dixie of tea and some rations.

I volunteered and so did a chap named John Forth.

Darkness had completely fallen by the time we re-entered the village and we had a job to locate our billet.

When we did eventually find it we got a shock. During our absence Jerry had lobbed a shell on the billet and three of my chums had become casualties. Our kip for the night was a washout. German artillery had levelled the place prior to their evacuation.

Even at this late stage in the war, danger lurked in harmless-looking farmsteads and villages, whose legal occupants had long since left or been butchered by German soldiers.

Orders came through from H.Q. to march again at dawn and on the evening of November 10th we anchored down in the vicinity of the village of Avesnes.

Next morning, November 11th, 1918, when L/Cpl. Dixon and I were busy cleaning and oiling the gun, Lt. Brookes—my Section officer—came along and in quite a casual manner said, 'No firing after eleven o'clock, an armistice has been declared'. For a moment or two his remark did not seem to sink in. We could not believe it was all over.

There was plenty of noise going on around us.

German ammunition dumps exploding, interwoven with occasional shell-fire, gave one the impression that the war was still on. But after eleven o'clock the shelling ceased and an eerie silence, apart from a few more dump explosions, confirmed the fact that IT WAS ALL OVER.

I am able to state with all truth that I did not see any hats thrown in the air, or hear any hurrahs; our one jubilation came when we discovered in a farmyard a portable boiler and two large tubs, which made it possible for our gun-team to enjoy an excellent bath, after which we were allowed to relax.

That night the whole of our machine-gun section had a good sleep among the hay in a loft adjoining the farm house.

Next morning a football appeared from somewhere or other and a game was arranged.

(A gunner of 46 Machine Gun Company)

PADDY

by G.M.M. (Ex 109 Machine Gun Company, 36th Ulster Division)

Paddy came from Belfast and had been a regular soldier with the Royal Inniskilling Fusiliers—'The Skins', as he called them.

He landed in France with the 36th (Ulster) Division in 1915 and never tired of telling us how Paddy Nugent (Major General O. S. W. Nugent, D.S.O.) had promised to take the Division back to Ulster in a rowing boat.

In 1916 Paddy was transferred to the Machine Gun Corps. When he joined my team I was rather pleased to have an old hand with me but I was soon to realize that, in addition to his accomplishments, he brought more than a few headaches!

A likeable soul, he was the laziest thing on two legs ever to land in France. Additionally he was the biggest scrounger in the British Army. Anything we wanted on the gun team suddenly and mysteriously appeared—thanks to Paddy.

He had no next-of-kin and when asked anything regarding them always referred to them as his 'next to skin'—an issue vest?

It was when we were in close support near St. Jean, on the Ypres Salient, that word came up that six boxes of ammunition were to be collected from the ration dump that evening.

Paddy, with two other lads named White and Black, from the Queen's Westminster Rifles, was detailed to bring the boxes to the gun-pit.

Shortly after evening 'stand-by' the three set off.

Time passed and White and Black appeared, each carrying a box of ammo and returned for the second trip. When they returned from this trip they said that there were two more boxes to come and left to collect them.

Eventually they returned, each carrying a box of ammo, followed by an unladen Paddy who went to great lengths to explain that he had 'bin kaaping an eye on the ammo, 'cos there wuz a crowd of thieving Skins loafing round to see wot they could pinch'!

Sad to relate Paddy never saw the end of the war—*he was blown to pieces early on November 11th, 1918—a few hours before the Armistice.*

8

The Mesopotamia Campaign

One of the immediate results of Turkey entering World War One as a combatant on the side of Germany, was to extend hostilities to the Persian Gulf area, where fighting soon broke out between Turkish and British forces.

The British Navy had, for many years, policed the Persian Gulf and reduced piracy, which once existed on a big scale, to nil. This fact encouraged the Sheiks of the area to give their support to the British when they were landing troops at a place called Fao—situated at the tip of the Persian Gulf.

In 1914 Mesopotamia was part of the Ottoman Empire, and the invasion of their lands was resisted with much vigour, but with the help of the British Navy, who were able to land supplies right up to the doorstep of the battlefield, British troops advanced and on November 21st, 1914, seized the port of Basra, on the western bank of the Shatt-el-Arab. Here the rivers Tigris and Euphrates meet before entering the sea, some 35 miles from the Persian Gulf and 270 miles from Baghdad.

This was the beginning of a campaign which eventually played an important role in the defeat of the Turkish Army, but at the time of the capture of Basra not much notice was taken of this event. The great battles being fought in France and Belgium and in Russia overshadowed the Mesopotamia venture.

Nevertheless, modest as the 'Mespot' campaign was at first, it had high strategical importance.

For some years before the outbreak of World War One, Germany had aimed to extend her sphere of influence in the far East. German engineers had supervised the building of railways to the north of Baghdad, and the ambition of German military minds was to continue this railway network from Baghdad to Basra, and use Baghdad as a powerful base from which to launch a descent through lower Mesopotamia to the Persian Gulf. The coming of war halted German ambitions in this direction, and the capture of Basra by British forces enabled the British Navy to make certain that sea communications to India remained open. In the early days of the Mesopotamia Campaign the bulk of supplies for that venture came from India.

Also, one of the great oil deposits of the world existed in the Persian Gulf area, and this had to be protected.

The capture of Basra ensured this, but after a few months, preparations were made to invade Mesopotamia proper. In April, 1915, the 6th Poona Division, under the command of General Townshend, pushed across the desert to Amara, a small town on the River Tigris 130 miles from Basra.

A Machine Gunner who served in the 6th Poona Division wrote:

When we arrived on the outskirts of Amara (April 29th, 1915) most of us were pretty well exhausted—having marched several miles in the heat of the day.

The battle of Amara commenced at dawn on May 31st and continued throughout the next four days and nights.

At dawn the heat was 110 degrees F, and at mid-day over 120 deg. There was no shade anywhere, only the blinding glare of the sun on the desert floor.

On the second day of the battle medical supplies ran out, and many wounded men were left lying out in no-man's-land under a scorching sun with no water left in their bottles. It was a scandal of the first magnitude.

Scorched sandy earth retained the heat of the day, so at night-time there was little coolness.

During the hours of darkness, fierce Arab tribesmen roamed the battlefield and robbed the dead and wounded lying out in no-man's-land.

At this stage of the war in Mesopotamia hostile tribesmen were a terrific menace to both Turkish and British troops.

During the night of June 4th the Turks abandoned their positions and retreating north towards Kut-el-Amara.

The appalling conditions under which British and Indian soldiers had fought at Amara took a heavy toll in casualties and there were twenty-seven cases of enteric fever, nine of which proved fatal. Dysentery was another illness that many of our chaps went down with. After a few weeks' rest, during which time the various battalions of the 6th Poona Division received some reinforcements in men and material, we advanced again.

By early September, 1915, Townshend's Invincibles—so named because nothing seemed to stop our advance—reached the outskirts of Kut-el-Amara, which is 230 miles from the Persian Gulf and 90 miles or so from Baghdad. In a matter of ten months, the Invincibles had marched and fought to within reasonable striking distance of Baghdad. This was a remarkable achievement under any circumstances, but more so when one considers that all supplies for the fighting troops came by river transport up the winding Tigris from the main base at Basra.

No railways existed between Basra and Baghdad, and the age of long-distance aircraft was a long way off in 1915.

THE FIRST BATTLE OF KUT

At Kut, twenty thousand Turks, occupying formidable defences, waited to oppose our advance. It was estimated that the Turks outnumbered us by two to one, but at dawn on September 28th, 1915, the Invincibles moved forward to the attack. The battle lasted throughout the heat of the day. Attacks and counter-attacks went on until late afternoon, when the whole of the northern defences of Kut were in British hands. By this time we were suffering from severe thirst and exhaustion, and General Delemain (Officer Commanding the forward battle area) was obliged to rest his men.

However, in the late evening his weary soldiers made a final attack. Turkish resistance was stubborn, but during the hours of darkness they evacuated all the remaining trenches they held and retreated north along the River Tigris.

British losses in killed and wounded amounted to 1,300. Turkish casualties were estimated at 4,000, and our infantry captured 14 guns and took 1,000 prisoners.

After the Kut battle most units were down to half strength, through sickness and casualties. Our Brigade was strengthened by the arrival of the 2nd Battalion Royal West Kents, who had been fighting on the Euphrates.

It was rumoured that we were not going to advance any further, but this proved to be all eyewash. After a rest period we went on again, reaching a place called Aziziyeh, 30 miles from Ctesiphon where the Turks held strong defensive positions across the Baghdad road. At Aziziyeh we rested until November 10th, when a Brigade of infantry, artillery and cavalry left the rest camp at Aziziyeh and moved forward towards Ctesiphon.

While at Aziziyeh I became a dysentery casualty, and was sent down river to Amara hospital, which spared me from being in the battle of Ctesiphon, where the Invincibles advance terminated.

Several Turkish Divisions, rushed out from Baghdad, forced General Townshend's small army to retreat 100 miles to Kut, where they were surrounded and besieged for over four months. A strong relief force failed to break through the Turks' lines encircling Kut, and on April 29th, 1916, the gallant Kut garrison, having reached starvation point, was obliged to surrender. With General Townshend were 240 British officers including five Generals, 270 Indian officers, and 9,000 other ranks. Casualties suffered by the relief forces on the Tigris during the months of March and April were estimated at 20,000.

Following the surrender of General Townshend and the recapture of Kut by the Turks, General Sir Stanley Maude became the new Commander-in-Chief of British and Indian forces in Mesopotamia.

The British hung on to their defensive positions at Sannaiyat, and the several miles of trenches on the opposite bank of the River Tigris facing Kut. This prevented the Turks from exploiting their victory of Kut.

Trench warfare developed on a big scale.

WITH 135 MACHINE GUN COMPANY

by an N.C.O.

This then was the situation when we (135 Machine Gun Company) arrived at the port of Basra in the early morning of a day in late September, 1916. It was the end of a most uncomfortable six weeks' sea voyage from Devonport, England.

On two occasions during the voyage our troopship had to run from threat of a U-Boat attack. Docking at Basra was welcomed as a relief from the perils of the sea, but we soon discovered new perils.

In 1916, Basra was a hell of a place. The heat was terrific, and swarms of big green flies, floating around in the humid air, clung to our sweat-soaked shirts as we unloaded our machine-guns and equipment from the troopship.

At mid-day the temperature reached 110 degrees F., and this in the month of September when, so we were told, the Mespot summer was on the wane. This led us to wonder what it must be like in the real summer months.

Actually Basra, being situated in swampy surroundings, has a more trying climate than you find further north, but climatic conditions in all parts of this far Eastern land were an extra battle British soldiers had to fight during the 1914–18 war against Turkey.

Our stay at Basra was for only a few days' duration, for which we were thankful.

A River Journey of 130 miles

Boarding a troop-carrying river boat, we began the 130 mile journey to Amara, which had been captured by Townshend's Invincibles in 1915 after a four days' battle which took place in the terrific heat of a Mesopotamian summer.

Our journey to Amara was not without interest. For the first time since leaving our troopship, it was possible to get a thorough wash and clean up. We got water from the River Tigris by slinging a canvas bucket over the side from the lower deck of the boat, taking care that someone hung on to one's waistline during the operation. This was necessary because of the swiftly running current of the mighty Tigris.

Once we stopped near the river bank within sight of an Arab village, and naked children came running to the edge of the water pleading for food. Arab women joined the children. We gave them a few tins of bully-beef and jam.

As we continued our journey, the surrounding desert became more eerie and began to swallow us up. We saw nothing but desert.

Upon arrival at Amara we were joined by machine-gunners of the 2nd Battalion Black Watch Regiment, who had already sampled Mespot as part of the force which tried to rescue the besieged Kut garrison. It was now ascertained that 135 Machine Gun Company was to form part of the 21st Brigade, 7th Indian Division. The Infantry Battalions in this Brigade consisted of the 2nd Black Watch, 1/8th Gurkhas, 20th Punjabis, and the 9th Bhopals.

Other British Units in this division were the 1st Battalion Seaforth Highlanders, 2nd Battalion Leicestershire Regiment, and 134 and 136 Machine Gun Companies, who had left Grantham at the same time as our 135 Company.

The remainder of the Infantry Units in this Division were Indian.

The 7th Indian Division had already fought in France and also as part of the relief force in Mespot. My chums and I felt somewhat proud to be part of such a famous Division.

Front Line Duty at Sannaiyat

It was late October, 1916, when we moved into the strongly fortified trenches at Sannaiyat, several miles below Kut which was in the hands of the Turks.

The trenches ran from the edge of an impassable marshland, known as the Suwaicha Marsh, right down to the edge of the River Tigris. On the opposite side of the river the system of trenches extended several miles nearer Kut.

The night we manned our guns for the first time in Mespot was so peaceful that it prompted me to say to Jock Fawcett (my No. 1 on the gun team), 'There don't seem to be a war on here'.

'Dinna ye get that idea, mon,' he replied. 'You'll see soon enough'.

Jock, a regular Black Watch soldier, had been in the 1st battle of Sannaiyat (April 10th, 1916). How right his comment turned out to be.

The heat grew less oppressive each day as we carried out duties alongside the lads of the 2nd Black Watch— and waited for we knew not what.

Christmas Day, 1916, came and went. We hardly noticed it. The first sign that the waiting period was almost at an end began about ten days after Christmas when the artillery on the opposite bank of the Tigris suddenly came to life.

At first the dull rumble of gun-fire came in spasmodic bursts, but as the days passed the rumble crescendoed like the approach of a terrible thunder-storm. During the hours of darkness gun-flashes dotted the landscape in the vicinity of Kut, and Very lights illuminated the sky above the Turkish positions. Occasionally the faint stutter of machine-gun fire echoed across the river.

But on our side of the river tranquility reigned supreme, and when our first spell of front-line duty ended in the middle of January we proceeded to rest camps behind the line.

Battle of Hai Salient

It was while we were at rest camp that the news reached us of the attack on Turkish positions in the Hai Salient.

The battle began on January 25th, 1917. It was a day of bitter fighting. Early in the attack the 39th Brigade failed to reach their objective. The North Staffords, Worcesters and Warwickshire Regiments suffered heavy casualties. Colonel Henderson, C.O. 9th Royal Warwickshire, was killed. He was awarded the V.C. posthumously.

In this action the 39th Machine Gun Company—supporting

the 39th Brigade—lost three out of four guns set up during consolidation of a position captured.

Next day the battle continued, the 14th Division taking over
from the 13th on the West Bank of the Hai. After about 10 hours
of very severe fighting the 82nd and 26th Punjabis succeeded in
re-taking the positions which had been captured and lost the
previous day—but at a high cost in lives, both of these units losing
half their numbers. In this action the 185 and 186 Machine Gun
Companies contributed a great deal to the ultimate capture of the
Turkish front-line trenches, which were over 1,000 yards in depth.

The Second Battle of Sannaiyat

The 1st battle of Sannaiyat had taken place on April 10th,
1916, when the relief column failed to break through the Turks'
defences. This time it would be different, said the planners, as
we got our final briefing before taking up battle positions in early
February, 1917.

The 21st Brigade, 7th Indian Division, supported by 135
Machine Gun Company, were to be the first to go over the top
from a point near the river. There was, however, not the slightest outward sign of the impending attack from our side of the
river, apart from the seemingly unending fatigues—taking up
ammunition and laying in water supplies. Water was more valuable than gold in this desert campaign.

The river was our only source of supply. Water drawn from
the Tigris was put into large canvas tanks and treated with a
chemical which smelt like ordinary disinfectant.

After standing for a few days it was considered suitable for
drinking. We filled our water-bottles with the liquid called
water in readiness for the coming attack. I well remember Cpl.
Darkie of No. 1 team remarking that everyone smelt like a
chemist's shop and that Johnny Turk would detect us a mile away.

I was withdrawn from my gun team and detailed to assist my
C.S.M. supervising ammunition supplies to the gun teams when
the attack got under way. Everything was now ready, and at
sunset on February 9th the first wave of attacking infantrymen
took up their positions in the front-line trenches and waited.

Just before zero-hour (daybreak) I walked along the communication trenches to the front line and wished Darkie, Jock,
and others of my section 'All the best'. The tension was terrific
as they waited alongside infantry of the 2nd Battalion Black
Watch Regiment for the signal to attack.

That was the last time I saw several of my chums.

My C.S.M. stood beside me in our H.Q. dug-out, watch in hand. Everywhere around us was perfectly still. The silence was unnatural, like the calm before a storm. A ray of light pierced night clouds on the desert skyline. The dawn of another day had arrived. The ray of light widened and simultaneously a big gun from well behind our lines fired a single shell.

Then all hell was let loose. A terrific bombardment by our artillery lit up the ground where the Turkish trenches were situated.

After about ten minutes this initial bombardment ceased, and leaning over the top of our dug-out I saw Black Watch and 20th Punjabi infantrymen—swarming over no-man's-land towards the Turks' front-line trenches.

By this time the British artillery had lifted their barrage beyond the Turks' front-line : the aim being to prevent enemy reserves from entering the battle.

Everything seemed to be going to plan until the middle of the morning, when the Turks counter-attacked.

Shells landed around our dug-out. One shell landed near the parapet of the Black Watch cook-house dug-out next door to us. My C.S.M. went to see the damage. Apparently, the two Black Watch cooks were in the process of making tea when the shell landed, scattering the dixies of boiling water. The cooks escaped unhurt but their language was shocking, said my C.S.M.

Our supposedly safe H.Q. dug-outs became most unhealthy places to be in. Every moment I thought a shell would land in the dug-out. Telephone wires were put out of action and we became isolated from the battle. Things did not appear to be going according to plan.

But British and Indian ammunition carriers continued to go forward over shrapnel-swept no-man's-land with boxes of ammo for our machine-gunners. Several of the ammo carriers did not return.

By mid-day the stream of wounded, which had been passing along the communication trenches since early morning, increased alarmingly. My C.S.M. decided to go forward to see—as he put it—'what the hell was going on'.

A Gurkha soldier with a badly injured shoulder pitched into my dug-out. A Black Watch cook from a nearby dug-out gave the little Gurkha a mug of hot tea, and we dressed his wound. Then he said 'I kill two Turkeymen', making a grim motion with his kukri knife which still bore traces of blood on it, 'then I get this', pointing to his shoulder. He continued : 'Corporal machine-gunner, him very brave man. He fire all the time, but too many

Turkeymen. Machine-gunners all dead'. From his description I knew it was "Darkie" and his team.

By nightfall on that fateful day, the attack had fizzled out, and we were back to where we had started. Our Brigade, (21st, 7th Indian Division) having suffered heavy losses, was withdrawn to a rest camp a few miles behind the front line.

The rainy season was on. Desert dust became treacle-like mud. We slept in tents that had seen better days, but there were compensations, for the only sound to disturb the tranquil surroundings was the occasional howl of a prowling jackal, a nightly feature of desert life.

Re-capture of Kut-el-Amara

Our peaceful rest spell ended and, marching at night, we re-entered the trenches at Sannaiyat. It was like returning to Bedlam. The steady bombardment of the Turkish positions at Kut which had been going on since our set-back at Sannaiyat on February 10th, became a terrific onslaught during the night of February 22nd. The Turkish guns retaliated. Casualties mounted up. We went to battle stations. Zero hour was at dawn on February 23rd, and as the hour approached the guns on both sides of the River Tigris suddenly became silent.

The resulting quiet was uncanny, portentous. Watches were out, seconds ticked away—and then as dawn began to break, a long line of Seaforth Highlanders and 92nd Punjabis sprang from their trenches and sped across the flat desert of no-man's-land towards the Turks' front-line trenches. The first wave was quickly followed by those tough little warriors the Gurkhas—(1/8th Battalion). In the early dawn light they looked like ghosts floating over to nowhere, but I knew, as I watched, that death stalked along every yard of the way.

Enemy shrapnel shells, bursting above the heads of the advancing infantry, soon tore big gaps in their ranks.

We moved forward and set up our machine-guns in a captured trench, in readiness to help repel any counter-attack.

Several miles away on the opposite side of the River Tigris the battle also raged. I detected pockets of white smoke drifting low in the sky near the Turks' trenches at Kut, and knew from past experience that those harmless-looking pockets of smoke were actually the outcome of shrapnel shells raining down red-hot jagged pieces of metal on infantrymen in the vicinity, and that the air would smell of death.

Turkish 'whizz-bangs' began to land along our trench, and one

such shell landed near No. 1 team, killing the officer in charge of
the section. We were 'sitting-duck' targets while we waited to advance again. I was glad when the order came, which was soon
after the 19th Brigade (7th Indian Div.) went over from Sannaiyat round about 10.30 a.m., supported by 134 Machine Gun
Company.

We reached the old Turkish backward positions, and began to
consolidate captured trenches. A Seaforth Highlander jumped
into our trench. 'How's it going, Jock?' asked Lt. Cross, my Section officer, as our medical orderly Joe put a fresh dressing on a
nasty wound in the Highlander's arm.

'Och, mon, they're on the run this time,' Jock assured us. His
prediction was correct, and as the day turned into night we moved
out into the open spaces of the desert.

February 23rd, 1917, was a red-letter-day in the Mesopotamia
campaign of World War One, for it was then that British and
Indian forces achieved a victory of momentous importance which
led to the final defeat of the Turkish Army in Mesopotamia.

One of the men who took part in the heavy fighting that preceded the victory was Sergeant Thomas Steele, serving with the
Seaforth Highlanders. At a critical moment when a strong enemy
counter-attack had temporarily regained some of the captured
enemy trenches, he rushed forward and assisted a comrade to
carry a machine-gun into position : he kept the gun in action
until relieved, being mainly instrumental in keeping the remainder of the line intact. Some hours later another attack enabled the
enemy to re-occupy a part of the captured trenches. Again Sergeant Steele showed the greatest bravery, and by his personal valour and example was able to rally troops who were wavering. He
encouraged them to remain in their trenches and led a number
of them forward, thus greatly helping to re-establish our line. On
this occasion he was severely wounded.

These acts of valour were performed under heavy artillery and
machine-gun fire.

For most conspicuous bravery and devotion to duty the award
of the Victoria Cross was made to this gallant Non-Commiss-
ioned-Officer.

ADVANCE ON BAGHDAD

Now that Kut was in British hands the advance to Baghdad
could begin. Right through the night we marched and when day-

light arrived I saw columns of troops spread out over a wide area. The pace was gruelling. At times we were on top of the scouting cavalry, continually in action with Turkish rearguards of their 18th Corps. The news reached us that British and Indian Sappers and Miners (Engineers) had thrown a Pontoon Bridge across the River Tigris from a point known as Shumuran Bend, several miles north of Kut. The width of the river was, at this time of the year, 330 yards—and there was also a treacherous undercurrent of 6 knots.

A machine-gunner of 185 Company—who experienced part of the fighting linked up with the building of the Pontoon Bridge at Shumuran Bend—recalls this historic happening. He writes:

It was about 5.15 a.m. on February 23rd, 1917—when the Engineers began to build the bridge. The Turks rumbled what was on, and fierce fighting occurred around a bridge-head established by the Norfolks and Gurkhas. The objective was to cross the river and cut off Turkish troops retreating from the Sannaiyat battle where the 7th Indian (Meerut) Division had broken through.

During the fighting around Shumuran Bend, heavy casualties slowed down the bridge-building but by mid-morning of the 23rd the Pontoon Bridge was built and the Norfolks were among the first to cross over. Our Machine Gun Company, and Nos. 39, 40, and 186 Companies found good targets—firing across the river. It must also be mentioned here that the Royal Flying Corps gave valuable help by spotting targets and bombing and machine-gunning Turkish rearguards.

While all this was happening on the Kut side of the river we, on the Sannaiyat side, raced forward.

British Naval Monitors (gunboats) nosed their way along the River Tigris and blazed away with their guns at columns of retreating Turks. I saw what looked at first sight like bundles of old clothes strewn about the desert floor, but upon passing some of these bundles, discovered them to be dead Turks. Flies swarmed around the bodies. A gruesome spectacle. Our spotter planes were kept busy, but in 1917 there were no heavy bombers to help the advancing fighting units. Day after day, night after night, we marched with little rest, until we reached the famous arch of Ctesiphon, when a halt was called. We were now only a short distance from Baghdad and our generals were perhaps a bit wary this time, for it was the place where, in the earlier part of the campaign, General Townshend had been held up by Turkish reinforcements rushed out from Baghdad. He was forced back to Kut, where after some months of siege, he had been obliged to surrender with the remnants of his force, which had reached starvation point.

We thankfully took off our packs and stretched our weary limbs on the floor of the desert. Many of the infantrymen who rested near us put their medical orderlies on overtime attending to swollen and bleeding feet.

The transport wallahs caught up with us, and after they had dished out a ration of bread, fried bacon, and good old English tea, our flagging spirits revived.

Again we marched. The great golden domes of mosques and tall minarets appeared on the horizon.

We passed huge dust heaps and mounds of earth; the remains of ancient cities, scattered about the face of the desert. All that remained of a once great civilisation . . . Was our civilisation heading for the same fate, I wondered? Was war a punishment to mankind for its sins? These thoughts passed through my mind as I marched in a dazed condition.

The marching pace became even more hectic. 'We should be in Baghdad in a couple of days if this pace is maintained', said my C.O., Captain McGregor-James.

I visualised a nice rest camp under palm trees by the banks of the River Tigris. This beautiful thought stimulated my tired body to fresh efforts, and my head cleared itself of dismal thoughts. But an unforeseen obstacle lay in the path of our final spurt. The Turks had decided to fight a rearguard action along the banks of the Dialah, which enters the mighty Tigris a few miles below Baghdad.

THE BATTLE OF THE DIALAH RIVER

The battle began on the night of March 7th, 1917. Men of the Lancaster Regiment (The King's Own) were detailed to make the first attempt to cross the Dialah, but even before the No. 1 pontoon could be launched, enemy machine-guns and artillery fired across the 50 yard wide river and wiped out the Royal Engineers assembling the pontoon. A second pontoon was launched and got half-way across when its occupants were all killed or wounded. A third, fourth, and fifth attempt to cross the river met with the same fate. Enemy machine-guns on the opposite bank dominated the battle zone. Daylight made further attempts impossible. I saw the pontoons with their dead and wounded floating down the River Tigris.

Next night (March 8th) the battle continued.

After an intense bombardment of the Turkish positions, men of the Loyal North Lancashire Regiment succeeeded in crossing the Dialah and gained a footing on the other side : but the supporting troops were not so lucky. Their boats and pontoons were blown to bits in mid-stream, leaving about 100 Lancashire soldiers isolated on the north side of the river. Throughout the night, the stranded men fought off attack after attack by a much stronger Turkish force. It was not until daylight on the 10th March that a rescue was effected. When we reached them, there were only about 30 exhausted survivors. The many dead lying round the parapets of the river-bound defences told their own grim tale.

The story of the Dialah crossing is comparable with that of the famous Lancashire Landing on the beaches of Gallipoli (April 25th, 1915) for the shores of both places are hallowed by the blood of many sons of the red-rose county, who fought and died to protect the British way of life—the way of right against might.

During the night of March 9th, while the brave few held on, the Wiltshires and East Lancs Regiments made a crossing higher up the river, which forced the Turks to abandon their defences. We continued our advance. Another halt was ordered on the outskirts of Baghdad. It was the early evening of March 10th, 1917. A terrific dust storm was raging. We were allowed a snack of bully-beef and biscuit, washed down with a swig of stale warm water from our water bottles. It was almost impossible to see the next man as we passed around our portion of rations, swallowing the dust with the bully-beef.

A few Turkish shells exploded near our resting site, but no-one bothered.

We were too weary to bother. The pace had been a hot one since we left Ctesiphon. The 1914–18 infantry soldier got very little transport to carry him. 'Marching! Marching! Marching! Always blooming well marching' became a famous marching song of weary troops. The song was sung to the tune of that well known hymn—'Holy! Holy! Holy! Lord God Almighty'.

Capture of Baghdad

The dust storm eased up with daylight. We were briefed as to our role in the final move to capture Baghdad.

My machine-gun team was detailed to go forward with a company of the 2nd Black Watch Regiment. Great infantrymen! Somehow one felt safe with them around.

The infantrymen skirmished forward carefully—but we met with little opposition from Johnny Turk, and by breakfast-time in England a section of the Black Watch seized Baghdad railway station. About mid-day the dust storm re-asserted itself. One's ears, nose, and throat, became simply blocked up with the stuff, but no-one seemed to care. It was a trifling matter now, for we had reached Baghdad, the goal of our mighty efforts. A red glow over the city suggested that the Turks had set fire to parts of it before they retreated north, but this turned out to be nothing serious. News reached us that the cavalry had entered the city outskirts on the opposite bank of the River Tigris. (Baghdad stands on both banks of the Tigris.) This proved to be correct, and by late afternoon of March 11th, 1917, Baghdad, that oriental city founded by the Caliphs in 763, and capital of a once-great empire, was entered by British and Indian troops. Two hundred and eighty-one years of Turkish domination had ended.

Baghdad had been in Turkish possession since the year 1636. Its capture was marked as an historic occasion of some magnitude. It was also a terrific morale booster to all Allied soldiers of World War One, similar to that brought about by the victory at Alamein in World War Two—a turning point in the war on land in favour of the Allied cause.

Before Baghdad was captured British and Indian soldiers marched and fought across 300 miles of desert; through choking dust storms, through the rainy season—when desert dust turned into treacle-like mud, and through suffocating heat—when water was at a premium. Seldom before or since has such a feat of endurance been accomplished.

THE AFTERMATH

Seventy miles of railway began at Baghdad and ended at Samarra. To make Baghdad secure from attack this railway had to be captured. The aim of our generals was to reach Samarra before the terrific heat of the Mespot summer arrived.

The 7th Indian Division (dubbed Cobbe's flying column) in which 134, 135 and 136 Machine Gun Company served, played a major role in bringing this about.

A Machine-Gunner who experienced the advance from Baghdad to Samarra writes:

The anticipated long rest at Baghdad turned out to be mere wishful thinking on our part and after about ten days spent in a bivouac camp on the banks of the Tigris, during which time reinforcements arrived for our depleted gun-teams and for the various Battalions in 7th Division, we marched again into the open spaces of the desert north of Baghdad.

We had been marching all day and it was early evening (March 23rd, 1917) when we came to a halt. Everyone was exhausted by the day's march. But one resurrects one's energy when shells and bullets begin to fly. The Turkish 18th Corps—still struggling to extricate itself from General Maude's advanced forces—now had the railway behind them and were able to bring up reinforcements to a prepared defensive position on high ground around Mouscheidi railway junction, which we now faced.

My Brigade (21st 7th 1/Division) received orders to clear the enemy out at once.

While we were preparing our machine-guns for action, several batteries of the Royal Horse Artillery galloped by us and, within minutes, their guns were hammering the Turkish positions.

A column of the 2nd Black Watch passed us in silence, covered in choking dust. We moved up in their rear.

Casualties began to mount up as the Turkish guns got our range. 'Jigger' of my gun team went down with a wound in the leg. An ammunition-carrier attached to our team picked him up and carried him to a safer spot.

Passing an artillery battery, I saw an officer fall from an observation ladder. Shrapnel from the Turkish guns had claimed another victim.

We made short, rapid spurts across the open desert spaces of no-man's-land. Arriving at the remains of railway outbuildings we ran into what looked at first sight like several Turkish soldiers calmly sitting with their backs to the wall of the building. We discovered they were all dead. The blast from an artillery shell had, apparently, killed them all as they sat there. At a point near the railway embankment we got our machine-guns into action in support of a company of the Black Watch who had run into a strong Turkish defence post.

Five-nine shells from the Turkish guns began to search for us, and as the shells exploded around us Lt. Cross, my section officer, ordered a move to the other side of the railway embankment. We moved only just in time, for the next big shell landed almost dead on the spot we had vacated. The embankment saved us.

NO ENEMIES IN DEATH

It was almost midnight when we occupied a section of captured Turkish trenches. It was then that I saw a young Turkish soldier, lying at the bottom of a trench. He had a horrible wound in the stomach. No immediate medical attention was possible for him. His screams and anguished appeals for water became unbearable. A Black Watch infantryman nearby shouted : 'For God's sake give him water and let him die in peace'. Another Jock unhooked his water bottle and, moved by pity, gave the wounded prisoner the drink he craved. And, don't forget, at that time it was never certain when the next water supply would arrive.

After taking a long drink this unknown Turk gave a deep sigh, opened his eyes wide, and gave us a smile to express his thanks. His enemies had become his friends.

After a moment he clutched the hand of his benefactor, slowly sank back and died in the arms of his supposed enemy.

The dim light from a torch held by my officer seemed to shine with an added lustre as my chum 'Dreamy' covered the young Turk with a spare coat, and we moved silently to the other end of the trench.

Next day Johnny Turk was buried alongside several of our lads. In death they were enemies no longer.

The battle of Mouscheidi Station had lasted only a few hours, but the 21st Brigade—especially the 2nd Battalion Black Watch and 1/8th Gurkhas—suffered heavy casualties.

Many of the casualties were men who had joined us at Baghdad. It was their first and last battle.

NIGHT MARCHES

After the battle of Mouscheidi we continued to advance along the railway line in pursuit of the retreating Turkish forces.

The temperature in the daytime reached 80 degrees F, so we rested by day and marched at night through unseen desert dust, which at times almost choked us.

Bengal Lancers and British Hussars, riding in single file, flanked our marching columns. Occasionally they swung in close to us, appearing like phantoms from the vast open spaces of the desert. Mile after mile we plodded alongside our Indian pack-mules. These hardy beasts carried our machine-guns, tripods, boxes of ammunition, and other equipment.

The monotony was sometimes broken when 'Inkey' (my gun-team mule) suddenly decided he had had enough, and it took the coaxing and threats of our Indian mule driver Johnny-Sahib to get him on the move again. 'What's wrong with him?' enquired my Section Officer during one of Inkey's tantrums.

'Him fed-up' said Johnny-Sahib, as we strove to catch up with the rest of the section.

Secretly I sympathised with Inkey. Often during those long night marches I felt like dropping out from sheer fatigue, but just when extra effort seemed impossible, a lone piper of the 2nd Battalion Black Watch, who seemed to sense the weariness of everyone, would strike up a lively Scottish air, which somehow gave me, and no doubt others, renewed energy.

Eventually we reached a small village on the outskirts of Istabulat (50 miles north of Baghdad) and passed along a narrow lane lined by Arabs who appeared, to my eyes, more perplexed than hostile. The Arab farmer was peaceful enough, and did not bother about who won the war, so long as he was left in peace to carry on his own way of life.

There were fresh water wells in the village, but we were not allowed to use this water for drinking purposes. However, a halt was made and a good wash was permitted : this amenity was in itself to be treasured. Company Sergeant Major Dewar told 'Fatty' (of my gun-team) it was now possible to see the colour of his face.

A DESERT BATTLE

The Turks held a string of fortified trenches and redoubts along several miles of high ridges which poked out of the flat desert round the ancient city of Istabulat. This was twelve miles from Samarra, where the railway terminated.

The 7th Indian Division were detailed to capture these ridges. A formidable task faced us. Three miles to the south of Istabulat the Division concentrated behind the ruins of the famous fortified line known to the Greeks as the "Median Wall", around whose mud bastions in long past ages every conquering race of the East fought for mastery. It was here, in the ghostly shadows of past history, that we prepared for the battle of Istabulat— the outcome of which would decide the fate of the Baghdad to Samarra railway.

The machine-gun companies of the division—134, 135, and 136—were detailed to support their respective Brigades in the coming attack, and an hour before the dawn on April 21st, 1917, we arrived at battle stations, where we lay prone or squatted around our machine-guns, waiting for the attack to commence.

My gun-team, No. 1 of 135 Company, occupied a support position directly behind a section of the 2nd Black Watch. There had been no artillery bombardment. It was to be a surprise attack. The eerie silence that surrounded us was occasionally punctuated by the howl of a jackal returning to his lair after a night prowl.

As dawn broke I saw a long line of the 2nd Black Watch infantrymen leave their slit trenches—which they had dug during the night of April 20th—and make for the first objective—a Turkish outpost. They reached it so quickly and silently that they captured it without a shot having been fired. Prisoners, looking extremely dazed and ill-clad, passed by us with a small escort of Black Watch men. Then the Turks discovered what was happening, and their guns opened up. The surprise attack was no longer a surprise. A battery of British 18-pounders took up a position a few hundred yards from our site and soon attracted counter-fire from the Turkish batteries.

The position we occupied became a death-trap. We could not move until we received orders to do so.

A Turkish heavy shell exploded among the 18-pounder battery. I heard the shouts of the gunners. Black Watch stretcher-bearers rushed over. The survivors kept their guns firing. Then an enemy shell skimmed the top of the incline we occupied and exploded with a terrific roar among our Indian ammo party, killing two and wounding several.

About the middle of the morning the Turks began to counter-attack. A sharp command rang out from our section officer— 'Advance!' We ran forward (carrying guns and tripods) into the open spaces of the desert, which seemed to stretch out for miles in front of the hills occupied by the Turks.

In no time at all high explosive shrapnel was bursting all around us. Sergeant K of No. 3 team went down with a piece of metal in his head, and died without a sound.

THE PHOTOGRAPH

After the second rush forward our machine-gun section was given a breather. I flopped down in a slight dip in the ground. There I saw, a few yards away, a dead infantryman of the Black Watch Regiment. He lay with his face turned towards me, a bullet hole in his forehead. My curiosity was aroused when I noticed something which looked like a photograph lying on the ground near his outstretched hand. I picked it up and read on the back of the picture 'With love—Mum'.

We were ordered to advance again and I ran like someone in a trance. Reaching a captured ridge we got our machine-guns into action. Almost immediately enemy artillery dropped five-nine shells around us. I expected every minute to be the last on this earth for me and my chums.

Shrapnel from the Turkish guns swept the top of the incline. Two gunners of No. 4 team were killed outright. The officer in charge of the section shouted to the two reserve gunners at the base of the incline to come up and get the guns going again. They did not appear to hear and the next thing I saw was the officer firing the gun. In a matter of minutes he rolled down the incline with a wound in the head.

Towards noon the Turkish counter-attack forced the Black Watch, who had captured a redoubt, to relinquish this position. Machine-guns of 135 Company fired thousands of rounds of ammunition at the Turks who had driven the Black Watch Regiment back into the open spaces of the desert.

It was during this period of fighting that Private C. Melvin—of the 2nd Battalion Black Watch Regiment—displayed great initiative and courage for which he was awarded the Victoria Cross. The Turkish counter-attack fizzled out, survivors retreating to their original positions.

In the middle of the afternoon the 9th Bhopals Regiment, supported by 134 and sections of 135 Machine Gun Companies, advanced across open ground in face of murderous fire from Turkish artillery and machine-guns.

Dead and wounded lay scattered everywhere. I witnessed the survivors storming ridges still in Turkish hands. Bayonets glittered in the evening sun.

Darkness came to shut out the ghastly sights. Stretcher-bearers moved around more freely. For many it did not matter.

Eventually the Turks surrendered their fortified trenches. The hellish noise of battle ceased and by midnight everything around us was peaceful.

We squatted by our machine-guns and waited for further instructions, just as we had done before the dawn of that deadly day. A lone jackal could be heard howling in the distance. Someone asked the time. My section officer looked at his watch. It was 3 a.m. Dreamy, one of our gunners, said it was his twenty-first birthday.

During the night of April 21st the Turks retreated some 4½ miles to a new position which ran along a ridge overlooking the open spaces in front of Samarra railway station.

The 28th Brigade, supported by 136 Machine Gun Company, moved forward and by mid-day occupied a point ready to attack the last defences of Samarra. A machine-gunner of 136 Company takes up the story :

The heat at mid-day was oppressive, and while the brigade rested, the ridge which was to be our objective was heavily shelled. It was late afternoon when the 2nd Leicesters led the assault, closely supported by the 51st Sikhs. Heavy casualties held up the attack. Several of our gun-teams suffered casualties while supporting the Leicesters. It was late at night before the attack could be renewed, after a terrific strafing of the Turks' positions by British artillery guns. When the barrage lifted the Leicesters and Sikhs surged up the slope.

It was a moonlight night. I saw the Turks leave their trenches and run back towards Samarra. Our guns had excellent targets.

The Leicesters and 51st Sikhs swept on beyond their objective for about a mile or so and surprised a battery of Turkish artillery, which surrendered without a fight.

Orders came instructing us to dig-in.

By this time the Leicesters and Sikhs had suffered heavy losses, and it was while they were preparing to consolidate their gains that the Turkish Commander began a counter-attack, throwing in all his reserves of about two thousand men.

The depleted Leicesters and Sikhs were obliged to fall back, and having no means of taking the captured Turkish guns with them had to leave them behind.

At this stage of the battle the 56th Punjabi Rifles went out to reinforce the hard-pressed Leicesters and Sikhs who were now caught in the open spaces in front of the ridge—the original Turkish front line. Fortunately the 56th Punjabi Rifles reached the ridge before the main Turkish onslaught could break through, but a large party of the enemy gained an important point near the railway embankment and shot down practically all our front-line troops who had not managed to get back to the cover of the ridge.

From the trenches on the ridge our machine-guns and the rifle fire of the Punjabis poured a hail of lead into the attacking Turks, but it did not prevent a strong party of the enemy from getting through a culvert to a spot 200 yards or so in the rear of our positions, and opening fire on the backs of the Punjabis. It was then that Lieutenant J. R. N. Graham of 136 Machine Gun Company answered an S.O.S. call from the hard-pressed Indian troops, and took out two guns with several men. One gun-team was knocked out on the way, but Lt. Graham brought the other gun to the threatened point.

I saw him carrying the gun over to the left of a trench, which was traversed and extremely narrow. He was forced to carry the gun over the open spaces as the trench was blocked with men—many of them wounded.

In the process he was wounded twice, but finally he got his gun into action. All his team had by this time become casualties and he fired the gun himself but was again wounded. When we eventually reached him he had collapsed from loss of blood. He had a wound in the chest, and his hand was bound up. We found another wound in his thigh, and he had stuffed a handkerchief under his puttee to staunch a wound in his leg.

When the stretcher-bearers got to Lt. Graham he was in a bad way, but he did survive, and subsequently was awarded the Victoria Cross.

The impetus of the Turks' counter-attack in front of Samarra on the 28th Brigade, 7th Indian Division, took them back on to the ridge which dominated the battle area, and it was only the gallant stand made by the 56th Punjabi Rifles, supported by 136 Machine Gun Company that saved the British from losing everything that had been won in twelve hours' hard fighting.

Lieutenant J. R. N. Graham of 136 Machine Gun Company contributed in no small way towards the ultimate defeat of the Turks at a crucial period of the battle.

British and Indian casualties in the two days' fighting at Istabulat and Samarra were over 2,000; the Turks left 600 dead on the battlefield, and about 250 prisoners were taken.

ON TO SAMARRA WITH 135 MACHINE GUN COMPANY

The day following the defeat of the Turkish force outside Samarra, we moved forward with the 21st Brigade, reaching Samarra railway station by noon on April 23rd.

The Turks had retreated north towards Tekrit, leaving the station undefended. Fire had destroyed a part of the main buildings, but many engines, trucks and other valuable rolling stock were found, which was to prove an asset in assisting transport on the railway from Samarra to Baghdad. Thus the whole of the 70 miles of railway running between Baghdad and Samarra, built by the Germans before the outbreak of war in 1914, had fallen practically intact into British hands.

By early evening on April 23rd—Samarra city, once the capital of the Caliphs, was captured.

Modern Samarra, built within the walls of the famous old city, was once a rival in importance to Baghdad.

The ruins of the old city stretch along the left bank of the River Tigris for a distance of nearly 20 miles.

In the days of its greatness, between the years 836 and 876, eight Caliphs ruled from Samarra, and according to historical records five of them suffered violent deaths.

These historical facts did not cut much ice with us, and after a quick look at the city (which was unsavoury in the extreme) defensive positions were dug several miles north of Samarra, and after each unit in the 7th Division had completed its allotted task we made camp a mile or so behind the new defences. We machine-gunners did little apart from taking our turn alongside the infantry lads of our brigade on trench night duty—purely a matter of routine precaution. The nearest Turk was now over 25 miles away at Tekrit, so there was little to worry about so far as Johnny Turk was concerned.

It was the terrific heat of the daytime that began to trouble us; and it was always our aim when we had been on trench night duty to get back to the cover of our tents before it became really hot.

This happened not long after daybreak when the sun popped up from behind the horizon looking like a huge fire-ball.

At night most of us slept on the floor of the desert outside the tents, but hot winds sweeping the open spaces made it difficult to sleep soundly.

Our food was poor stuff, consisting of a bread ration of two slices per man per day, two ounces of cheese, an occasional bacon ration, and perhaps a lime-juice issue.

The main meal of the day was mostly a stew of bully-beef thickened with crushed army issue biscuits contributed by each member of the gun team from his personal stock.

Corporal Crisp (apt name) of my gun-team made it his task to see that everyone did contribute.

We always took the main meal after sunset.

A drink of tea (char) was all one bothered about at mid-day. Our cooks were heroes.

Because of the poor food, dust and heat, skin complaints were common. The slightest cut turned septic.

By July the desert was a vast expanse of shimmering heat. The inside of our tents became like bakehouse ovens.

We passed the days lying under mosquito nets, and tried to keep up our morale by cracking jokes. In between we would moan about the lousy climate.

One afternoon, when we were all in our tents, trying to keep cool under the nets, a message arrived from H.Q. instructing No. 1 Section 135 Machine Gun Company to prepare to move within fifteen minutes on a 'reconnaissance'. I was in this lot.

Air patrols had spotted a Turkish force moving towards our lines. 'What!' we shouted. 'Is this a joke?'

'Has someone gone raving mad,' demanded Sergeant Jock, 'asking us to move out in this heat?'

We soon discovered it was official. Each man filled up two water bottles from the section supply, and packed the usual iron rations of bully and biscuits. We loaded the pack mules with guns and ammo, and marched. A squadron of Bengal Lancers passed us at the trot, closely followed by an armoured car escort. A halt was not allowed until a distance of about five miles had been covered. The heat was stifling. We were joined by a battery of Light Artillery whose gunners were riding on the gun-carriages. The horses and their riders looked exhausted with the heat.

Someone came to my officer asking for a volunteer to take the place of a machine-gunner in an armoured car, who had collapsed. I volunteered. I had not been inside an armoured car before, but in or out, a machine-gun was the same to me—or so I thought. I soon found out my mistake.

In very quick time the armoured car joined up with the advanced scouting cavalry. Scouting around for what seemed hours, I saw nothing but miles of barren desert through my peep hole. Then, suddenly, a loud bang shook the car. The officer in charge said it was a Turkish shell, and it was time we turned around and made tracks towards the infantry lads of the 20th Punjabi Regiment.

We had, it seemed, done our job. The heat in that armoured car was like a furnace, and I was thankful to reach the infantry when we were allowed to get out of this heat trap. Another chap took my place in the car.

The Turks did not advance when they discovered we knew all about their movements. It all seemed stupid to me, for they must have found the going just as tough as we did on a mid-afternoon patrol in 120 degress.

Perhaps one of their Generals had had one over the eight,

suggested my C.O., when we arrived back in camp next morning.

Our gun-team was excused duty for the next few days and nights. We needed this rest, for that afternoon patrol was something of a nightmare to unlucky ones detailed for the job.

A few nights later, turning in to sleep (if possible), I sat on a scorpion. I had no clothes on to protect me, and the scorpion, resenting my action, promptly bit me on the backside. As I brushed it off it took another nip at my knee. None of our chaps had previously been bitten, although we knew that these nasty blighters, as well as centipedes, existed in many parts of the desert. I felt encouraged when Sergeant Jock, who had seen several years' service in India, informed me that the Mespot scorpion was not so deadly as the Indian black scorpion; nevertheless, the bite left me in a state of nervous tension for many hours. All that night I walked about, trying to get some relief from the pain of it. Joe—our medical orderly, gave me a swig of neat whisky from the 'comforts for the troops' box', which I never knew existed until that moment, but it was some twelve hours before the pain subsided, and by that time I felt like a wet rag.

Each night after this incident, Dreamy and Jock spent quite a time looking for scorpions with the aid of a hurricane lamp. Several were caught, and Dreamy put them into an empty jam jar, to study their habits. I often watched with him, and saw how they fought each other to the death. It was cruel, but helped to pass away the monotonous days. We had no papers or books, and letters from home were few and far between. We seemed to be a forgotten legion.

A pay parade was one event that helped to cheer up the troops. A few rupees enabled us to buy melons and dates from Arab farmers, who had set up a small market near the river. When the Tigris subsided during the summer months these experts grew melons on the banks.

Sergeant Jock, Fatty and myself paid a regular visit to one old Arab, who enjoyed our friendly banter. We in turn got quite a lift from our visits to Abdul, as we called him.

One day, as the summer began to wane, Abdul packed up and said good-bye to us. His pockets were full of rupees. We wished him a safe journey, and he assured us that if it were the will of Allah he would reach his home safely. He lived in a village many miles distant.

In late September, 1917, reinforcements for the Infantry Regiments and our Machine Gun Companies of the 7th Indian Division arrived from England and India. We were told about the food rationing at home.

We went out on an exercise with the 2nd Black Watch, 1st Seaforths and 2nd Leicester Regiments as a rehearsal for the advance to Tekrit, which I knew was soon to take place, and when we halted for a breather I talked to several Jocks. Despite the terrific trials of the past months, these men looked as hard as nails. They reminded me of the famous Foreign Legion about whom I had read in adventure books, long before my Army days.

The Turkish air forces were now growing active, and we saw many dog-fights, as combats in the air were called.

Air control was of vital importance to artillery batteries, but up to this stage of the campaign we had experienced no bombing from the air. However, a few days after our return from the exercises, we were out on a food convoy escort when an enemy plane dropped a few light bombs near us. Not much damage was done, but this light air-bombing was a sign of the things to come.

HOW BRITISH TROOPS STORMED THE SALADIN TOWNS OF TEKRIT

During the summer months of 1917 the Turkish army on the Tigris front had held on to Tekrit, some 30 miles north of Samarra. According to reports coming in from air reconnaissance, they occupied an elaborate trench system in front of the town, some seven miles in circumference, with their flanks protected by the river. In the middle of October the 21st Brigade (7th Indian Division) left their camp at Samarra and marched twenty miles to Daur where a brisk engagement with Turkish outposts took place. They quickly withdrew to their main defences in front of Tekrit when threatened with encirclement by British Cavalry. An ex-machine-gunner of 135 Company, who experienced the battle of Tekrit, tells his story :

Ten miles separated us from the Turks at Tekrit—as we prepared for the main advance.

The day before the assault—November 4th, 1917—we overhauled our machine-guns, filled ammunition belts, packed spare ammo boxes, drew iron rations, filled our water bottles—water was more precious than riches—and did many other vital fatigues. The day's effort, to be followed by a long night march, deserved an interval of quiet. The sun, still looking like a ball of fire, was dipping below the horizon when we sprawled alongside our guns and equipment waiting for the order to move.

My old and trusted friend, Jock, relaxed a few yards from me, gazing into empty space, as one often does when there is nothing particular to bother about.

Dreamy (my No. 2 gun pal) propped up on an elbow, talked quietly to another gunner. 'Fatty' No. 3 on the gun was flat out on his back, fast asleep, by the side of the gun team mule, Inkey who wore a bored expression and stood motionless for a change.

Everything was gloriously peaceful.

The peaceful interlude ended when we were paraded before our C.O. and given a final briefing on our part in the coming battle. It was our duty to carry out our instructions to the best of our ability, said the C.O.

Duty seemed a queer word to me at that moment, for I knew it meant killing or being killed.

We marched in comparative silence throughout the night of November 4th, and by the middle of the next morning arrived at our battle stations, where we rested for a while.

Shortly before mid-day the 8th Brigade, which included the 132 Machine Gun Company, began the assault on the centre of the Turkish position, and while this was taking place the 21st Brigade, supported by 135 Machine Gun Company, advanced on the flanks of the Turks' positions near the Tigris.

Reaching a suitable point we hastily dug shallow gunpits with our entrenching tools and got our guns into action.

A Turkish observation plane flew low over us and very soon enemy shells came thudding over. One such shell exploded with a terrific roar near No. 3 gun team. When the smoke cleared two of the team lay dead. My officer moved us along to a dip in the ground, where we lay still for a while.

The Turkish guns ceased firing in our direction. Our counter-artillery fire had perhaps knocked them out.

The din of battle from other parts of the line became intense during the early afternoon, but, as is always the case in any battle, one only knows about happenings in one's own vicinity. An order came from H.Q. instructing us to move in closer to a rough track which we had been raking with fire for several hours. It was now early evening. Turkish guns were withdrawing along that road.

All section guns were ordered to open fire and the road became a death-trap for the poor devils trying to pull out from the battle. Through the field glasses one could see horses and men strewn around.

The Turkish light artillery shelled us with their Whiz-bangs, and we had to move our positions. Dreamy got a piece of shell splinter in his right hand but, the wound having been bound up, he continued to help get the spare ammo from the boxes.

When darkness came the fighting quietened down and the infantry consolidated the positions captured.

At dawn next day, we swarmed over to the other part of the Turkish lines in our battle sector. Johnny Turk had evacuated most of his defences.

The cavalry (13th Hussars and 13th Lancers) made a charge on one part of the Turkish line still holding out—similar to those made in the days before trench warfare. I saw lances and swords flashing in the pale autumn sunlight, as horses thundered by our shallow gun-pits.

As far as Johnny Turk was concerned, this was the final straw to break the camel's back. The battle of Tekrit was over. Entrenched positions, prepared by the Turks during the summer months, were demolished in less than two days, but at a cost of many lives, especially among the 8th Brigade infantry regiments —1st Manchesters, 59th Rifles, 47th Sikhs, and 132 Machine Gun Company—who had borne the brunt of the battle in the centre of the attack.

Although Tekrit was occupied on November 6th, and over 300 prisoners were taken, the main Turkish force, depleted of course, was able to get away north to a new position at Fatha Gorge, where the river Tigris cuts through the hills. The battle of Fatha Gorge came later the following year.

It is interesting to reflect that Tekrit was the birthplace of Saladin, a once-renowned Sultan of Egypt and Syria.

In the years of his greatness he fought Richard the Lionheart and his crusaders.

When British troops captured Tekrit and practically all of Mesopotamia in 1917 they completed what England's King Richard set out to do over 700 years previously.

A GRIEVOUS LOSS

On November 19th, 1917, just twelve days after the capture of Tekrit, General Sir Stanley Maude, Commander-in-Chief of the army in Mesopotamia, died in Baghdad of cholera.

So said the official report, but rumour got around that he was poisoned while attending a courtesy entertainment in Baghdad. Cholera was *not* an epidemic in this campaign.

DESERT DENTISTRY

Dentists (Army) did not accompany front-line troops in Mesopotamia. The nearest from Tekrit was some 100 miles away at Baghdad.

Another gunner of 135 Machine Gun Company contributes this story :

A few days after the battle of Tekrit, I was detailed as part of a machine-gun escort to a food convoy. We had to cross the desert to a distant outpost, and hostile Arabs were still troublesome.

We started out at the crack of dawn. I had been awake the previous night with toothache, and the pain was acute as we got moving across the desert. The escort party did not reach camp again until early evening, and I went straight to our medical orderly and asked if he could extract the offending tooth. He said he could not, but I might be lucky if I went across to the Black Watch camp and asked to see their M.O.

I found the Black Watch doctor talking to a medical orderly in a tent reserved for receiving the sick. The Black Watch doctor was not a big man in stature, but I well knew he was used to dealing with big problems, and taking out a tooth would be child's play to him. I hoped !

'We can take a tooth out, canna we, Jock?' he laughingly enquired of his orderly. 'I should think so, sir,' said the orderly, with a sickly grin.

The doctor took command. 'Sit down a wee minute while I sterilise these pliers. Boil up some water, Jock.'

Jock fetched an old black-looking kettle, and disappeared towards another part of the camp hospital. After what seemed hours he arrived back with the boiling water. The doctor poured some of this into a basin, plunged the pliers into the water, rolled up his shirt sleeves and approached me.

'Hold his head back, Jock . . . Oh, yes, I can see the big bad wolf. Hand me those pliers . . ."

Gripping the offending tooth with his instrument, he had it out in no time. Holding it up for me to see, he asked if there were any more I wanted out.

'I don't think so,' I replied weakly.

Jock gave me a drink of water, and then, with the doctor's instructions to come and see him again if I had any more trouble, I made my way out of the tent, feeling a little wobbly but happy to be rid of my bad tooth.

The doctor and orderly, grinning all over their faces, watched me leave for the walk back to my camp. I felt so grateful that I turned on reaching the end of the line of tents, and waved a last 'thank you'. They returned the compliment and then disappeared into their desert hospital tent. I never saw them again.

After the capture of Baghdad (March 11th, 1917) General Maude's forces spread out southwards as far as the northern banks of the river Euphrates, and on September 27th and 28th, 1917, a British Division under Sir H. T. Brooking captured the Turkish stronghold at Ramadi, some 60 miles along the Euphrates from Baghdad, and took 3,500 prisoners including the Turkish Commander, Ahmed Bey, and his entire staff.

In this action the 13th Light Armoured Motor Battery (heavy section of the Machine Gun Corps) fighting alongside the 6th Cavalry Brigade, contributed in no small way to the British victory—which made Baghdad safe from a Turkish counterattack down the river Euphrates. Machine Gunners of the 42nd Brigade (130 Company) also distinguished themselves at Ramadi.

After Ramadi a lull in the Euphrates operations occurred, and it was not until March 1918 that General Brooking's 15th Division moved to attack Khan-Baghdadi, where the Turks held entrenched positions on hills overlooking the plains, interwoven with broken undulating country with ravines.

THE BATTLE OF KHAN-BAGHDADI

Ex-machine-gunner No. 33516, of 130 Machine Gun Company, 42nd Brigade, 15th Division remembers and he writes:

A few days before the advance on Khan-Baghdadi we had a pep-talk. If we did not give Johnny Turk a proper hiding this time we should have a hell of a job getting to Aleppo, we were told. After the pep-talk a field Church service was held. Prayer before battle idea!

A 40-mile march faced us. We started out in good shape but very soon the terrific heat and dust whittled down some of our early enthusiasm.

The word went round that we must stick it and leave the water bottle alone. We were a long way from the river and there was no water in the desert. Hostile Arabs did the knife trick on chaps who fell out, then stripped their victims of clothes and left him for the Piards (wild dogs) and the birds, with wing spans like that of an aeroplane. We knew that this sort of thing had happened in the past—so 'stick it' we did.

For long spells I marched automatically, with my head down by the side of the mules.

Once I imagined I saw the old village church and the apple orchard of my home in Yorkshire.

We marched in comparative silence. The dust made one keep one's mouth shut, but when we halted at the end of the day we indulged in a 'ramsammi' (sing-song) and did a little scrounging. In our Brigade were three Gurkha Battalions. The 1/5th, 2/5th and the 2/6th, and better comrades none could wish for. Often they passed on to us some of their excellent chappattes, rice and tea.

Water was the big problem and one's thirst was never satisfied. As the march progressed our mules seemed almost human. Ben, the gun-mule, was a veteran of the Indian Frontier. Steady and reliable. He made no fuss when we pinched his 'conner' (split peas) which we put in our bully-beef stew. In return we gave Ben some of our biscuit ration and this seemed to please him. Shells, low-flying aeroplanes, or anything else unusual never worried Ben. No prancing about like Talkie, the spare mule, who wanted some holding at such times.

Madhu, the No. 2 mule, was O.K., but we had to hobble him to put on a saddle.

Jenny, No. 3 mule, was a good 'un, and liked someone to ride her when free to do so. Driver Achar Singh, a Sikh, thought the world of Jenny, and when she was wounded in the shoulder with shrapnel, he threw himself on the ground and prayed to Allah for her recovery. His prayer was answered.

No. 4 mule was also a good one. Her driver, Chadju Singh, called her Blossom. I well remember how Chadju and Blossom were gluttons for work.

Now a word about my gun-team mates. No. 1 on the gun was L/Corporal Sagar from Halifax, Yorks. Harry had seen service with the 49th Division in France, where he got a Blighty wound, and after recovery was sent to join our Machine Gun Company at Clipstone, where I first met him.

No. 2 on the gun was myself, and No. 3 was Bill Miners, a Welshman. Bill never grumbled about anything, and was always ready to assist anyone needing help. A grand personality. There were also Joe Witt and Percy White, both from the Dorset Regiment, and last, but not least, Jimmy Wickham, mule supervisor.

This then was our little lot as we advanced towards Khan-Baghdadi, in the early hours of March 26th, 1918.

We were resting in a ravine when the first enemy shells came whizzing over. They did not explode. 'Duds!' we chorused. Taffy Owens (of No. 16 team) who had been at Mons in 1914, came running over to us with a warning that the supposed duds could well be gas shells. He was wrong.

Johnny Turk, to his eternal credit, never used gas shells at Gallipoli or in Mesopotamia.

Mr. Crashe, our section officer, gave orders to unload the mules before we advanced again. We were soon carrying guns, tripods, and equipment over the rough no-man's-land.

Harry was about 15 to 20 yards in front, tripod over his shoulder. I followed with the gun, and behind me came Bill Miners with the spare parts box and ammo box. The rest of the team plodded along at the rear with ammo boxes, etc. There seemed to be a hell of a rise in front of us. 'That is where the Turks are,' said someone.

We rested again and while doing so spotted a cutting in the hill. Shells were bursting thereabouts. Captain Smith, 2nd in command, shouted some instructions from well behind us, but we did not hear what he said, and Harry and I dashed across the open spaces to within about 50 yards of the cutting in the hill, where we took cover behind a big boulder.

Harry shouted to the rest of our team to come on, which they did, and all but one made it.

Sheltered from enemy shell fire we moved rapidly through the cutting, and coming out at the other side found ourselves at the base of the hill occupied by the Turks. We moved up the hill. Section Sergeant Collins, known as Todge, joined us, and suggested to Harry that he should endeavour to mount his gun by a pile of stones a further distance ahead. Corporal Prior, who had also got through to us, was against the idea as he thought the stones were deliberately put there by Johnny Turk's artillery men, who had ranged the spot.

'Come on, let's chance it,' said Harry, and picking up the tripod and the gun, we ran like hell and mounted our gun.

Bill Miners was soon up with the ammunition and he and others went back for more, directly we saw our target. And what a target! From our position we were able to enfilade a section of Turkish trenches at a range or not more than 500 yards.

We saw the Gurkhas advancing up the hill under a hail of enemy shrapnel. The fire from our machine-gun kept the heads of the Turks down, as the Gurkhas advanced.

Harry kept shouting 'Get some more ammo !'

The gun behaved like an angel, with never a stoppage.

By late evening the Gurkhas and 1/4th Dorsets had captured the ridge and they continued to advance until darkness set in, but we stayed put and relaxed. News reached us that Turkish resistance had collapsed and that Nazmi Bey had surrendered with the whole of his force of over 5,000 men. The battle of Khan-Baghdadi was over.

After a few days' rest we began the trek back to a basecamp near the river Euphrates. On the way we came across a couple of acres of melons.

Like the song says, 'Sonny-boy, they were sent from heaven'. We had a good fill and then loaded up sandbags with more melons. At the time they seemed like the most beautiful fruit, or whatever they really are, in the whole wide world.

For gallantry in action at Khan-Baghdadi, L/Cpl. Harry Sagar, of 15 Gun Team, and Walt James, of 16 Gun Team, were awarded the Military Medal, and Captain Smith was awarded the Military Cross.

I, No. 33516, got a leave to India, which suited me nicely.

MEMORIES OF MESOPOTAMIA

(by former Private No. 37529, M.G.C. 129 Company, 34th Brigade, 15th Indian Division)

When the Company arrived at Basra in the autumn of 1916 very few of us had started to shave. One who did was Archie Nash, from Newmarket (?). Although camped first near a canal, the only usable water was brought by donkey. Archie had a small shaving mug. The form was for Archie to shave each morning, then his mug of water was passed around for each of us to have his morning wash, performed by dipping two fingers in the mug and rubbing them round the face.

In 129 Company were two Liverpool chaps, Tom Maudesley and Micky Dooly. These two came from different parts of Liverpool and hardly spoke the same language. Nevertheless, they very soon got on well together. Micky Dooly was, of course, Irish, very Irish, and how he loved to tell a story.

One night in the 80 Lb tent he shared with nine others at Basra he started to relate an adventure he had had. It went on and on . . . one after another his companions fell asleep, but still Micky went on with his story. In the very early hours a

Londoner named Williams awoke to hear Micky saying, "Well, to cut a long story short . . . !'

Late in 1916, 129 Machine Gun Company moved with the 34th Brigade from Khamiseyeh to Nasiriyeh—30-odd miles of desert and mud—in square formation with supplies and transport inside a perimeter of combat troops. This precaution was necessary because of hostile Arabs—a threat to our supplies.

One of the big headaches in Mesopotamia was protecting the lines of communication from raiding Arabs, both on the Tigris and the Euphrates fronts. Nasiriyeh was on the Euphrates and its capture in September 1915 firmly secured the Basra area, the main British base for the campaign.

Nasiriyeh, when 129 Machine Gun Company arrived there in late 1916, was actually on the lines of Communication along the Euphrates battle front, but there was never any chance to relax.

We found the conditions there much the same as elsewhere around this area—plenty of mud directly the rainy season set in, and lots of water which one couldn't drink.

Of course, being part of the 15th Division, which the Lancashire lads of 13th Division called the 'fishing Division'—those amenities which troops elsewhere enjoyed were completely absent. No canteens, no Y.M.C.A.'s, but 129 M.G.C. were drumming up experts and needed no such frills. Indeed, the only Y.M.C.A. I recall was encountered when en route from Nasiriyeh and Kurna and Amara via Makina. And there, our chaps, spurning the chances of a meal there, did their usual drumming up on the broken ground outside the Y.M.C.A. tents.

Guard Mounting

One charming feature of 129 Machine Gun Company was that daily an extra man paraded with the evening guard mounting. The smartest man on parade was chosen for the 'honour' of being orderly at Coy. office for 24 hours. Even in the rainy season —in the worst possible conditions—the guard mounting was a spic and span affair : clean, creased KD, scrubbed equipment, etc. Yet, remarkably, no-one deliberately evaded the 'honour' of becoming orderly for a day despite the fact that no-one liked the job. As the chosen orderly I was called one night to take a letter to another unit in the Division. I learned on enquiry that this unit was the other side of the Euphrates, some miles away, and in the darkness and mud it was a foolhardy commission, unless absolutely vital. But in 129 Coy. one did as required without question, and I set off on foot with a hurricane lamp. After crossing the pontoon bridge, seeing what appeared to be tents, I went in that direction intending to ask my way, to be suddenly confronted by a silent Gurkha soldier sentry with kukri knife at the ready. I was in an ordnance depot. The Gurkhas were, I think, amused but it was a very bad moment for me. I finally got to my destination, delivered the letter, was told 'No answer', and set off to return.

To avoid the Gurkhas I started to cross what appeared in the darkness to be open ground, but suddenly and literally fell over a low bivouac type of tent of carpets. By the light of my lamp I saw an arab woman was lying there alone. She was in no way put out by my arrival and indeed showed hospitality by patting her pillow in invitation to share her bed.

Scared somewhat, I just ran and saw that what I had taken for open ground was in fact an Arab encampment.

I regained my own unit just before dawn, very wet (it had rained throughout the night), very tired, and oh, so angry.

SMILER

I remember many chaps who served with me in 129 Machine Gun Company. The tall lean gunner, Owen, Bill Chappell, and Mike Hunt, but outstanding in my memory is P. G. Smale—we called him Smiler. I have every reason to remember him. His efforts on my behalf undoubtedly saved my life.

A Territorial soldier when war broke out in 1914, Smiler went with his regiment, the 6th Devonshires, to India. When volunteers were called for to reinforce the 6th Poona Division (Townshend's Invincibles) serving in the Persian Gulf area, he—with many other valiant soldiers of Britain's part-time Army—answered the call, joining the 2nd Battalion Royal West Kents (34th Brigade) and taking part in the capture of Nasiriyeh on the Euphrates front. Then he was in the advance to Kut, and on to Ctesiphon where the British advance terminated, followed by the retreat of 100 miles back to Kut, where after months of siege Townshend surrendered with his survivors. But Smiler was not among those unfortunate devils who were surrounded by a Turkish force.

During the great retreat from Ctesiphon, A and C Companies of the Kents, the 14th Hussars, a couple of guns of S Battery, Royal Horse Artillery, and some Indian stragglers, escaped the net, thanks to the C.O. of the Hussars who took over and managed to get his party back to Sheik Saad where the 13th Division, which had fought at the Dardanelles, and the 7th Meerut Division from France, were assembled.

It will be seen then that Smiler was an old soldier with battle experience when we first met in the autumn of late 1916 I believe he was the only one amongst us who had been with Townshend's force and escaped capture.

Smiler was the sort who could never resist helping someone less tough than he was, and suffering as I was because of wrongly diagnosed illness, I was struggling with normal duties on the move up from Amara and at Iron Bridge, west of Baghdad.

I was rapidly falling apart. Smiler scrounged all sorts of delicacies to make me eat, and saw to it that I was spared rough work—was a real nursemaid in fact. Of course, some collusion with the rest of the company was necessary, but I certainly would have died then but for him. Finally the C.O. (Major Campbell) saw to it that I was given a new diagnosis with the result that I was admitted to hospital with very bad dysentery, and did not walk again until in a convalescent hospital in Bombay. Thirteen months elapsed before I rejoined the company at Tekrit in late 1917

Former No. 37529, of 129 Machine Gun Company, finished up as a Major after serving six years in Iraq Levies and 27 years in the Colonial Police.

Smiler came through the war safely and became a much respected citizen of his home town of Handkey, Barnstaple, Devon.

LAMB

In the Eastern Campaigns of World War One, the Light Armoured Motor Battery (LAMB) of the Machine Gun Corps carried out a vital role, and the following story comes from an officer who served as second-in-command, and then as C/O of 13th LAMB.

20th Battery Motor Machine Gun Service, equipped with Clyno motor cycles and Vickers mounted sidecars, was awaiting posting to France from Bisley in 1916 when it was ordered to take over eight Rolls Royce armoured cars and proceed to Mesopotamia at once.

Our new title was to be 13th Light Armoured Motor Battery. We were to be commanded by the late Charles Cowan, a truly remarkable and gutful character, who had already been invalided out of the Canadian forces, after the Ypres shambles. He had fiddled his way into the British Army without a medical.

We embarked at Devonport in September 1916 and sailed for Basra. From there all vehicles, including heavy workshop lorries and some dozen Ford light vans, were towed up the winding Tigris on barges to Sheik Saad, then near the front line.

At this stage of the appallingly badly-run campaign, Kut, on the left bank, was still held by the Turks to whom General Townshend and some 10,000 unfortunate British and Indian troops had surrendered the previous April.

13th LAMB joined the 20th Cavalry Division and were, I think, the only mechanised troops therein. For a few weeks we reconnoitred and occasionally fired on Turkish and Arab cavalry on the right bank whilst infantry and gunners continued to blast tightly-held Kut on the left bank. On or about February 22nd, 1917, Gurkhas and Norfolks made a gallant and costly pontoon rowing crossing at Shumuran Bend from the right to left bank and held a bridge-head whilst the Royal Engineers threw a 1,000 yard pontoon bridge across—a truly remarkable feat considering the 6 knot current and heavy enemy fire.

On February 23rd, 13th LAMB was ready to cross but, on account of our weighty cars and the risk of breaking the bridge, was barred. However, rafts were soon made and the first two cars towed across.

Within a few miles we were up with the Cavalry and Royal Horse Artillery, endeavouring to cut off the Turks now in retreat from Kut. This was our first action and it at once became painfully obvious that visibility inside a turret was very restricted and, owing to a complete absence of landmarks in the featureless desert and no maps, we were almost driving blind. In fact, in this first action one car (Cowan's) nearly ran over some entrenched Turks, one of whom enterprisingly lobbed a hand grenade under the front wheels blowing out part of the sump. The gallant Rolls however was able to reverse out so that I, in the second car, could attach a tow rope and drag the damaged car out of range when it inevitably seized up. It also became very apparent, at this early stage, that a stoppage-prone Maxim gun (Boer War model) was an inadequate armament against trenches.

General Crocker and his staff saw the point and thereafter used us mainly as reconnaissance or long penetration troops. Repeated appeals for some Lewis Guns as additional weapons were unsuccessful it being pointed out that these were 'not included in LAMB establishment'!!

En route from Kut to Baghdad we were busy harrying the Turk

but were again delayed whilst a pontoon bridge was thrown across the River Dialah, but on March 11th, 1917 we entered Baghdad well in the vanguard. We grabbed what we thought a good billet just north of the city wall. This had been Turkish Cavalry barracks. It was infested with fleas and we soon moved over to the North-West Gate which took all our vehicles and men comfortably and, although swarming with cats, was flealess.

From Baghdad on we were constantly in touch with the enemy, sending cars across the Euphrates where a similar situation prevailed. We must have saved many hundreds of Cavalry horses in doing this essentially mobile job.

One must pay tribute to these eight Rolls Royces, some of which we discovered still had London number plates on the rear tank and in 1928 were seen operating on the North West Frontier. It was over 129 degrees F. in the shade that summer of 1917— and even hotter inside the cars in the completely shadeless desert.

Water in the radiators never boiled unless we shut the front flaps when in close action.

One of our unusual jobs soon after Baghdad, when the Turks had been driven well north, was to take a convoy of T model Fords laden with food and supplies to the Russians who were said to be joining us via The Caucasus and Persia.

With one Rolls leading and another taking up the rear we made Kasri-Shirin and handed out stores.

I was then in command of 13th LAMB, Charles Cowan having at last agreed to be invalided home.

I therefore reported to the picturesque Russian General who invited me to lunch with him and his equally flashily-dressed officers. In atrocious French I endeavoured to convey my Welsh pleasure at the troops' singing outside. His reply was that these were revolutionary songs and that he and his officers were very uneasy!

After this short episode we were in all 'shows' both on the Euphrates and the Tigris.

When away from any irrigation nullahs, we were able quietly to drive out away from the river for some ten miles then run some 20 miles parallel with it, turning again to come well behind the Turk lines bringing eight guns to bear on enemy troops often obligingly in marching order.

Returning from one of these forays we came unexpectedly on a troop of Turkish cavalry dismounted and at ease in about the only small hollow within miles.

A quick surrender, and we returned to Headquarters with

Turks aboard and their horses in tow. We tried to retain one for our amusement but had to give it up to the Cavalry.

After this LAMB batteries galore began to appear, so the War Office had at last woken up to the fact that 'Mespot' was an ideal terrain for this new arm, rather than the Gallipoli Beaches or France.

Several rescues of RFC officers were effected and, in one case, Francis Nutter of 13th LAMBS brought back an RE8 and crew, by hitching the tail of the machine on to the back of the car. The most sensational was the break-through of one battery some hundred miles towards Mosul where they picked up Colonel Tennant and Major Hobart, who were on their way to captivity under escort and were literally grabbed from under the noses of the Turks.

Colonel Tennant was the commander of the Royal Flying Corps in Mesopotamia, and Major Hobart was the Brigade Major of the 8th Brigade. They were taken prisoners on March 25th, 1918, when the plane they were in, flying in low cloud over Khan Baghdadi, was shot down. Neither was hurt, which was something of a miracle.

FATHA GORGE

Following the defeat of the Turkish Forces at Tekrit (November, 1917) the bulk of the remaining Turkish Army on the Tigris had concentrated around Fatha Gorge, a position of great natural strength, some 35 miles from Tekrit.

Fatha Gorge had been thoroughly prepared for a protracted defence. The enemy's right flank from the Fatha Gorge to Sherghat was not only artificially defended, but also naturally protected by two formidable ranges of hills known as the Jebel Makhul and the Jebel Khanuka.

The Turks had reinforced the Fatha Gorge stronghold with a second line of defence astride the two hills mentioned, as well as trenches to defend the line of the Lesser-Zab river—a bridge at El Humr giving them free movement between both banks of the Tigris.

In early October, 1918 preparations were made to launch an assault on the Turkish positions at Fatha Gorge.

The conduct of these operations was entrusted to Lieut. General Sir A. S. Cobbe, V.C., K.C.B., C.S.L., D.S.O., Commanding

I Corps, who had placed at his disposal, in addition to the 17th and 18th Divisions, the 7th and 11th Cavalry Brigades.

The task facing Lieut. General Cobbe and his troops was an immense one. No railway existed between Tekrit and Fatha. To remedy this situation the 56th Brigade was brought from the Euphrates front to construct a railway line in advance of Tekrit. Another setback to General Cobbe's plans was a serious outbreak of influenza which occurred at this time, and greatly reduced the fighting strength of all units.

Special influenza camps had to be improvised in order to free medical units in the field for the reception of wounded. It is a curious fact, said the official report, that directly operations started there were practically no further cases of influenza.

Notwithstanding the difficulties General Cobbe and his staff encountered before the date fixed for the advance on Fatha Gorge, all preliminary moves were completed by the morning of October 23rd and contact with the enemy was made on the right and left banks of the Tigris.

On October 24th the 11th Cavalry Brigade, which had concentrated at Ain Nakhaila on the previous day, after a 45-mile trek through waterless country, reached the Lesser-Zab river, some twenty miles above its confluence with the Tigris, at about 3 p.m.

The Turks were holding the right bank in some strength, but in spite of opposition a crossing was forced over a deep ford in the neighbourhood of Uthmaniya with surprisingly few casualties. The 17th Division, on the right bank, was keeping in touch with the Turks, but was meeting with great difficulties.

An ex-officer of 257 Machine Gun Company, 17th Machine Gun Battalion (17th Division) tells of the task which faced the forces of General Cobbe, in what proved to be the final battle of the Mesopotamia Campaign of World War One :

> The 1st Corps, of which we were part, received orders to advance on Fatha, one evening in late October, 1918. We moved from our camp at Istabulat just after midnight, leaving our tents behind in charge of a fair number of flu' victims plus any spare Indians, to await those of us who were lucky enough to return.
>
> In the early morning of October 24th a very weary Company reached the battle zone. We moved out across no-man's-land via Jift (a desert dump of a place) to contact Johnny Turk at Fatha

where he was well entrenched on both sides of the Tigris. The heaviest fighting took place mostly during daylight hours, I believe at Divisional strength, with many Cavalry skirmishes along all flanks each side of the river, and whenever possible across the Lesser-Zab. Many miles were covered and lots of actions became confused both in front and on the flanks of the 17th Division which was on the right bank; 257 Machine Gun Company was given the job of clearing the Jebel Hamrin, Jebel Makhul, and Jebel Khanuka. These hills were steep, with only a few goat tracks. Johnny Turk held them stubbornly from prepared entrenchments for at least 15 miles from Fatha northwards.

The Jebels sloped down to the plains and the river at Sherghat. When we reached the top of each set of Jebels we found ourselves on the extreme left flank of the Division with nothing but open desert for miles on our left and sand and yet more sand.

After clearing the Turks, with the aid of the 10th Gurkha's and some 1st Battalion H.L.I. lads to whom we had to give overhead indirect fire from three Machine Gun Companies of our Division, as there was no mountain artillery available for us 'up there', the Turks were forced back down to the Tigris along which those who were not obliterated or captured could retreat to Mosul.

257's greatest difficulty at this stage of the attack was lack of supplies owing to extended lines of communication. This is where I came in, as my C.O. (Captain E. A. McKnee) ordered me to collect Private Thomas Black and Private Charles Henry Bond and Private Harold Stanbury plus three mules and find, somewhere, he didn't know where, supplies of food and ammunition and water, if possible, for the whole of 257 Machine Gun Company, who were really desperate.

So we set off, heading south, at 10 p.m. receiving covering fire from our own guns until we were safely 1,000 yards down along the hills. In the dark I headed, by compass, for Jift, but never found it so I headed for a railhead which I knew had various dumps. We had spent the previous summer helping to extend the railway from Samarra to Tekrit so I was in luck once we got within a few miles of Tekrit.

We began our journey back so as to arrive at Company headquarters 'On top of the Jebel' (as the song goes) about midnight, to be greeted with flares and nasty artillery fire from Johnny Turk, until rescued by some of our own chaps who had spotted our difficulty. However, to see their faces in the dark when they saw the supplies, plus about twenty mules fully laden which, on my instructions, the three Privates with me had 'found' at Tekrit, was truly wonderful after our round trip of about 40 miles in two nights and one day of travelling with only about two hours' sleep during that one day, in the heat.

Owing to the complete exhaustion of men and animals due to the heat, lack of water, and their previous exertions, the 17th Division was in no fit state to pursue a Turkish force dislodged from a position three miles south of Sherghat. In this action the 2nd Battalion Royal West Ken Regiment was prominent, capturing 200 prisoners and 11 machine-guns.

Closing on the Enemy

The position now was that a stubborn and not yet defeated enemy lay between General Cassel's Cavalry force, which had cut the Mosul road (the main avenue of retreat for the Turks) and the 17th Division. The troops were urgently in need of rest —the 17th Division had been marching and fighting for the preceding four days under the most arduous conditions. The 11th Cavalry Brigade had been continuously in action for 72 hours, and all had made very long marches. Nevertheless it was imperative to call on the troops for renewed exertions in order to close in on the enemy and force his surrender.

During the night of October 28th/29th, 1918, the Turks, ably led by many German officers as well as their own, made repeated attempts to break through to the north, but were each time repulsed. During this fighting the Guides' Cavalry and the 1st Battalion, 7th Gurkha Rifles, distinguished themselves by their staunchness.

In spite of exhaustion, darkness, and abominable roads, the troops of the 17th Division responded magnificently to the calls made on them, and by 11 a.m. on the 29th had driven back the Turkish rearguard on to the main body, which was holding a position north of Sherghat. During these operations units of the R.F.C. did great work spotting for the guns, sorting out the wheat from the chaff in positions held by the Turks, and also bombing Turkish forces whenever possible.

Meanwhile a serious threat from Turkish reinforcements (5th Division troops) moving down from the Mosul direction developed against Cassel's right flank. These troops established themselves with guns and machine-guns on the high bluffs near Hadranija, but were promptly dealt with by the 7th Cavalry Brigade. The 13th Hussars galloped across the open ground, dismounted under the bluffs, and, led by their colonel, carried the position by assault, many Turks being accounted for with the bayonet. Mounted pursuit by the remainder of the 7th Cavalry Brigade cleared away any further menace from the north, and resulted in the capture of 1,000 prisoners, with two guns and 12 machine-guns.

The end came on October 31st when Ismail Hakki, the Turkish Commander, surrendered with 11,000 of his men, including 643 officers, 51 guns, 130 machine-guns, over 2,000 animals, three paddle-steamers, and large quantities of gun and rifle ammunition, bombs, a complete bridging train, and war material of all kinds. So ended the last battle to be fought by a Turkish Army in the Mesopotamian Campaign of World War One.

Throughout this last battle machine-gunners of the Machine Gun Corps played an important role and the following awards were made for this action.

ORDER OF THE DAY
No. 125

Awarded the Military Cross

Temporary Second Lieutenant Alfred George Abolson, 257 Machine Gun Company, Machine Gun Corps, for conspicuous gallantry and devotion to duty. Exhausted after a forced march of 60 miles and suffering from ill health, he conducted his section over 1,500 yards of shellswept ground up to a ridge exposed to heavy fire, rallying and taking with him a Lewis gun team who were beginning to withdraw. He at once came into action and enfiladed the enemy's advancing line and was thereby largely instrumental in breaking up their counter-attack.

Lieutenant Edward John Cheesman, 257 Machine Gun Company, Machine Gun Corps, and The Dorsetshire Regiment for conspicuous gallantry and devotion to duty. Although wounded in five places, he succeeded in getting rations and ammunition to his company at night under heavy fire. He never spared himself and his conduct throughout the operations was most praiseworthy.

Lieutenant Dougal McLeod Douglas, Machine Gun Corps and The Northumberland Fusiliers, for conspicuous gallantry and devotion to duty. In an attack on a strong enemy position he commanded a section which operated on the left of an infantry battalion. He placed his guns so skilfully that not only did he succeed in driving back the whole enemy right wing, but silenced many hostile machine-guns which were harassing our advance.

o

Awarded the Military Medal

113339	Private Thomas Black, 257 Machine Gun Company.
113337	Private Charles Henry Bond, 257 Machine Gun Company.
113529	Lance-Corporal John William Bracken, Machine Gun Corps.
61167	Sergeant Alfred Bernard Card, Machine Gun Corps.
46512	Lance-Corporal Alec Dawson, Machine Gun Corps.
62110	Sergeant William John Hales, Machine Gun Corps.
61183	Corporal John William Havers, Machine Gun Corps.
97658	Private Frank Hicks, Machine Gun Corps.
113581	Lance-Corporal William Hindmoor, Machine Gun Corps.
91032	Corporal David Thomas Lewis, Machine Gun Corps.
113348	Private Harold Stanbury, 257 Company, Machine Gun Corps.

(The above is a copy of the original document)

The casualties among British and Indian forces in the Mesopotamia Campaign of World War One amounted to 100,000, of whom one-third were killed or died of wounds or sickness.

The many British and Indian cemeteries dotted throughout Mesopotamia (now Iraq) remain as a permanent reminder of the men who never came home again.

WITH A MACHINE GUN IN THE SINAI DESERT

The passing of the years has dimmed very little my recollections of the crossing of the Sinai desert, writes an ex-machine-gunner of 162 Machine Gun Company :

After taking part in the evacuation of Gallipoli in December, 1915, our Division, 54th East Anglian (T), was ordered to Egypt to help strengthen the Suez Canal defences.

At the time the so-called Egyptian campaign was referred to as a side show of the war, but history has shown that the successful defence of the Suez Canal saved the jugular vein of our Empire from being severed.

After the battle of the Canal in 1915, the defeated Turks escaped with their guns across 130 miles of desert to Beersheba, and pockets of the enemy still roamed the desert throughout the year of 1916. From defensive posts our machine-guns often accompanied fighting columns into the mountains amid the arid wastes of Sinai—waterless, red rocks 2,000 feet high, glaring sun, plagues of flies and mosquitos, with heat of 122 degrees in the shade, and there was precious little shade. In 1916 preparations were set going to cross the Sinai Peninsula from a place called El-Kantara, a filthy little village on the Suez Canal. From Kantara a railway was eventually built across one hundred miles of waterless desert.

This stupendous achievement was accomplished in stages. After each advance a pause would ensue until sufficient supplies were collected at the rail head.

Miles of wire roads were also laid over the thick sand. Water, non-existent in the desert, was brought by rail in tank trucks from the base at Kantara.

Water pipe-lines were laid from rail head to the fighting men. Camels and mules were also used to take supplies to scattered front-line units. It was estimated that hundreds of miles of water piping were laid by British engineers during the crossing of the Sinai desert. A desert previously almost destitute of human habitation was subdued and made habitable, with sufficient lines of communication protected by hundreds of miles of barbed wire.

During these operations our 162 Machine Gun Company did many outpost duties alongside the 1/5th Bedfords, 1/4th Northants, and 10th and 11th London Regiments (162 Brigade 54th "T" Division).

Often, especially during night-time, one's nerves became a little on edge. The surroundings were so silent, an unnatural silence, a deceptive silence.

It was always on the cards that from the seemingly empty desert hostile Arabs might attempt to cut the throat of a sentry, so one could never relax for a moment.

Many Arabs were in the pay of the Turks.

This hard-graft soldiering continued until January 9th, 1917, when British and New Zealand troops reached the town of Rafa, where a ten-hour battle took place.

The Turks were defeated and retired to Gaza.

Habitable country now lay ahead, but alas! many of those who had experienced the desert hardships were not destined to see the green fields and orange groves of Palestine. They perished in the Gaza battles of 1917.

WITH 135 MACHINE GUN COMPANY IN PALESTINE

In December, 1917, the 7th Indian Division was withdrawn from the Mesopotamia battle front and sent to Palestine to take part in what has been described as 'Allenby's Final Push'. An ex-machine gunner of 135 Company, 21st Brigade, 7th I/D, recalls this historic event; he writes:

On a day in late January, 1918, we arrived at Ismailia, a small town situated on Lake Timseh on the Suez Canal. After a few weeks' sorting ourselves out, we boarded a troop train en route for the Palestine battle zone. Packed like sardines in a tin we travelled in open trucks to the railway junction of Ludd, not far from the port of Jaffa, where we regrouped, and after many weary-ing fatigues, getting our equipment and guns ready for front-line duty, we marched. The marching was a different kettle of fish from that which I had experienced in Mesopotamia. The frag-rance of orange blossom, the green hills and valleys, made march-ing pleasant. 'Our luck's in', said my team mate, Jock.

The 7th Indian Division were to take over from a Division being transferred to France.

I had not seen green grass for over a year, and it was a nostalgic reminder of dear old Blighty.

For several weeks we did what we called 'exercises' with the infantry of the 2nd Black Watch and other units in the 21st Brigade. On several occasions during these stunts we slept on the beaches of the Mediterranean Sea, under cover of steep cliffs. The steady gentle swish of incoming waves, which never encroached beyond a safe point from our beach beds, created an atmosphere soothing to the mind.

The existing tranquillity made war seem unnatural.

THE TWO SISTERS

In early March, 1918 we manned our machine-guns for the first time in the line, on the Palestine Front.

It was a quiet affair. We didn't fire a single shot, but the next time our spell of trench duty came round it was a very different story.

The Turks occupied two hills, about a mile from our lines, which we named the Two Sisters because they were so much alike.

These hills had to be captured, said General Allenby, and the 21st Brigade, 7th Indian Division, was detailed for the task. 135 Machine Gun Company received orders to support the attack, which was to take place on April 3rd, 1918.

Until now the machine-gun sections had always gone forward with the attacking infantry, but this time we were to be used as a covering barrage fire, from a distance behind the infantry. The night before the attack, each machine-gun team crept out into no-man's-land and dug slit trenches with a shallow platform from which the guns would be fired. Our teams were spaced out at about thirty-yard intervals. Sixteen guns would operate under the fire control of section officers, from centrally placed dug-outs. Sergeant Jock, my usual team leader, and Fatty were loaned to number two team because of illness in that team, and I was put in charge of number one, two members of which were new lads, recently out from England.

Long before dawn we were wearied by our digging efforts. It was a race against time. 'Let's get some rest in', said Dreamy. I insisted on another pile of sandbags in front of our trench. Then we slung out a roll of barbed wire about forty yards in front of us, fixed our zero-discs in front of the gun, set the clinometer ready for the opening firing range . . . and dropped down to await the dawn.

The first streaks of light appeared in the sky. It was the signal to stand by for the attack.

A gun, well behind our lines, boomed out and a big shell screamed over our heads. This was the cue for many artillery guns to open fire. I could see the shells exploding all along the tops of the Two Sisters. It was a fantastic sight. No sooner had one barrage fire cleared itself of smoke than another took its place. The trenches on those hills seemed alight. Could anything possibly live, I wondered, in the Turkish positions?

After about ten minutes of this fierce bombardment, the first wave of Black Watch infantry lads made for the Turkish trenches under cover of another artillery barrage.

It was at this stage that the machine-gun sections opened fire with a covering barrage of bullets, from sixteen guns each firing at the rate of at least 500 rounds per minute.

The Turkish artillery guns began to reply. Shells landed around our gun pits. The din was indescribable, the smell of battle sickening. The infantry reached their first objective, so it seemed to us, but we soon discovered it was not going all according to plan. Battles never do. It was about the middle of the morning that Johnny Turk made a counter-attack. Enemy shells strafed our positions and the next thing I knew was that I was buried up to the neck. Our gun pit was completely wrecked. The other members of my team were buried alive. I could not move : my arms were pinioned to my sides, my ribs seemed to be near breaking point. 'Dinna ye get excited, mon,' shouted a voice from the open ground above, as I struggled to free myself. 'I'll soon have ye out'.

It was dear old Jock, carrying a spade. Braving the shells and bullets now flying about like pins on a skittle board, he jumped into the hole and dug like one possessed with supernatural strength.

Free once more, I slumped down, utterly exhausted. Another gunner from the nearest pit joined in helping to release the others of my team, three in number, who had all about had it as far as doing anything more in the attack was concerned.

The Turkish artillery lifted its barrage to reserve trenches behind us. During this break stretcher bearers got my chums away to a nearby ravine, where a field dressing station was situated. Our lives had undoubtedly been saved by the extra sand-bags I had insisted on putting out the previous night!

I was just feeling a little better when the Turks, counter-attacking, reached our wire. My gun still lay in the dirt. Jock made a dive for it, and somehow got it to work in a matter of minutes. A miracle in itself. I acted as his number two, and fed the gun from rescued boxes of ammunition in the trench. Directly the attacking Turks realised there was a machine-gun behind our stretch of barbed wire, they showed no further inclination to come forward.

By late evening our infantry had consolidated their positions on the Two Sisters hills, and everywhere became as quiet as an English park. I owed my life to Jock.

BUTTERCUP HILL

A few weeks after the 'Two Sisters' affair, 135 Machine Gun Company moved to another section of the front line, where we took over from 162 Machine Gun Company of the 162 Brigade, 54th ('T') Division.

The trenches we occupied extended along the edge of an orange grove. In front of our positions a big field, covered with buttercups and greenish long grass, sloped upwards towards the Turkish trenches at the top of the incline, a distance of about a mile. In peacetime one would imagine Buttercup Hill (as we named it) to be a pleasant place for having a picnic with the family. The surroundings were typically English, with the added beauty of many orange trees.

In our section of the line, doing duty with us, was a company of the 1/8th Gurkhas Rifles. These fearless Indian Army soldiers are noted for their skill with the Kukri knife. Small and sturdy men, they all seemed so much alike in looks to us Tommies that we could not tell one from another. We had great respect and admiration for them.

The Turks were always jumpy, especially at night-time when they knew the Gurkhas were facing them.

The conditions existing in this part of the line suited the Gurkhas, and after a few days' settling in at Buttercup Hill they decided to let Johnny Turk know that there was a war on. By this time the heat, during daytime, was sufficient to induce most troops in the line to take it as easy as possible, but the Gurkhas were an exception, and in broad daylight, usually mid-morning, about twenty of them, led by a young English officer, would leave our trenches for excursions to the top of Buttercup Hill. They would fan out immediately upon reaching the long grass of the field in front of us, and it would then be impossible to follow their movements. Nothing would be seen or heard for quite a while, and then a terrific banging and crashing heard coming from the Turkish trenches at the top of the hill notified us that our Gurkha comrades had arrived.

After about another half hour, we would see them returning, popping up out of the long grass like a lot of Jack-in-the-Boxes. As they passed us, several would grin and point to the hill, drawing their blood-stained knives in a mock action across throats. It made me feel cold, even in the heat of the summer day.

TWO STARLESS NIGHTS IN THE HOLY LAND

The oranges had become ripe for eating, and each day we picked as many as we fancied. Jaffa oranges straight from the tree are indescribably luscious. We drank the juice instead of water.

At night—well, on most nights—the stars shone so brightly you could see clearly right across no-man's-land. But the night before we were due to be relieved by No. 2 and 4 gun teams, dark clouds blotted out the stars for the first time in weeks.

Decidedly it was a suitable night for raids, and when the sentry on the gun reported a strange tapping noise on the wire fences —erected some hundred yards or more in front of us, the atmosphere became a little jittery. Our nearest infantry lads (20th Punjabis), who had taken over from the 1/8th Gurkhas, were in trenches on our right flank, but several hundred yards separated us.

Our section officer decided against sending up a Very-light, but Taffy, a new man on our team, and in civvy street a Welsh miner, volunteered to crawl out to the wire to see what was happening. Taffy knew the dangers but he readily slid over the top of our trench and was soon swallowed up by the darkness. We waited anxiously. It was a tense situation. The tapping noise stopped, and, after what seemed an age (actually it was about half an hour) Taffy popped up in front of our gun-pit. We hauled him into the trench.

'What was it?' our officer asked, almost before Taffy had recovered his wind.

'What a joke', spluttered Taffy. 'It was a stray mule tapping his hooves against the barbed-wire posts.'

The next night was dark too, when Nos. 2 and 4 gun teams relieved us. We filed out along the communication trenches and marched in comparative silence until we reached the H.Q. rest camp. There we dumped our kits and made a bee-line for the sleeping tents.

We were putting down our blankets when a terrific noise was heard, apparently coming from the trenches we had just left.

Everyone rushed outside. 'It looks like a raid on our old gun pit,' said Jock, the sergeant.

Very-lights lit up the starless sky over no–man's-land. Shells screamed over our heads. Joe, our medical orderly, ran past us on his way to the trenches.

'It's number two team,' he shouted. We could do nothing.

When it became quiet again I went with Jock to the Orderly Room to seek information. I noticed, as we waited, that the stars had broken through the clouds.

The information was that No. 2 team had been wiped out. A Turkish raiding party had attacked our old gun-post before the new occupants had properly settled in. Cutting the wire in front, they had crept up close before throwing their hand-grenades and the sentry had only been able to fire a short burst before the bombs landed among them. Everyone in the gun-pit had been killed outright.

ALLENBY'S FINAL PUSH

Not long after the ghastly spell of front-line duty at Buttercup Hill, 135 Machine Gun Company accompanied the 21st Brigade to another post, at a distance from the coastal strip. The area was alive with malaria flies, and as we stood in the trenches, the bloody things (in Jock's apt description) kept biting at our necks, especially at night-time.

Several of our gunners got an attack of malarial-fever, which left our gun-teams undermanned.

Our new positions faced a formidable range of hills, not too far distant, but far enough to allow Infantry patrols to go out at night without being too conspicuous.

The Turks were getting fed up with the war. We had our troubles but theirs were more formidable. News had reached us of the German retreat on the Western Front, and no doubt Johnny Turk had also got the message of the impending defeat of Germany. Every night Turkish soldiers were surrendering to our patrols in order, as one prisoner said, to get a meal from our side of the fence. It was a sure sign of the cracking up of Turkish morale, said my C.O., but I knew Johnny Turk to be a tough fighter, and that the men who defended the hills at which we gazed each day would not surrender without a stand.

The hot summer months ended, and General Allenby was ready with his plans for the Final Push.

In the third week in September an attack on the Turkish line was launched along a fifty-mile front from the Mediterranean to the Jordan. On the coastal strip, where we fought, a breach in the Turkish line of twenty miles was made during the first day of the fighting. It was during this advance that my luck gave out. Reaching a low range of hills in the early evening we received orders to rig-up our machine-guns in readiness to help repel a possible Turkish counter-attack.

We had just snatched a bite of bully beef, and enjoyed a mug of tea our section cook got to us, when the gods of war decided it was time I respected them a little more.

A Turkish whizz-bang (light artillery shell) burst in front of our shallow gun-pit, and I got a shell splinter in my arm and the finger of my right hand.

Joe, our medical orderly, after attending to my wound, sent me to the Field Ambulance and I missed the next part of the Big Push.

CORPORAL JONES AND A FUTURE FIELD MARSHAL

Frederick Harry Jones, late of 161 and 163 Machine Gun Companies, has a special reason for remembering General Allenby's Final Push in the Palestine Campaign of World War One: He writes:

A desperate request had come through from 161 Machine Gun Company for ammunition. I seized a poorly-conditioned stray pony that had not had its feet severed: a trick of Johnny Turk when in retreat. It was loaded with the belt-boxes and I was given very broad ideas about where the line might be. Going up ridge after ridge and down among broken rocks I plodded on, while Johnny threw over black shells. Thanks be, he seemed to be out of shrapnel. Almost incredibly, at long last, with me and my priceless charge almost on our knees, I stumbled right on top of 161 Coy's position.

The first living soul I encountered was the O.C. Company, Major Harding, M.C. He knew me, and said 'Cpl. Jones! Where the hell have you come from? Am I glad to see you.'

I was just in time to have a grandstand view of the attack carried out by the 6th Essex (T) battalion on a Turkish built-up rock position. The Essex lads took the position at the point of the bayonet.

Then I had to find my lonely way back to our base-line on foot. Major Harding kept the pony.

Footnote

The Major Harding of the then 161 Machine Gun Company is now Field Marshal Lord Harding of Petherton, G.C.B., C.B.E., D.S.O., M.C., and the much respected President of the Machine Gun Corps Old Comrades' Association.

Like Field Marshal Montgomery of World War Two fame, Lord Harding experienced front-line warfare in the 1914–18 Great War. It is true to say that both men came up the hard way, which did, in no small way, help them to understand the trials and tribulations of the ordinary soldier both in times of peace and war.

WITH THE 1st ARMOURED MOTOR BATTERY, MACHINE GUN CORPS

Bisley—British East Africa—Libyan Desert—Palestine

When I enlisted in 1915, motor cyclists were required for service in the newly formed Machine Gun Corps. Being an experienced motor cyclist I volunteered and was duly posted to Bisley, a village in Surrey, where the 1st Armoured Motor Battery was formed. My Regimental number was 1812. Training at Bisley was keen and thorough, but the diet we got was not up to the standard of our training routine, and like most young soldiers I was always hungry.

There was no such thing as supper; well, not officially! But one day a quiet rumour floated around that anyone wanting supper could get this at Hut ? at 9 p.m.

Our pay of 1/- per day did not leave much scope for an evening meal outside camp, so my chum and I decided to look into this supper rumour. The price per head was a mere 3d (no change given) and the number was limited to the first 300 arrivals. 'Just up our street', said my chum and we joined the crowd already assembled outside the specified hut at 8.45 p.m.

Two quartermasters stood outside the closed doors of the hut taking the cash and counting the number in the queue. Directly the stipulated number had been reached the doors opened and in we filed.

In anticipation of something good, we had brought along our own enamel plate, pint mug, and a knife.

Each of us received a pint of cocoa, one thick slice of bread, a lump of cheese, and a lump of butter. All went down well and we did not grumble at the price. Supper over, we were ordered to depart by the rear doors and without noise.

During the training period at Bisley my friend and I attended many of the unofficial supper sessions. We often wondered how much cash was collected from our rations, and if any charitable fund received any benefit!

A Memorable Sea Voyage

In January, 1916 we were issued with tropical clothes, and one dark night the entire unit marched to Brookwood (Surrey) railway station where we entrained for Devonport.

Early the following morning we filed on board the troopship *Huntsgreen*. Our destination was somewhere out east but we did not know where.

Hammocks were dished out and some of the crew showed us how to knot each hammock to the hooks running along the beams in the sleeping-quarters below deck. It was a real work of art, for if one hammock got out of line it upset the whole lot.

Next we were allocated to dining tables, 20 men to a table.

Our troopship sailed at noon. A strong gale blowing in the English Channel kept everyone quiet. The storm got worse when we reached the Bay of Biscay. Giant waves, smashing against the ship, sounded like claps of thunder. The *Huntsgreen* pitched and rolled alarmingly. No-one was allowed on deck. There were about two thousand troops on board, and everyone was sea-sick. I was ill for twenty-four hours, and most of the others in my section were sick for another twenty-four hours. When I had recovered I began to feel hungry.

'What about some grub?' I asked the N.C.O. in charge of my section dining table.

'Go away and don't you dare bring any food near me,' he bellowed. An order I decided not to obey, and picking up a dixie I went to the galley deck where three boilers were steaming and ship's cooks waiting for orders.

'You are the first applicant for food,' said the Head Cook, and told me to help myself, as no-one else seemed to want to eat. I did so, and my first load was a whole leg of mutton, and about eight lbs. of potatoes in their skins.

The ship was still in the storm, although not quite so severe, but somehow I managed to take my load down below to my section's dining table.

I made a second journey to the Galley and brought back four large loaves, six 1 lb. tins of corned beef, a 6 lb. tin of jam, and other small items. Then up I went again and collected a goodish supply of tea, butter and margarine. Having finished my collection of grub, I had a good feed myself and everything left over was put on a shelf under my section's dining table.

I was the only one of my section table chums who ate anything that day, the others could not bear the sight of food. That night I slept well in my hammock.

Next morning the sea was much calmed. Seasickness eased up and by tea time most of the section wanted to eat, so I fished out the store of food I had collected the previous day, and we had a real party.

Seasickness has no respect for ranks, and during the storm in the Bay of Biscay officers had retired to their bunks, but with calmer conditions on board they popped up again and we held our first parade. It was then that our C.O. informed us that our destination was British East Africa.

Our troopship reached Cape Verde, the most westerly point of Africa, where a short stop was made in the harbour. Fresh fruit was brought on board.

Then on we sailed through a smooth sea and glorious sunshine. This continued for three weeks. Our ship rounded the Cape non-stop, and two days later we berthed at Durban, the seaport of Natal, South Africa.

The order 'No troops allowed to go ashore' was a disappointment to us, and was received with disgust by the locals. Not to be outdone in showing their hospitality, the people went back into the town and returned with Zulus pulling rickshaws filled with cigarettes, newspapers, fruit, etc. which was a delight to us after almost five weeks at sea.

Old soldiers who passed through Durban in World War One have never forgotten the generosity of its people.

We put to sea again and several days later reached Mombasa where we disembarked. It was now February, 1916. The heat was terrific as we unloaded our vehicles and arms. Two days later we went by rail to a place called Voc, 120 miles from Mombasa.

The Germans were now only 10 miles away across the border. Real slogging work started as we advanced south.

Our armoured lorries had solid tyres and we had to dig them out about every half mile. There were no roads and jungle had to be cleared to make a passsage.

First Contact with the Enemy

At last we made contact with the enemy near a place called Taveta, a small town surrounded by hills and thick jungle. Bullets sprayed around us, but we could see nothing. It was impossible to get to close grips with our armoured vehicles.

It was decided to camp rough that night and make a dash forward early next morning. In the silence of a tropical dawn we moved forward and reached Taveta in a few hours without opposition. During the night the Germans had vanished to the south. Our scouts could find no trace of them, so on we went.

This chasing of an elusive enemy continued for several weeks, with occasional sorties when we did overtake them. The Germans were on foot and this enabled them to pass through the forests faster than we could with our armoured cars and ox-waggons. This sort of warfare went on until October, 1916, when we reached Morogora, on the Central railway. Whilst there we were told that the monsoon was due shortly.

With native help we made a waterproof shelter camp, and had only just completed this, when down came the rain. It never ceased raining for the next three weeks. No one could move, neither our men nor the Germans. After two months of monsoon weather, the sun appeared again and very quickly dried up the land.

In early January, 1917, we continued to advance southwards until we reached the Rufiqi River which, after the rains, was 800 yards wide. The Germans were entrenched on the opposite bank.

After two days on the river outposts we were relieved by a Punjabi Regiment, and we got orders to retire and proceed to Dar-es-Salaam, the capital of German East Africa before it surrendered to the British in September, 1916.

We began our journey. Our Battery consisted of four armoured lorries, various food trucks, and twenty-four gunners on Triumph motor cycles.

Gunner Draper and I were the last two motor cyclists of the column because we were mechanics. We carried all the necessary repair tools and the First Aid Kit.

We found our first case about noon. Gunner Maclachland was lying in the track, ill with malaria. We gave him quinine and water, got him to his feet, put him on his motor cycle and told him to go on. We followed and Mac kept going for about an hour before collapsing again. He was now too weak to control his motor cycle. It started to rain heavily and very soon the track turned into a sea of mud. We talked things over and decided that either Draper or I must catch up the Battery and get help.

We tossed up to decide which of us should remain behind with Mac. Draper went off. I put our motor cycles under a tree, dosed Mac again, and waited. The rain continued and as darkness approached—and no sign of help—I decided we must move, for the East African jungle is no place to picnic at night time. I remembered a native village (we had been over this ground previously) about a mile away on the other side of a small river. I wrapped Mac in his waterproof sheet, picked up the two rifles and First Aid bag, and after much encouragement, mingled with a few strong words, induced my patient to make the effort to move.

We reached a wooden bridge—a temporary affair—which was now shaking and leaning over about 40 degrees.

It was now completely dark, and I did not fancy our chances all that much, but told Mac we had got to crawl over the bridge before it was washed away. He responded like the stout heart he was and we scrambled over, only just in time. After a short rest we made for the village, about 300 yards from the river bank, and reached the first house, a hut affair. I rattled the cane door and shouted in Swahili, 'Open the door.'

A voice replied 'Who is it?'

'Two British soldiers, open the door or I will use the gun,' I shouted. The door was opened and an old woman let us in. The hut consisted of two rooms and in the entrance room was a centre pole and a small heap of hot ashes on the earthen-floor—which was the fireplace.

I asked the woman for food and water. She brought both. I then laid Mac on a waterproof sheet alongside the warm ashes, and gave him more first aid, after which he went to sleep. I then propped myself against the side of the hut and dozed off. In the meantime the woman had gone into the other room. My slumber was of short duration, being broken by voices coming from the other room.

Suddenly I heard a scratching noise overhead where a pole ran across horizontally. I looked up and saw two bright eyes reflecting the dim light. I jumped up and as I did so a queer sort of animal leapt to the floor near me.

I was somewhat scared and shouted. The old woman came in and I pointed to the animal. She laughed, bent down and picked it up. It was a mongoose, which the natives kept as pets, as British folk keep cats. 'You sleep safely, mongoose kill snakes' said the woman. I was learning, and promptly went into another doze. Mac continued to sleep soundly.

Some time later, when it was still dark, the woman re-entered and quietly said 'Simba' which in Swahili means lion. I listened and heard a low growl which came nearer every second. I seized my rifle, loaded it, and waited. A growl came from outside the door of the hut, but apparently the lion sensed nothing to grab, and after a few moments the growl faded away as the animal passed on.

The woman said 'Good', and went back into the other room.

Dawn came. I got up and opened the door and looked round. In the mud outside, barely six feet away, was the perfect imprint of the lion's feet.

The rain had ceased and the sun was shining. I put various oddments of our kit outside in the sun, woke up Mac and gave him some more quinine.

A little later on that morning I heard the welcome noise of a car engine. Draper and one of our officers were searching for us. I went to meet them and gave the officer details of what was happening. We got Mac into the heavy truck and after making him comfortable drove down to the river.

The wooden bridge had been swept away, but lower down the bank where the river was shallow and only about 30 yards wide, our heavy Ford truck made a safe crossing.

As we proceeded to the spot where our motor cycles were left the previous day, I saw a large notice-board on the side of the track. It was put there for the guidance of pre-war visitors. The reading on the notice-board, in Swahili and German, warned : 'Do not camp in this area. This is a Leopard Preserve.'

As I read, I remembered that Mac and I had halted on this very spot, but we had seen no leopards. The heavy rain had probably kept the animals under cover, I was told later.

Eventually we rejoined our battery, some three miles ahead, just in time to enjoy a hearty breakfast, and Mac was well cared for in the sick-bay truck.

The Battery now formed up and we proceeded on our journey. During the next four days, we trudged through the East African forests, reaching Dar-es-Salaam without seeing any signs of the enemy.

Three days after our arrival at Dar-es-Salaam we were informed that the battery was to proceed to the Libyan Desert for patrol duties. We went on board the troopship *Huntsgreen* which had brought us out from Devonport over a year ago.

Our first stop was at Aden where we buried five men who had died on the boat. Eventually we docked at Port Suez, and then went by train to Cairo detail camp, where we enjoyed 7 days' rest before moving on to the port of Alexandria.

From Alexandria we went by boat to Mersa-Matruh and then on to Sollum (2 nights' sailing). There was no water at Sollum.

A trawler brought coal once a week and a distilling plant was erected on shore to make fresh water.

Ration per man was two pints per day for every purpose.

Desert Patrols in 120°F.

We were now supplied with original Ford T cars—with a Vickers machine-gun mounted on each car.

Half of the patrol cars were based at Siwa for two weeks, and half at Sollum. Change-over took place each 14 days. There was ample water at Siwa.

The main object of our patrols was to map out the desert, and catch camel caravans carrying arms and other war material to the Senussi Tribes, who had staged an uprising in the early part of the 1914–18 war.

We always caught these caravans, and after practice could read camel tracks in the sand, and even tell what time they traversed our route during the night.

In the daytime the heat was terrific, but often at night the desert was frosty. The sudden extremes in temperatures were most trying.

After six months of patrol duties we met with a serious setback. Our supply trawler was torpedoed and sunk by enemy action. We ran out of vital supplies as a result.

The revolt of the Senussi tribes had, by this time, been terminated, so we received orders to motor back to Kantara, on the Suez Canal.

Upon arriving there we were issued with six armoured Rolls-

Royce cars and dispatched to Palestine where General Allenby was preparing for his Big Push against the Turks.

It was now late February, 1918.

Mopping-up Operations in Palestine

When the attack got going we raked up Turks along their eastern front. It was now all movement and action.

On several occasions—when water supplies ran out—I wondered if we should ever reach base again. Often we were split up into small reconnoitring parties, probing deep into the desert, when this happened; but our Libyan experience stood us in good stead.

I remember most vividly the utter stillness of the desert at night time, the dawn patrols, and the blood-red sunsets. Each day we scoured the desert for Turkish troops and hostile Arabs who had escaped from General Allenby's net around the battlefields of the lush pastures of Palestine and in the Jordan Valley.

In October, 1918, British troops captured Damascus, the capital of Syria, and our armoured cars got a look at the place. We also saw Galilee, the town where Christ spent His boyhood—and where He did much of His active ministry.

I remember the sort of wonderment I felt as I tried to visualise all this.

Such a contrast to a patrol of armoured cars carrying weapons of destruction, I thought. It seemed to me, as I looked at historic landmarks mentioned in the Holy Bible, that Christ's teaching on the brotherhood of man had not yet been understood, and for a few moments I felt sad to know this was so.

Allenby's forces continued to push on northwards, and in late October, 1918, our Armoured Division joined up with other forces at the gates of Aleppo, where the Turkish Army finally surrendered.

During my three years' service with the Machine Gun Corps heavy sections I had travelled thousands of miles over sea and desert and through the forests of East Africa. I experienced few battles of any size—but, nevertheless, it had been no picnic. I was, of course, one of the lucky ones.

MEMORIES OF THE END IN PALESTINE AND SYRIA (1918)

My old unit (135 Machine Gun Company) were on the road to Tripoli in Syria when late one afternoon in October, 1918, I reported to the Company Orderly Room, a few miles behind the actual front line. I was received with much good-humoured banter.

'The war's as good as over', joked C.S.M. Dewar.

'You have certainly missed some marching this time,' said Captain McKenzie, 2nd in command.

'Makes up for all the marching I didn't miss in Mespot,' was my reply in similar vein.

Sergeant Jock appeared, and we greeted each other like long-lost brothers. I was then informed that Dreamy of my team had stopped a shell splinter in his ankle, only the day after I was hit, and that Fatty, my other gun-team chum, had gone sick during the march. Jock and I were the only remaining original members of my gun-team.

The end of General Allenby's Final Push had almost come when we reached the hills of Tripoli, where we camped down.

Other units of the 7th Indian Division, which included 134 and 136 Machine Gun Companies, helped to capture Beirut, the seaport town on the Mediterranean, 60 miles from Damascus, capital of Syria, already in British hands.

By the end of October and early November, 1918, Syria as well as the whole of Palestine had been set free from the Turkish yoke. Battlefields, named in the Bible, had been crossed over by British forces, British cavalry had galloped across the actual field of Armageddon, and occupied the sacred place of Nazareth. Armageddon, overlooking the great plains of Esdraelon, south-west of Nazareth, was the battlefield where Barak defeated the Canaanites, and Gideon the Midianites : there Saul was slain by the Philistines, and in 1799 Napoleon defeated the Turks on this same battlefield.

During General Allenby's final push, two entire Turkish armies were wiped out. Historians have since stated that the British advance through Palestine and Syria in 1918 was probably the most swift and most successful of the 1914–18 war.

November 11th, 1918

I was returning to the camp guard tent, after night duty, when the news arrived. An armistice had been declared. The war was over.

The whole camp went mad with joy.

No more night patrols in no-man's-land, lonely sentry duties, screaming shells, and calls for stretcher bearers.

No more 'over the top'.

It was as though a great weight had suddenly been lifted from my mind, and another kind of world discovered—a world of sanity and peace.

Principal Contributors

LIEUT. COLONEL G. S. HUTCHISON, D.S.O., M.C. (33rd Battalion Machine Gun Corps).

W. G. MARTIN (168 Machine Gun Company and 12th London Regiment).

BILL COMMERFORD (126 Machine Gun Company and 1/10th Manchester Regiment).

W. G. HALL (New Zealand-Machine Gunner with Gallipoli Brigade —No. unknown).

TOM HAMILTON (11th Enniskillens, 36th Ulster Division).

N. DUBBURY (50th Machine Gun Company).

A. G. MORRIS (142 Machine Gun Company).

P. G. ACKRELL (62nd and 58th Machine Gun Company).

LT. F. JACKSON (166 Machine Gun Company).

WILLIAM SHUTTLEWORTH (151 Machine Gun Company).

J. GADSBY (142 Machine Gun Company).

C. E. CRUTCHLEY (135 Machine Gun Company and 1/4th Northants Regiment (T)).

A. C. HANNANT, M.M. (3rd Cavalry Squadron Machine Gun Corps).

SELBEY G. DAVEY (74th Machine Gun Company).

H. A. SALISBURY (46th and 47th Machine Gun Companies).

FRANK GILL (98th Machine Gun Company).

W. C. TOPHAM (205 Machine Gun Company).

A. WHITE (142 Machine Gun Company).

ANON. (PER MRS. ANN SLOPER) (56th Machine Gun Company).

W. J. BAXTER (142 Machine Gun Company).

G. M. MANUELL, M.B.E. (109 Machine Gun Company).

J. R. (25th Division Machine Gun Company).

ALFRED HENSHER (17th Battalion Machine Gun Corps).

J. W. AVERY (41st Machine Gun Company).

WILFRED GANDY (3rd Battalion Machine Gun Corps).

S. G. MORRIS (16th Battalion Machine Gun Corps).

R. FAWCETT (136 Machine Gun Company).

COLONEL SIR GEORGE WADE M.C., J.P. (137 Machine Gun Company).

F. MELLOR (130 Machine Gun Company).

MAJOR E. H. RICHES (129 Machine Gun Company).

F. H. ROOD (1st Armoured Motor Battery Machine Gun Corps).

CAPTAIN E. J. CHEESMAN (257 Machine Gun Company).

S. FORSYTH (162 Machine Gun Company).

F. H. JONES (161 & 163 Machine Gun Company).

D. R. PARSONS (184 Machine Gun Company).

W/COMMANDER R. C. WILLIAMS (13th Light Armoured Motor Battery Machine Gun Corps).

ANON. (58th Division M.G.C.).

BRIGADIER A. LOW, C.B.E., M.C. (10th Brigade Machine Gun Corps).

S. G. SMALE (129 Machine Gun Corps).

F. L. GOLDTHORPE (185 Machine Gun Corps).

Special thanks also to—

MAJOR D. O. DIXON (Hon. Secretary, M.G.C. Old Comrades Association) who supplied Editor with items from the "Boy David" Journal.

To LIEUT. FRANK PALEY and the REV A. J. WHITTET for the loan of the History and Memoir of the 33rd Battalion Machine Gun Corps.

To MRS. ANN SLOPER for items she supplied to the book.

To A. E. ROBERTS of the M.G.C. Executive Committee O/C Association.

For reasons of space it has not been possible to include the names of all those who have interested themselves in the compiling of this book, but the compiler extends his grateful thanks to such helpers.

The Machine Gun Corps Old Comrades Association

An Old Comrades Association still exists, and there are also many associate members.

Most of the Old Comrades are now over 70 years of age, but continue to meet annually at the Corps Memorial—'The Boy David' by Derwent Wood, R.A.

This unique statue stands in a favoured spot at Hyde Park, Corner, London.

The President of the M.G.C./O.C.A. is

Field Marshal Lord Harding of Petherton, G.C.B., C.B.E., D.S.O., M.C.

Vice President—H. R. Bailey, Esq.

Chairman—Colonel Sir George Wade, M.C., J.P.

Hon. Secretary—Major D. O. Dixon, 11 Bywater Street, Chelsea, London, SW3 4XD.

Units Mentioned

Index

Abbots, Jock, 67
Abolson, 2nd Lieutenant Alfred George, 207
Abrahams, Gunner, 60
Achar Singh, Driver, 195
Achi-Baba, 27, 32
Achiet-le-Grand, 149–50
Adams, Lieutenant, 110
Aden, 222
Ahmed Bey, 194
Ain Nakhaila, 204
Airaines, 53
Albert, 61, 137, 148
Albion, battleship, 29
Aleppo, 194, 223
Alexandria, 23, 82, 222
Allan, Captain, 118
Allen, Private, 142
Allenby, General Edmund, 210–11, 215, 223–4
Alt, Lieutenant-Colonel, 19
Amara, 167–8, 170, 198, 200
Amiens, 134, 148
Anafarta Hills, 33
Ancre, river, 77
Andrew, Major W. C., 140
Antelope Trench, 76
Anzac Cove, 28, 33
Anzim-Saint-Vaast, 127
Applin, Colonel, 93
Arbuthnot, Lieutenant, 89–90
Armentières, 48, 107, 121
Arques, 133
Arras, 16, 91, 113, 124, 132; battle of, 80, 83–7, 90
Arthurs, Private, 145
Asnex, 38
Aubers Ridge, 143
Aulnoye, 160–1
Avesnes, 164
Ayres, Private, 142
Aziziyeh, 168

Bachant, 163
Baghdad, 166, 168–9, 175–8, 180, 182, 186–7, 192, 194, 200, 201–2; capture of, 178–9, 194
Bailleul-Ravensburg, 111
Bairnsfather, Bruce, 97
Baldwin, General, 37
Bapaume, 75, 104, 125, 137, 161–2

Barbed Wire Square, 90
Barker, Corporal, 126
Barking Creek, 19, 128–9
Barnes, Sergeant, 50–1
Barrass, Private, 110
Bartlett, Artificer H., 53
Basra, 166–70, 197–8, 201
Bates, Corporal, 109
Batty, John, 66–7, 71, 73
Bawn, Corporal, 138–9
Bazentin-le-Grand, 62–5, 72–3
Bazentin-le-Petit, 50, 72
Beard, Sergeant, 52, 84
Beaumont Hamel, 38, 49
Becque, 146–7
Beersheba, 208
Beirut, 224
Bellerby, Captain J. R., 107
Belton Park, Grantham, 103, 112–13
Bennett, Billy, 90
Bennett, Lieutenant, 76
Bennett Trench, 76
Berlaimont, 159–60
Bethune, 134
Bidder, Lieutenant-Colonel, 107
Bienvillers, 86
Billing, Private, 86
Birdwood, General Sir William, 35, 37
Bisley, 216–7
Black, Private Thomas, 205, 208
Black Watch Trench, 52
Blackwood, 62
Blendecqes, 20
Boast, Lance-Corporal, 110
Bodmin Copse, 109
Bogle Farm, 146
Bohain, 154–5, 157; Wood, 157
Bond, Private Charles Henry, 205, 208
Booth, Captain F. C., 160
Bouchavesnes, 143
Boucly-Villevesque, 133
Boullens, 137
Boulogne, 20, 103
Bourlon Wood, 88, 119–20, 125, 127
Bouvet, battleship, 27–8
Bracken, Lance-Corporal John William, 208
Bradbury, Private, 51